D0120005

PARENTING AFTER PARTNERING

Relationships between adult partners following divorce or separation can be fragile, and the issues which have divided the parents are often hard to disentangle from the ongoing relationships between parents and children. There is a small group who have ongoing difficulty and who need professional help and legal intervention to make arrangements for ongoing parenting. This volume brings together a wealth of new empirical research from the USA, Central, North Western and Southern Europe, and Australia on the nature and importance of children's relationships with parents after parental separation, on the kinds of conflicts which develop, and on the range of professional interventions which support parents and children through these difficult times.

Oñati International Series in Law and Society

A SERIES PUBLISHED FOR THE OÑATI INSTITUTE
FOR THE SOCIOLOGY OF LAW

General Editors

William LF Felstiner   Johannes Feest

Board of General Editors

Rosemary Hunter, University of Kent, United Kingdom
Carlos Lugo, Hostos Law School, Puerto Rico
David Nelken, Macerata University, Italy
Jacek Kurczewski, Warsaw University, Poland
Marie Claire Foblets, Leuven University, Belgium
Roderick Macdonald, McGill University, Canada

Titles in this Series

Social Dynamics of Crime and Control: New Theories for a World in Transition edited by Susannah Karstedt and Kai Bussmann

Criminal Policy in Transition edited by Andrew Rutherford and Penny Green

Making Law for Families edited by Mavis Maclean

Poverty and the Law edited by Peter Robson and Asbjørn Kjønstad

Adapting Legal Cultures edited by Johannes Feest and David Nelken

Rethinking Law Society and Governance: Foucault's Bequest edited by Gary Wickham and George Pavlich

Rules and Networks edited by Richard Appelbaum, Bill Felstiner and Volkmar Gessner

Women in the World's Legal Professions edited by Ulrike Schultz and Gisela Shaw

Healing the Wounds edited by Marie-Claire Foblets and Trutz von Trotha

Imaginary Boundaries of Justice edited by Ronnie Lippens

Family Law and Family Values edited by Mavis Maclean

Contemporary Issues in the Semiotics of Law edited by Anne Wagner, Tracey Summerfield, and Farid Benavides Vanegas

The Geography of Law: Landscapes, Identity and Regulation edited by Bill Taylor

Theory and Method in Socio-Legal Research edited by Reza Banakar and Max Travers

Luhmann on Law and Politics edited by Michael King and Chris Thornhill

Precarious Work, Women and the New Economy: The Challenge to Legal Norms edited by Judy Fudge and Rosemary Owens

Juvenile Law Violators, Human Rights, and the Development of New Juvenile Justice Systems edited by Eric L Jensen and Jørgen Jepsen

The Language Question in Europe and Diverse Societies: Political, Legal and Social Perspectives edited by Dario Castiglione and Chris Longman

European Ways of Law: Towards a European Sociology of Law edited by Volkmar Gessner and David Nelken

Constitutional Politics in the Middle East: With Special Reference to Turkey, Iraq, Iran and Afghanistan edited by Saïd Amir Arjomand

Parenting after Partnering

Containing Conflict after Separation

Edited by
Mavis Maclean

Oñati International Series in Law and Society

A SERIES PUBLISHED FOR THE OÑATI INSTITUTE
FOR THE SOCIOLOGY OF LAW

·HART·
PUBLISHING
OXFORD AND PORTLAND OREGON
2007

Published in North America (US and Canada)
by Hart Publishing
c/o International Specialized Book Services
920 NE 58th Avenue, Suite 300
Portland, OR 97213-3786
USA
Tel: +1 503 287 3093 or toll-free: (1) 800 944 6190
Fax: +1 503 280 8832
E-mail: orders@isbs.com
Website: www.isbs.com

© Oñati IISL 2007
First Printed 2007 and Reprinted 2009

All rights reserved. No part of this publication may be reproduced, stored in a retrieval system, or transmitted, in any form or by any means, without the prior permission of Hart Publishing, or as expressly permitted by law or under the terms agreed with the appropriate reprographic rights organisation. Enquiries concerning reproduction which may not be covered by the above should be addressed to Hart Publishing at the address below.

Hart Publishing, 16c Worcester Place, Oxford, OX1 2JW
Telephone: +44 (0)1865 517530 Fax: +44 (0)1865 510710
E-mail: mail@hartpub.co.uk
Website: http://www.hartpub.co.uk

British Library Cataloguing in Publication Data
Data Available

ISBN: 978-1-84113-781-0 (hardback)
ISBN: 978-1-84113-782-7 (paperback)

Typeset by Compuscript, Shannon
Printed and bound in Great Britain by
CPI Antony Rowe, Chippenham, Wiltshire

Contents

List of Contributors

Benoit Bastard, Directeur de Recherche at COS, CNRS, Paris.

Laura Cardia Vonèche, Senior Researcher, Institute for Public Health, University of Geneva.

Rachel Carson, Doctoral Candidate at Griffith Law School, Australia.

John Dewar, Professor, Deputy Vice-Chancellor, Griffith Law School, Australia.

Belinda Fehlberg, Professor, The Melbourne Law School, Australia.

Malgorzata Fuszara, Director of the INSS, Institute for Applied Social Studies, University of Warsaw.

Joan Hunt, Senior Research Fellow, Department of Social Policy and Social Work, University of Oxford.

Rosemary Hunter, formerly Associate Professor of Law and Director of the Socio-Legal Research Centre, Griffith Law School, Australia. Since October 2006 she has been Professor of Law, University of Kent.

Jacek Kurczewski, Professor Sociology of Custom and Law at the University of Warsaw. From 1991–93 he was Deputy Speaker and member of the Polish Parliament and from 1997–98 he was Director of the International Institute for Sociology of Law in Onati, Spain.

Michael E Lamb, Professor, Faculty of Social and Political Sciences, University of Cambridge.

Agurtzane Goriena Lekue, Assistant Professor, Faculty of Law, University of the Basque Country, San Sebastian.

Mavis Maclean CBE, Director of the Oxford Centre for Family Law and Policy in the Department of Social Policy and Social Work, University of Oxford, and a Senior Research Fellow in the Faculty of Law. She is former President of the RCSL, a Fellow of the IISL, and Academic Adviser to the Ministry of Justice, formerly the Department for Constitutional Affairs.

Vanessa May, Research Fellow, University of Manchester.

Katrin Mueller-Johnson, Lecturer in Applied Criminology, Faculty of Law, University of Cambridge.

Helen Rhoades, Senior Lecturer, Melbourne Law School, University of Melbourne, Australia.

Grania Sheehan, Senior Research Fellow, Griffith Law School, Australia.

Carol Smart, Professor of Sociology, University of Manchester.

Liz Trinder, Reader, University of Newcastle.

Introduction:
Conflicted Contact between Parents and Children after Separation

RELATIONSHIPS BETWEEN ADULT partners are becoming increasingly fragile, while the relationships between parents and children even after parental separation seem to have become more enduring. Taking the United Kingdom as an example, current estimates suggest that almost one in three children in England and Wales will experience parental divorce before the age of 16 and an increasing number will be affected by the separation of cohabiting parents for whom statistical data is still hard to find (Hunt, 2004). Children living in lone parent families in England and Wales in 9 cases out of 10 live with their mothers, but in 9 cases out of 10 stay in contact with their fathers (Attwood et al, 2003). But the continuation of a meaningful relationship between parents and children after separation may be difficult to establish and maintain, and in some cases, about 10 per cent across a number of jurisdictions, it becomes highly conflicted and requires public intervention and legal regulation.

Sadly, the issues which have divided the parents are hard to disentangle from the ongoing relationships between parents and children, both for the parents who live with their children and for those who no longer share a common household. In addition there may be new arguments arising from new adult relationships, and the presence of new step-siblings. Though parents aim, hope and try to make adult transitions as easy as possible for their children and most succeed, there seems to be a small group who have ongoing difficulty and need professional help and legal intervention to make arrangements for ongoing parenting which is now widely accepted as desirable, provided that arrangements are safe and in the best interests of the child. It should, however, be noted that the research evidence about the desirability of ongoing contact with non-resident parents is far from clear. American meta analysis (Amato and Galbraith, 1999) found that the two elements consistently associated with child well-being were the economic contribution of the father and the closeness of the mother–child relationship. Furthermore, a recent study of step-families in England and Wales found that the quality of relationships in the primary home was a stronger predictor of a child's well-being than continuing contact with a non-resident parent (Smith, 2001). Pryor and Rodgers in their overview of the research literature found that 'the mere presence of fathers is not enough ... it is the aspects of parenting encompassing monitoring, encouragement, love and warmth that are consistently linked with well being' (Pryor and Rodgers, 2001).

This volume brings together new socio-legal research from the United States, central, north western and southern Europe, and Australia on the nature and importance of children's relationships with parents after parental separation, on the kinds of conflicts which develop, and on the range of professional interventions which support parents and children through these difficult times. We are grateful to the WELL CHI Network for their early support for the project, and to the International Institute for the Sociology of Law in Onati for enabling us to take the work forward at a workshop in September 2005. The revised papers now constitute the fourth volume in a series made possible by the Institute, to whom we are most grateful for their hospitality, and the opportunity to continue our cross-national work on issues of family law and policy.

Feelings in this area run high. Our contributors, Benoit Bastard and Laura Cardia Voneche convened a meeting in Paris in 1999 on contact centres where delegates were besieged in the Ministry of Labour by a group of militant fathers, demanding better access to their children. This was my first personal experience of such movements, but these have now developed worldwide. In Australia the extreme group known as the 'Blackshirts' have picketed the homes of mothers with care, and in the UK a militant group known as 'F4J', now disbanded, carried out high profile stunts including scaling the walls of Buckingham Palace and handcuffing the Minister for Children at a family law conference in Manchester in November 2005. Some of the individuals concerned are skilled in media management, but their behaviour appears disturbed as well as disturbing.

But the fathers' groups encompass far more than extreme minority activity. There is a larger movement, reflecting the changing work–life balance. Some mothers are becoming more involved in the workplace, and some fathers are becoming more involved in the home, though in the UK at least there is little indication that parents have become interchangeable. (Gershuny's time budget studies show a small increase in the leisure time spent by fathers with their children, and data on the employment of women with young children shows that it remains largely part time and low paid.) In the UK there is a broad spectrum of fathers' groups, including 'Fathers Direct', who make a positive contribution to improving the skills of fathers, especially those taking responsibility for young children on contact visits. But there is concern about the way this increased paternal interest in playing a larger part in children's lives has become expressed in the language of adult rights rather than child welfare. The existing statutory framework in England and

Wales for all matters relating to children coming before the courts is the Children Act 1989, which is expressed in terms of parental responsibility rather than rights, and assumes that this responsibility is independent of the civil status of the parents. The court is only there in private law matters to assist in resolving disputes about where a child will live and who they will remain in touch with, and will only intervene if it is in the best interests of the child to do so. Case law makes it clear that continuing contact with both parents after a separation is thought to be desirable, unless there are specific reasons for this to be contrary to the child's welfare, for example in the case of parental substance abuse or domestic violence. There has been considerable pressure on government from the fathers' pressure groups to change the legal framework to reflect the conceptualisation of contact as a matter of parental rights, rather than, as it is at present, the right of the child to see a parent. Such a change was resisted by both mothers' groups concerned about domestic violence, and by other groups concerned about the interests of the children and hearing the voice of the child. In preparing consultation papers and legislation, the Children and Adoption Bill 2006, the Government has upheld the 1989 Children Act emphasis on the welfare of the child as the paramount consideration in any decision affecting that child, and concentrated on developing ways of establishing and supporting contact in practice. The Government has rejected the calls for a formula to define what might be meant by reasonable contact, or any demands that children should share their time 50/50 between both parents, holding to the view that every family is different and each case should be considered individually. A similar position has been adopted in both Canada where a commission set up to examine the issue concluded that there should be no 'one size fits all' solution, and in Australia where a parallel commission entitled its report *Every Picture tells a Story* (chapter eight; Rhoades and Boyd, 2004).

This approach also underpins the Parenting Guidelines adopted in a number of American states, which look to developmental criteria to determine contact patterns, but most states emphasise that these are not prescriptive in individual cases (chapter one; Kelly and Lamb, 2000; Gould and Stahl, 2001). The issues being debated range from what contact should be suggested or prescribed for conflicted parents, to how such arrangements should be put into effect and monitored and supported. There has been concern from non-resident parents in the UK about the way that resident parents can obstruct a contact order with impunity. This is due in part to the lack of services to establish and support contact, and in the very few cases of implacable failure to comply with an order the difficulty of finding a sanction which will impact on the parents but not on the children. It must be emphasised that no jurisdiction has yet found a solution to these problems. In Denmark where contact disputes cannot be taken to court—ie the problem is not accepted as amenable to a legal solution—problems remain.

And in France where the Government has come out strongly in favour of 50/50 parenting there is resistance from the public, and a suggestion that this is an attempt to get around the increased rate of divorce which is not welcome to the Government or the Church by making joint parenting a requirement after divorce and thus preventing any real separation between parents (Bastard and Voneche, 2005: chapter 6).

This volume brings together a wealth of new multidisciplinary empirical material, and presents data and views from a variety of perspectives. I am grateful to those who write in English although it is not their first language, and though a little editing is sometimes helpful in this volume as in our previous work we try to maintain the individual character of the differing perspectives. The purpose of the volume is to stand back from the kinds of arguments currently sadly being employed as ammunition in the 'gender war', and to take a broader and deeper look firstly at how relationships between parents and children after separation are characterised in different countries, and among different family settings; secondly to examine in detail what kinds of conflicts currently emerge between parents in both opposite sex and same sex settings after separation; and finally to look at the policy response and the development of new forms of intervention to support parents and children through these difficulties. The final section includes three chapters from Australia, which reflects the recent high level of research activity in this field in that jurisdiction in preparation for the major changes to family law brought into effect in July 2006.

Part I, 'The Changing Landscape of Relationships', begins with a chapter from Professor Michael Lamb, a leading American expert in the psychology of child development, now working in Cambridge, UK. He has carried out empirical studies focusing on the relationship between fathers and children after separation. He opens our volume by reviewing current understanding of the importance of the relationships between children and both parents (chapter one, Lamb). In chapter 2 we present an analysis by the family sociologists Benoit Bastard from CNRS, Paris, and Laura Cardia Voneche, University of Geneva, of why patterns of contact after separation are so variable given the growing consensus (see chapter one) on the need for both parents to have a strong ongoing relationship with their children after separation. From their recent research they conclude that the way parents function after separation is related to the way they functioned during the partnership, rather than whether they remain amicable after separation. They believe that the norm of shared parenting after separation, though supported by government, may be simply irrelevant for parents who did not share the role during their relationship. The first part ends with chapter three from Malgorzata Fuszara and Jacek Kurczewski from Poland, where traditional family values associated with the Roman Catholic Church remain strong. They begin by reminding us of the complexity and practicality of parental roles found by anthropologists, and set these alongside their recent interviews with a small group of lesbian mothers in Poland who now challenge traditional concepts of gender and parenting as well as gender and partnering.

Part II, 'The Conflicts associated with Post-separation Parenting', presents empirical data on the precise nature of the conflicts, which develop between opposite sex parental couples after separation in England and Wales and in Spain. In chapter four sociologists Vanessa May and Carol Smart describe how ongoing conflict about contact is a part of the ongoing conflicted relationship between the former couple, and how difficult it is for this to be resolved in a legal setting. In chapter five Liz Trinder from East Anglia gives us the psychologists' view of attempts to help courts with this task through the provision of conciliation services within the courts, but again she highlights the intractable nature of these disputes even when parents first approach the courts. She traces a gender difference in the nature of the conflict. The women expressed concern about welfare issues, whether the father is able to keep the child warm and fed during visits, ie the quality of parenting. The fathers expressed concerns about losing control of the situation and being excluded from the former family setting. Both parents and children showed high levels of distress. In chapter six Agurtzane Goriena Lekue describes recent changes in Spain where the government now supports equal and shared parenting, but referring to empirical work the parenting behaviour of the fathers and the labour force participation of the women do not fit with these official assumptions of equality.

Part III, 'Professional Intervention' is concerned with what is or could be done about these problems in a number of jurisdictions. Katrin Mueller-Johnson in chapter seven gives a detailed account of the development of contact services in Germany. Here, despite a strong legal framework to support shared parenting, sanctions to prevent either parent making contact difficult for the other, powers to compel a reluctant parent to exercise contact with the child, and a wide range of supportive services, even so there are a small number of protracted and intractable contact disputes.

The final three chapters report policy and developments in Australia, where contact has been a high profile issue recently, culminating in the Family Law Amendment (Shared Parental Responsibility Act) which came into effect in July 2006. In Australia, as in England and Wales, the paramount presumption in any case affecting children has been the welfare of the child. But this principle has been subject to increasing criticism as essentially unclear. Helen Rhoades from Melbourne Faculty of Law sets the policy scene, describing the move from the child protection approach of the early 1990s to the emergence of fathers groups demanding a right to time with their children on a basis substantially equal to that of the mother. She raises important concerns about the impact of the legislation on the protection of children from domestic violence and abuse, and about the failure of the reforms to give children an effective voice in proceedings.

The policy debates in Australia stimulated an active research agenda, and a major evaluation was undertaken of one of the key elements of the reforms, the establishment of Children's Contact Services (CCSs), which aim to support families in conflict by offering assisted handovers (enabling parents to exchange children without coming face to face with each other) and supervised contact (enabling children to be with their contact parents under the supervision of service staff). The services are seen as the courts' way of responding in the short term to pressure from fathers for more contact in risky cases. However, Grania Sheehan and colleagues John Dewar and Rachel Carson from Griffith University, Brisbane, in chapter nine describe how families who enter the system tend to stay there for long periods of time, and how this has made it difficult for the service to deal with the growing number of cases.

In chapter ten, Professors Belinda Fehlberg of Melbourne Law Faculty and Rosemary Hunter formerly at Brisbane, now at the University of Kent, present data on the referral process into the service in Victoria and Queensland, describing the propensity of the courts to make interim orders, and the anxieties expressed about the ability of services to protect children at risk of violence or abuse.

The book closes, in chapter eleven by Joan Hunt from Oxford, with an overview of current forms of intervention in litigated contact disputes throughout the world. The picture she presents is surprisingly consistent across jurisdictions, in that only a small proportion, around one in ten, of parents have an ongoing problem, but these parents are highly conflicted and difficult to help. Pressure to reach an agreement at the door of the court can certainly lead to agreement and more contact (see Trinder, chapter five) but such an agreement does not necessarily lead to a reduction in stress for the children. Education in post-separation parenting, as originally developed in the UK and Canada, has been enthusiastically received, but rarely systematically evaluated. Services for higher conflict families, such as the Australian Contact Orders Pilot, was accepted by the Government after an ambitious but not unproblematic evaluation programme. Therapeutic mediation in Alameda County, California, has aroused great interest, but again lacks independent evaluation. Compliance programmes to support contact have also been widely attempted, but seldom effectively evaluated.

This may appear to be a dispiriting note on which to end a volume which brings together the existing evidence on whether contact matters, why it is so difficult, and what might be done to help. But Joan Hunt reminds us that although those developing new ideas and services do not always achieve independent review and evaluation, nevertheless there are many and varied ideas waiting to be tried and tested. It is hard to avoid the conclusion that parenting is difficult. Parenting after separation in co-operation with someone you are no longer close to is even more difficult. But children need as much 'good' parenting as they can get.

REFERENCES

Amato, P and Galbraith, J (1999) 'Non resident Fathers and Children's Well-being; a Meta Analysis 61(3) *Journal of Marriage and the Family*.

Attwood, C et al (2003) *2001 Home Office Citizenships Survey; People, Families and Communities* (London, Home Office).

Bastard, B and Cardia Voneche, L (2005) 'Can Co-parenting be Enforced? Family Law Reform and Family Life in France' in M Maclean (ed) *Family Law and Family Values* (Oxford, Hart Publishing).

Gould, J and Stahl, P (2001) 'Never Paint by the Numbers *Family Court Review* October 2001.

HM Government (2005) *Parental Separation; Children's Needs and Parents' Responsibilities: Next Steps* Cm 6452 (London, The Stationery Office).

Hunt, J (2004) 'Child Contact with Non-resident Parents' *Family Policy Briefing 3*, (Oxford, DSPSW).

Hunt, J (2005) 'International Review of Interventions to Support Parents in Conflicted Contact' *Family Policy Briefing 4* (Oxford, DSPSW).

Kelly, J and Lamb, M (2000) 'Using Child Development Research to Make Appropriate Custody and Access Decisions for Young Children' 38 (3) *Family Court Review* July 2000.

Pryor, J and Rodgers, B (2001) *Children in Changing Families* (Oxford, Blackwell).

Rhoades, H and Boyd, S (2004) 'Reforming Custody Laws; a Comparative Study 18 (2) *International Journal of Law Family and Policy*.

Smith, M et al (2001) *A Study of Step Parents and Step Parenting* (London, Thomas Coram Research Unit).

House of Representatives Standing Committee on Family and Community Affairs, *Every Picture Tells a Story: A Report on the Inquiry into Child Custody Arrangements in the Event of Family Separation* (Australian Government Publishing Service, Canberra, 2003).

Part 1

The Changing Landscape of Relationships

1

Improving the Quality of Parent–child Contact in Separating Families

MICHAEL E LAMB

INTRODUCTION

S OCIAL SCIENTISTS IN general and psychologists in particular, largely agree that parent–child relationships play a crucial role in shaping children's development and adjustment. As a result, considerable efforts have been made to examine the developmental course of these relationships, the features ensuring that some relationships have more positive effects on children's development than others, and the effects of separations and relationship disruptions on children's subsequent adjustment. My goal in this chapter is to briefly summarise what we know, citing the secondary rather than primary literature for the most part in order to minimise the length and density of the text. I begin by discussing the development of infant– and child–parent relationships, and the factors that affect the strength and quality of these relationships. I then turn to research concerned with the effects of divorce on children, with special focus on the ways in which harmful effects can usually be minimised by promoting the maintenance of children's relationships with both of their divorcing parents. Many of these issues have been discussed in some detail elsewhere, and readers may want to consult these articles for fuller coverage (eg Kelly and Lamb, 2000, 2003; Lamb, 2002a, 2002b; Lamb and Lewis, 2005; Trinder and Lamb, 2005).

THE DEVELOPMENT OF PARENT–CHILD RELATIONSHIPS

As described by Bowlby (1969), and largely confirmed by subsequent research (for detailed review, see Thompson, in press), infant–parent attachments pass through four broad developmental phases, during the first three of which infants learn to discriminate among adult carers and gradually develop emotional attachments to them.

In the first two months (phase 1), infants indiscriminately accept care from any carer and use a repertoire of innate signals, including crying and smiling, to bring and keep potential carers close to them. The relief of distress from hunger or pain and the growing interest in and response to social signals from adults are the building blocks for more discriminating attachment processes but frequent interaction is needed in order to continue the process of attachment formation because infants at this age have very primitive memories and cognitive abilities.

Around 2–7 months of age (phase 2), infants begin to recognise their parents and other carers and prefer interaction with them. They also begin to anticipate carers' responses to their signals although they do not yet understand that people (including carers) continue to exist when they are not present. Infants of this age initiate and enjoy social interactions and start to show signs of 'attachment in the making'. Infants in this phase do not typically protest separations from their parents, but require frequent contact with their parents for attachment formation to continue. Importantly, research has shown that fathers are as competent to care for their infants and toddlers as mothers, given opportunity and experience (Lamb, 1997, 2002a; Parke, 1996).

In the third phase of attachment development (between 7 and 24 months), attachments become increasingly apparent, as infants seek to be near and to interact with preferred carers, by whom they are more easily soothed than by strangers. Contrary to Bowlby's initial speculation and widespread 'common sense', there is considerable evidence that most infants in two parent families form attachments to both parents at about the same age, around 6–7 months (see Lamb, 2002a, for a review) even though fathers typically spend less time with their infants than mothers do (Pleck and Masciadrelli, 2004). This indicates that, although a threshold level of interaction is crucial for attachments to form, time spent interacting is not the only critical dimension. Infants begin to protest when separated from their primary attachment figures around 6–7 months of age, react warily to strangers, and, in a rudimentary way, start to recognise that parents continue to exist even when they are not present. Over the ensuing months, infants and toddlers become able to tolerate longer separations from their parents or attachment figures, although such separations may remain stressful. Most infants come to 'prefer' the parents who take primary responsibility for their care (typically their mothers), but this does not mean that relationships with their less-involved parents are unimportant. In fact, many toddlers and preschoolers seem to 'prefer' their 'traditional' fathers, especially in emotionally undemanding situations (Lamb, 2002a). There is no evidence that the amounts of time infants spend with their two parents affect the security of either attachment relationship although they do affect the relative formative importance of the two relationships. Nonetheless, both relationships remain psychologically important despite disparities in the two parents' levels of participation in child care.

According to attachment theorists, infants form attachments to those who have been available regularly and have responded to their signals and needs (Lamb, Thompson, Gardner and Charnov, 1985). All carers are not equivalently sensitive, of course, and individual differences in responsiveness affect the quality or security of the attachment relationships that form. The quality of both maternal and paternal behaviour is reliably associated with the security of infant–parent attachment (DeWolff and Van IJzendoorn, 1997; Van IJzendoorn and DeWolff, 1997). The association between the quality of paternal behaviour and the quality of infant–father attachment appears to be weaker than the parallel association between maternal behaviour and the security of infant–mother attachment but the quality of both mother–child and father–child interaction, however, remains the most reliable predictor of individual differences in psychological, social, and cognitive adjustment in infancy, as well as in later childhood (Lamb and Lewis, 2005; Thompson, in press).

According to Yarrow (1963; Yarrow and Goodwin, 1973), separation responses become increasingly intense as attachments to parents and other important carers strengthen between 6 and 24 months. Most infants early on demonstrate a preference for those individuals who provide most of their care and are more likely to seek out their preferred parents for comfort when distressed (see Lamb, 2002a, for a review). Non-preferred parents remain emotionally important, however, and are sought out for other social and emotional needs, and when primary carers are not available, for comfort. Preference for primary carers diminishes with age and often disappears by 18 months of age (Lamb, 2002a). Although infants and toddlers may resist transitions between parents in the second year, just as they sometimes protest (even more strongly) daily transitions to out-of-home care providers, they generally comfort quite quickly once the transition is accomplished. This is particularly likely when both parents have the opportunity to engage in normal parenting activities (feeding, playing, soothing, putting to bed, etc) while attachments are being established and consolidated.

Infants and toddlers need regular interaction with their 'attachment figures' in order to foster, maintain, and strengthen their relationships (Lamb, Bornstein and Teti, 2002; Thompson, in press). This means that young children need to interact with both parents in a variety of contexts (feeding, playing, soothing, putting to bed, etc) to ensure that the relationships are consolidated and strengthened. In the absence of such opportunities for regular interaction across a broad range of contexts, infant–parent relationships may weaken rather than grow stronger. When toddlers are separated for as little as a few days from all of their attachment figures (for example, both parents) simultaneously, intense distress and disturbances that persist for six months after reunion have been reported (Bowlby, 1973; Heinicke, 1956; Heinicke and Westheimer, 1966; Robertson and Robertson, 1971). Reactions are muted, but not eliminated, when children are cared for by other attachment figures or sensitive substitute carers during the separation (Robertson and Robertson, 1971). Extended separations from either parent with whom the child has formed a meaningful attachment are thus undesirable because they unduly stress developing attachment relationships (Bowlby, 1973). The loss or attenuation of important attachment relationships may cause depression and anxiety, particularly in the first two years, when children lack the cognitive and communication skills that would enable them to cope with loss. The absence of regular contact slowly erodes relationships, such that, over time, parents who do not interact regularly with their infants effectively become strangers.

In the final phase of attachment formation, which begins around age two, toddlers better understand why parents come and go, and can enter with their parents into some joint planning around daily activities (Greenberg, Cicchetti and Cummings, 1990; Thompson, in press). The increased cognitive and language abilities of 2–3 year-olds enable them to tolerate longer separations from their parents without undue stress. However, their very primitive sense of time prevents them from conceptualising much beyond today and tomorrow, inhibiting their ability to understand and cope with lengthy separations of several weeks or months.

Relationships with parents continue to play a crucial role in shaping children's social, emotional, personal and cognitive development into middle childhood and adolescence (Lamb and Lewis, 2005). Indeed, the quality of both mother–child and father–child interaction remain the most reliable correlates of individual differences in psychological, social, and cognitive adjustment in infancy, as well as in later childhood (Lamb and Lewis, 2005; Thompson, in press). Not surprisingly, therefore, children in both two-parent and single-parent families appear better adjusted when they enjoy warm positive relationships with two actively involved parents (Amato and Gilbreth, 1999; Hetherington, 1999; Lamb, 1999, 2002b; Thompson and Laible, 1999). Children are better off with insecure attachments than without attachment relationships, because these enduring ties play essential formative roles in later social and emotional functioning. There is also a substantial literature documenting the adverse effects of disrupted parent–child relationships on children's development and adjustment, with a linear relationship between age of separation and later attachment quality in adolescents. The weakest attachments to parents are reported by those whose parents separated in the first five years of their lives (Woodward, Fergusson and Belsky, 2000).

THE EFFECTS OF PARENTAL SEPARATION OR DIVORCE

Researchers have clearly demonstrated that, on average, children benefit from being raised in two biological or adoptive parent families rather than separated, divorced, or never married single parent households (Amato, 2000; Aquilino, 1996; Clarke-Stewart, Vandell, McCartney, Owen and Booth, 2000; Hetherington, 1999; Hetherington and Kelly, 2002; McLanahan, 1999; McLanahan and Sandefur, 1994; McLanahan and Teitler, 1999; Simons and Associates, 1996; Simons, Lin, Gordon, Conger and Lorenz, 1999), although within groups there is considerable variability, and the differences between groups are relatively small. Indeed, although children growing up in fatherless families are on average, disadvantaged relative to peers growing up in two-parent families with respect to psychosocial adjustment, behaviour and achievement at school, educational attainment, employment trajectories, income generation, involvement in antisocial and even criminal behaviour, and the ability to establish and maintain intimate relationships, the majority of children with divorced parents enjoy average or better social and emotional adjustment as young adults (Booth and Amato, 2001; Hetherington and Kelly, 2002; Kelly and Emery, 2003). Only a minority of children in single-parent families are maladjusted; the majority evince no psychopathology or behavioural symptoms, although they are likely to experience psychic pain for at least some time (Emery, 1998; Hetherington and Kelly, 2002).

Such individual differences force us to identify more precisely both the ways in which divorce/single parenthood may affect children's lives and the factors that might account for individual differences in children's adjustment following their parents' separation.

Four interrelated factors appear to be especially significant. Typically, first, single parenthood is associated with a variety of social and financial stresses with which custodial parents must cope, largely on their own. Single parent families are more economically stressed than two parent families, and economic stresses or poverty appear to account (statistically speaking) for many effects of single parenthood (Hetherington and Kelly, 2002; McLanahan, 1999).

Secondly, because single mothers need to work more extensively outside the home than married or partnered mothers, parents spend less time with children in single-parent families and the levels of supervision and guidance are lower and less reliable than in two-parent families (Hetherington and Kelly, 2002; McLanahan, 1999). Reductions in the level and quality of parental stimulation and attention may affect achievement, compliance, and social skills while diminished supervision makes antisocial behaviour and misbehaviour more likely (Hetherington and Kelly, 2002).

Thirdly, conflict between the parents commonly precedes, emerges or increases during the separation and divorce processes, and often continues beyond them. Inter-parent conflict is an important correlate of filial maladjustment just as marital harmony, its conceptual inverse, appears to be a reliable correlate of adjustment (Cummings et al, 2004; Johnston, 1994; Kelly, 2000). The adversarial legal system tends to promote conflict around the time of divorce although both pre-divorce and post-divorce conflict can be harmful to children and Kelly (2000) has argued persuasively that some of the 'effects of divorce' are better viewed as the effects of pre-separation marital conflict. Anger-based marital conflict is associated with filial aggression and externalising behaviour problems (Jenkins, 2000), perhaps because such parents and children have similar difficulty regulating negative affect (Katz and Gottman, 1993).

Fourthly, divorce commonly disrupts one of the child's most important and enduring relationships, that with the father. As Amato (1993; Amato and Gilbreth, 1999) has shown with particular clarity, however, the bivariate associations between father absence and children's adjustment are much weaker than one might expect. Indeed, Amato and Gilbreth's (1999) meta-analysis revealed no significant association between the frequency of father–child contact and child outcomes, largely because of the great diversity in the types of 'father-present' relationships. We might predict that contacts with abusive, incompetent, or disinterested fathers are likely to have much different effects than relationships with devoted, committed, and sensitive fathers. As expected, Amato and Gilbreth (1999) found that children's well-being was significantly enhanced when their relationships with non-residential fathers were positive and when the non-residential fathers engaged in 'active parenting'. (Positive relationships with custodial mothers were also beneficial, of course.) Dunn, Cheng, O'Connor and Bridges (2004), Simons and Associates (1996), Hetherington, Bridges and Insabella (1998) and Clarke-Stewart and Hayward (1996) likewise reported that children benefited when their non-resident fathers were actively involved in routine everyday activities. Similarly, higher levels of paternal involvement in their children's schools were associated with better grades, better adjustment, fewer suspensions, and lower dropout rates than were lower levels of involvement (Nord, Brimhall and West, 1997). Another meta-analysis indicated that, on multiple measures of emotional and behavioural adjustment and academic achievement, children in joint custody were better adjusted than children in sole custody arrangements, and were in fact as well adjusted as children whose parents remained married (Bauserman, 2002). The clear implication is that active paternal involvement, not simply the number or length of meetings between fathers and children, predicts child adjustment. This suggests that post-divorce arrangements should specifically seek to maximise positive and meaningful paternal involvement rather than simply allow minimal levels of visitation. As in non-divorced families, in other words, the quality of continued relationships with the parents–both parents–is crucial (Kelly and Lamb, 2000).

Stated differently and succinctly, the better (richer, deeper, and more secure) the parent–child relationships, the better the children's adjustment, whether or not the parents live together (Lamb, 2002a, 2002b).

Overall then, a number of factors help account for individual differences in the effects of divorce, and because they are intercorrelated, it is difficult to assess their relative importance. As shown later, however, thoughtful interventions can take advantage of these intercorrelations, initiating processes that minimise the adverse effects on children's adjustment by striving to promote healthy relationships between children and both of their parents, whether or not they live together.

MINIMISING THE ADVERSE EFFECTS OF DIVORCE

Even though children's best interests are usually served by keeping both parents actively involved in their children's lives, many custody and contact arrangements may not foster the maintenance of relationships between children and their non-resident parents. It is no less important to maintain both child–parent attachments when the divorced parents had 'traditional' roles before divorce than when they shared parenting responsibilities more equitably. Our focus should remain on the children's best interests, not 'fairness' to the parents.

Writing on behalf of 18 experts on the effects of divorce and contrasting parenting plans, Lamb, Sternberg and Thompson (1997: 400) observed a decade ago that:

> To maintain high-quality relationships with their children, parents need to have sufficiently extensive and regular interactions with them, but the amount of time involved is usually less important than the quality of the interaction that it fosters. Time distribution arrangements that ensure the involvement of both parents in important aspects of their children's everyday lives and routines ... are likely to keep nonresidential parents playing psychologically important and central roles in the lives of their children.

In order for parents to have a positive impact on their children's development, it is important that parents be integral parts of their children's lives. This remains especially important as children get older and greater portions of their time are occupied outside the family by virtue of friendships, extracurricular activities, sports, and the like. At all ages, it is important for parents to know teachers and friends, what's happening at school, how relationships with peers are going, what other activities are important or meaningful to the children, etc, and to be aware of daily ups-and-downs in their children's lives. It is hard to do this without regular and extensive first-hand involvement with their children in a variety of contexts, especially when children become less communicative as they enter adolescence.

As Kelly and Lamb (2000; Lamb and Kelly, 2001; Lamb, 2002b) reiterated, the ideal situation is one in which children with separated parents have opportunities to interact with both parents frequently in a variety of functional contexts (feeding, play, discipline, basic care, limit-setting, putting to bed etc). The evening and overnight periods (like extended days with naptimes) with non-residential parents are especially important psychologically for infants, toddlers and young children. They provide opportunities for crucial social interactions and nurturing activities, including bathing, soothing hurts and anxieties, bedtime rituals, comforting in the middle of the night, and the reassurance and security of snuggling in the morning that 1–2 hour long visits cannot provide. According to attachment theory, as noted earlier, these everyday activities promote and maintain trust and confidence in the parents, while deepening and strengthening child–parent attachments, and thus need to be encouraged when decisions about access and contact are made.

One implication is that even young children should spend overnight periods with both parents when both have been involved in their care prior to separation, even though neo-analysts have long counselled against this (Kelly and Lamb, 2000; Lamb and Kelly, 2001). As Warshak (2000) has pointed out, the prohibition of overnight 'visitation' has been justified by prejudices and beliefs rather than by any empirical evidence. When both parents have established significant attachments and both have been actively involved in the child's care, overnight 'visits' will consolidate attachments and child adjustment, not work against them. The results of recent research by Pruett and her colleagues (2005) show that regular overnight visits were associated with better adjustment on the part of toddlers and young children. Parents who have been actively involved before divorce but are then denied overnight access to their children are excluded from an important array of activities, and the strength or depth of their relationships suffer as a result.

Solomon and Biringen (2001) have challenged our conclusions regarding the beneficial effects of overnight visits for many young children, citing the results of a study by Solomon and George (1999a, 1999b). These researchers did not find that overnight visits with non-custodial fathers affected the security of infant–mother attachments, however, or that overnights were more problematic for pre-schoolers than for infants and pre-schoolers. In addition, many of the infants and toddlers they studied had never lived with their two parents and may thus not have formed attachments to their fathers before the overnight visits commenced; their situation is much different from that of infants and toddlers who have established attachments to two involved parents prior to separation/divorce. Different steps are needed when promoting the formation rather than the maintenance of attachments. Solomon and George (1999a: 27) also noted that some of the infants in their study had experienced extended and repeated separations from their fathers, which, as noted above, would have stressed these relationships further.

To minimise the deleterious impact of extended separations from either parent, furthermore, attachment theory tells us there should be more frequent transitions than would perhaps be desirable with older children (Kelly and Lamb, 2000). To be responsive to young children's psychological needs, in other words, the parenting schedules adopted for children under age two or three should actually involve more transitions, rather than fewer, to ensure the continuity of both relationships and to promote the children's security and comfort. From the third year of life, the ability to tolerate longer separations begins to increase, so that most toddlers can manage two consecutive overnights with each parent without stress. Although practical considerations (such as the parents' work schedules and the distances between their residences) must, of course, also be taken into account, decision makers and parents should do their utmost to ensure that arrangements address children's psychological needs as well as possible.

Interestingly, psychologists have long recognised the need to minimise the length of separations from attachment figures when devising parenting plans, but they have typically focused only on separations from mothers, thereby revealing their presumption that young children are not meaningfully attached to their fathers. To the extent that children are attached to both their parents, however, separations from both parents are stressful and at minimum generate psychic pain. As a result, parenting plans that allow children—especially very young children—to see their fathers 'every Wednesday evening and every other weekend' clearly fail to recognise the adverse consequences of weeklong separations from non-resident parents. It is little wonder that such arrangements lead to attenuation of the relationships between non-resident parents and their children. Instead, it is desirable to promote continued involvement by both parents, striving when necessary to increase the participation of those parents (typically fathers) whose limited prior involvement may initially make overnight contact inappropriate.

RESTRICTING CONTACT IN RESPONSE TO MARITAL CONFLICT

Of course, there are some cases in which the possible benefits of keeping both parents involved are outweighed by the costs of doing so. Conflict-filled or violent relationships between the parents are most likely to trigger such cost-benefit analyses because, as noted earlier, high conflict is reliably associated with poorer child outcomes following divorce (Johnston, 1994; Kelly, 2000; Maccoby and Mnookin, 1992) and exposure to family violence can have harmful effects on children's adjustment (Sternberg, Baradaran, Abbott, Lamb and Guterman, 2006; Wolfe, Crooks, Lee, McIntyre-Smith and Jaffe, 2003). Children in high conflict families who have frequent contact with their fathers are more poorly adjusted than those in low conflict families (Amato and Rezac, 1994; Hetherington, 1999; Johnston, 1994; Johnston, Kline and Tschann, 1989; Maccoby and Mnookin, 1992). Interparental conflict should thus be avoided wherever possible, but litigation-related conflict and conflict triggered by the high levels of stress around the time of divorce do not appear to have enduring consequences for children. As a result, their occurrence should not be used to justify restrictions on children's access to either of their parents. Maccoby and Mnookin (1992) further cautioned that minor or isolated instances of domestic violence should not affect decisions regarding custody and visitation. The high conflict found harmful by researchers such as Johnston (1994; Johnston and Roseby, 1997) typically involved repeated incidents of spousal violence and verbal aggression that continued after divorce at intense levels for extended periods of time, often in front of the children, between parents with substantial psychiatric problems and character disorders. As a result, Johnston has emphasised the importance of continued relationships with both parents except in those relatively uncommon circumstances in which intense, protracted conflict occurs and persists. According to Maccoby and Mnookin (1992), somewhere around a quarter of divorcing families experience high levels of conflict around the time of divorce, and perhaps 10 per cent of them may have conflict that is sufficiently severe and sufficiently intractable that it is probably not beneficial for the children concerned to have contact with their non-resident parents (see also Johnston, 1994).

Significant numbers of children have warm and supportive relationships with parents who have violent relationships with one another, so we must be careful when reports of parental conflict are allowed to influence decisions about parent–child contact (Holden, Geffner and Jouriles, 1998; Maccoby and Mnookin, 1992; Sternberg and Lamb, 1999). According to Appel and Holden (1998), 60 per cent of the children whose parents were violent with one another were not themselves victims of physical child abuse, suggesting that decision-makers need to assess the relationships with parents directly and not simply assume that children must have been abused because their parents were violent with one another. Unfortunately, however, mere allegations of conflict or even marital violence can be powerful tools in an adversarial system, frequently resulting in reduced levels of court-approved contacts between fathers and children (Sternberg, 1997). Disagreements about the occurrence, nature, and perpetrators of violence are quite common, furthermore, and do not always reveal self-serving biases (Braver and O'Connell, 1998; Sternberg, Lamb and Dawud-Noursi, 1998).

Research on the impact of post-divorce as opposed to pre-divorce conflict on children's adjustment has yielded mixed results. Some investigators have found that marital conflict is a more potent predictor of post-divorce adjustment than post-divorce conflict (Booth and Amato, 2001; Buehler,

Krishnakumar, Stone, Anthony, Pemberton, Gerard and Barber, 1998; King and Heard, 1999; Kline, Johnston and Tschann, 1991), whereas Hetherington (1999) found that post-divorce conflict had more adverse effects than did conflict in married families. Booth and Amato (2001) reported no association between the amount of post-divorce conflict and later adjustment in young adults. The varied findings may reflect the use of different measures, a failure to differentiate between types of conflict after divorce, parental styles of resolution, and/or variations in the extent to which children are directly exposed to anger and conflict. High conflict is more likely to be destructive post-divorce when parents use their children to express their anger, and are verbally and physically aggressive on the phone or in person. By contrast, when parents continue to have conflict, but encapsulate it and do not put their children in the middle, children appear unaffected (Buchanan et al, 1991; Hetherington, 1999).

In addition, most experts agree that conflict localised around the time of separation and divorce is of less concern than conflict that was and remains an intrinsic and unresolved part of the parents' relationship and continues after their divorce (Cummings et al, 2004; Cummings and O'Reilly, 1997). Similarly, conflict from which children are shielded also does not appear to affect adjustment (Hetherington, 1999) whereas conflict that includes physical violence in more pathogenic than high conflict without violence (Jouriles, Norwood, McDonald, Vincent and Mahoney, 1996; McNeal and Amato, 1998).

The quality of the relationships between non-residential parents and their children is also crucial when determining whether to sever or promote relationships between divorced parents and their children. Regardless of the levels of violence, there are many families in which non-resident fathers and children have sufficiently poor relationships—perhaps because of the fathers' psychopathology, substance abuse, or alcohol abuse—that 'maintenance' of interaction or involvement may not be of net benefit to the children, but we do not know how many relationships are like this. Unrepresentative data sets, such as those collected by Greif (1997) in the course of research designed to study fathers and mothers who lose contact with their children after divorce, suggest that perhaps 10–15 per cent of parents do not have either the commitment or individual capacities to establish and maintain supportive and enriching relationships with their children following divorce. Taken together, Johnston's and Greif's estimates suggest that, at most, 15–25 per cent (depending on how greatly the two groups of parents overlap) of the children whose parents divorce might not benefit from regular and extended contact with their non-resident parents. Stated differently, of course, this suggests that more than three-quarters of the children experiencing their parents' divorce could benefit from having and maintaining relationships with their non-resident parents. Instead of 'standard' parenting plans, therefore, individual circumstances should be examined to ensure that the arrangements made are sensitive to the parents' and children's strengths, schedules and needs.

Because conflict can have such powerful effects on children's adjustment, it is often worthwhile taking steps to minimise both the conflict and children's possible exposure to it. Many of the recent legal innovations in the UK have had this as their goal, but although many have face validity, few of these interventions have been evaluated to date (Trinder and Lamb, 2005). Experience in the US, where litigation is much more common and the tensions thus tend to be ratcheted higher, suggests a couple of strategies that appear to reduce opportunities for harmful conflict and exposure to it.

First, many jurisdictions and agencies have developed brief courses, like those being implemented in the UK, that explain the effects of divorce on children to parents and provide training regarding behaviours and strategies to minimise conflict and children's exposure to it. At least in the short term, these courses appear to be effective (eg Pedro-Carroll, Nakhnikian and Montes, 2001).

Secondly, professionals can make sure that individual 'parenting plans' are clear enough that there are fewer ambiguous issues that the parents can argue about. Orders that refer vaguely to 'liberal visitation' invite argument whereas a concrete agreement specifying when and where visits will take place and exactly how exchanges will occur limit these opportunities. Even in a legal culture like the UK's that emphasises 'private ordering', courts (and solicitors) should encourage couples to articulate their expectations in as much detail as possible.

Thirdly, because exchanges provide opportunities for discussion and argument, it may be worth ensuring that exchanges take place in neutral settings and at times that limit contact between the parents (eg mother drops children at school, from where father picks them up at the end of the day). Increasing numbers of cities and towns now have centres where children can be brought by one parent to reunite with the other without need for the parents to encounter one another directly. Such arrangements may be especially helpful when either the parents or children are fearful, and have been shown to increase the frequency of contact between nonresident parents and their children while reducing levels of conflict between the parents (Flory, Dunn, Berg-Weger and Milstead, 2001).

Fourthly, when there are sufficient resources (private or public), parenting co-ordinators can play an important role in keeping the lid on possible conflict and encouraging the parents to start making joint decisions in their children's interests.

Although the role was only invented within the last decade, parenting co-ordinators have become quite popular in a number of jurisdictions in the US and Canada. Groups in California, Oregon, and Colorado have had the most experience, although parent co-ordinators are being appointed increasingly in North Carolina, Massachusetts, the District of Columbia and Maryland (Baris, Coates, Duvall, Johnson and La Cross, 2001). In each case, the judiciary has been enthusiastic and other professionals involved with these families have indicated in surveys that parent co-ordinators can be very effective, especially when working with conflictful families (Coates et al, 2004). Jurisdictions with the most experience have revised and refined the role more precisely, so that recent analyses of the topic provide very detailed and thoughtful guidelines (eg AFCC Task Force on Parenting Coordination, 2003; Sullivan, 2004) although there has been little systematic research on the long-term effectiveness. In the short term, however, Johnston and her colleagues (unpublished) have reported dramatic decreases in the rates of litigation (court appearances) after parent co-ordinators were appointed. Several articles in a special issue of Family Courts Review (2001, volume 39, issue 3) on the most problematic post-divorce families make clear that parent co-ordinators are among the most important interventions available to smooth the post-separation and divorce transitions, and this point was underscored in the recent article by Coates and her colleagues (2004).

CONCLUSION

In all, basic research on early social development and descriptive research on the multifaceted correlates of divorce have together yielded a clearer understanding of the ways in which divorce affects children and of how the welfare of many children could be enhanced by changes in common practices. Most importantly, we know that children benefit from support-ive relationships with both of their parents, whether or not those parents live together. We also know that relationships are dynamic and are thus dependent on continued opportunities for interaction. In order to ensure that both adults become or remain parents to their children, post-divorce parenting plans need to encourage participation by both parents in as broad as possible an array of social contexts on a regular basis. Brief dinners and occasional weekend visits do not provide a broad enough or extensive enough basis for such relationships to be fostered, whereas weekday and weekend daytime and night time activities are important for children of all ages. In the absence of sufficiently broad and extensive interactions, many fathers drift out of their children's lives, placing their children at risk psychologically and materially. It is not clear exactly how much time is necessary to ensure that both parents stay involved in their children's lives; Braver and O'Connell (1998) have suggested that at least one-third of the non-school hours should be spent with the non-resident parent and most experts would agree that 15 per cent (every other weekend) is almost certainly insufficient.

To date, unfortunately, policy makers, judges, and solicitors have not been very attentive to the importance of promoting children's relation-ships with both of their parents. Representative statistics are not readily available, but there is general satisfaction in the UK with post-separation arrangements that ensure 'regular contact' without sufficient effort made to ensure that the contact is sufficient to ensure that children are able to maintain meaningful relationships with their non resident parents, who are overwhelmingly fathers. The default arrangements recommended by most solicitors typically involve 'every other weekend' visits, rather than arrangements that allow non-resident fathers to really be involved in their children's lives. Furthermore, reasoned discussion about the potential benefits of greater involvement by non-resident parents has been drowned out by poisonous rhetoric from groups and individuals mired in gendered concerns about fairness for parents rather than children's best interests.

REFERENCES

AFCC Task Force on Parenting Coordination (2003) Parenting coordination: implementation issues *Family Court Review* 41, 533–64.

Amato, PR (1993) 'Children's adjustment to divorce: Theories, hypotheses, and empirical support' *Journal of Marriage and the Family* 55, 23–38.

Amato, PR (2000) 'The consequences of divorce for adults and children' *Journal of Marriage and the Family* 62, 1269–87.

Amato, PR and Gilbreth, JG (1999) 'Non-resident fathers and children's well-being: A meta-analysis' *Journal of Marriage and the Family* 61, 557–73.

Amato, PR and Rezac, S (1994) 'Contact with residential parents, inter-parental conflict, and children's behavior' *Journal of Family Issues* 15, 191–207.

Appel, AE and Holden, GW (1998) 'The co-occurrence of spouse and physical child abuse: A review and appraisal' *Journal of Family Psychology* 12, 578–99.

Aquilino, WS (1996) 'The life course of children born to unmarried mothers: Childhood living arrangements and young adult outcomes' *Journal of Marriage and the Family* 58, 293–310.

Baris, MA, Coates, CA, Duvall, BB, Johnson, LT and La Cross, ER (2001) *Working with high conflict families of divorce: A guide for professionals* (New York, Jason Aronson).

Bauserman, R (2002) 'Child adjustment in joint-custody versus sole-custody arrangements: A meta-analytic review' *Journal of Family Psychology* 16, 91–102.

Booth, A and Amato, PR (2001) 'Parental predivorce relations and offspring post-divorce well-being' *Journal of Marriage and Family* 63, 197–212.

Bowlby, J (1969) *Attachment and loss: vol 1 Attachment* (New York, Basic Books).

Bowlby, J (1973) *Attachment and loss: vol 2 Separation: Anxiety and anger* (New York, Basic Books).

Braver, SL and O'Connell, E (1998) *Divorced dads: Shattering the myths* (New York, Tarcher, Putnam).

Buchanan, CM, Maccoby, EE and Dornbusch, SM (1991) 'Caught between parents: Adolescents' experience in divorced homes' *Child Development* 62, 1008–29.

Buehler, C, Krishnakumar, A, Stone, G, Anthony, C, Pemberton, S, Gerard, J and Barber, B (1998) 'Interparental conflict styles and youth problem behaviors: A two-sample replication study' *Journal of Marriage and the Family* 60, 119–34.

Clarke-Stewart, KA and Hayward, C (1996) 'Advantages of father custody and contact for the psychological well-being of school-age children' *Journal of Applied Developmental Psychology* 17, 239–70.

Clarke-Stewart, KA, Vandell, DL, McCartney, K, Owen, MT and Booth, C (2000) 'Effects of parental separation and divorce on very young children' *Journal of Family Psychology* 13, 304–26.

Coates, CA, Deutsch, R, Starnes, H, Sullivan, MJ and Sydlik, B (2004) 'Parenting coordination for high-conflict families' *Family Court Review* 42, 246–62.

Cummings, EM, Goeke-Morey, MC and Raymond, J (2004) 'Fathers in family-context: Effects of marital quality and marital conflict' in ME Lamb (ed), *The Role of the Father in Child Development* 4th edn (Hoboken, NJ, Wiley) 196–221.

Cummings, EM and O'Reilly, AW (1997) 'Fathers in family context: Effects of marital quality on child adjustment' in ME Lamb (ed), *The Role of the Father in Child Development* 3rd edn (New York, Wiley) 49–65.

DeWolff, MS and van IJzendoorn, MH (1997) 'Sensitivity and attachment: A meta-analysis on parental antecedents of infant attachment' *Child Development* 68, 571–91.

Dunn, J, Cheng, H, O'Connor, TG and Bridges, L (2004) 'Children's perspectives on their relationships with their non-resident fathers: influences, outcomes and implications' *Journal of Child Psychology and Psychiatry* 45, 553–66.

Emery, RE (1998) *Marriage, Divorce, and Children's Adjustment* 2nd edn (Thousand Oaks, Sage).

Flory, BE, Dunn, J, Berg-Weger, M and Milstead, M (2001) 'An exploratory study of supervised access and custody exchange services' *Family Court Review*, 39, 469–82.

Greenberg, MT, Cicchetti, D and Cummings, EM (eds) (1990) *Attachment in the Preschool Years: Theory, Research, and Intervention* (Chicago, University of Chicago Press).

Greif, G (1997) *Out of Touch: When Parents and Children lose Contact after Divorce* (New York, Oxford University Press).

Heinicke, C (1956) 'Some effects of separating two-year-old children from their parents: A comparative study' *Human Relations* 9, 105–76.

Heinicke, C and Westheimer, I (1966) *Brief Separations* (New York, International Universities Press).

Hetherington, EM (1999) 'Should we stay together for the sake of the children?' in EM Hetherington (ed), *Coping with Divorce, Single Parenting, and Remarriage* . (Mahwah, NJ, Erlbaum) 93–116.

Hetherington, EM, Bridges, M and Insabella, GM (1998) 'What matters? What does not?–Five perspectives on the association between marital transitions and children's adjustment' *American Psychologist* 53, 167–84.

Hetherington, EM and Kelly, J (2002) *For Better or for Worse: Divorce Reconsidered* (New York, Norton).

Holden, GW, Geffner, R and Jouriles, EW (eds) (1998) *Children Exposed to Family Violence* (Washington, DC American Psychological Association).

Jenkins, JM (2000) 'Marital conflict and children's emotions: The development of an anger organization' *Journal of Marriage and the Family* 62, 723–36.

Johnston, JR (1994) 'High-conflict Divorce' *The Future of Children* 4, 165–82.

Johnston, JR, Kline, M and Tschann, J (1989) 'Ongoing post-divorce conflict in families contesting custody: Effects on children of joint custody and frequent access' *American Journal of Orthopsychiatry* 59, 576–92.

Johnston, JR and Roseby, V (1997) *In the Name of the Child: A Developmental Approach to Understanding and Helping Children of Conflict and Violent Divorce* (New York, Free Press).

Jouriles, EN, McDonald, R, Norwood, W, Vincent, JP and Mahoney, A (1996) 'Physical violence and other forms of interpersonal aggression: Links with children's behavior problems' *Journal of Family Psychology* 10, 223–34.

Katz, LF and Gottman, JM (1993) 'Patterns of marital conflict predict children's internalizing and externalizing behaviors' *Developmental Psychology* 29, 940–50.

Kelly, JB (2000) 'Children's adjustment in conflicted marriage and divorce: A decade review of research' *Journal of the American Academy of Child Psychiatry* 39, 963–73.

Kelly, JB and Emery, RE (2003) 'Children's adjustment following divorce: Risk and resilience perspectives' *Family Relations* 52, 352–62.

Kelly, JB and Lamb, ME (2000) 'Using child development research to make appropriate custody and access decisions for young children' *Family and Conciliation Courts Review* 38, 297–311.

Kelly, JB and Lamb, ME (2003) 'Developmental issues in relocation cases involving young children: When, whether, and how?' *Journal of Family Research* 17, 193–205.

King, V and Heard, HE (1999) 'Nonresident father visitation, parental conflict, and mother's satisfaction: What's best for child well-being?' *Journal of Marriage and the Family* 61, 385–96.

Kline, M, Johnston, J and Tschann, J (1990) 'The long shadow of marital conflict: A model of children's postdivorce adjustment' *Journal of Marriage and the Family* 53, 297–309.

Lamb, ME (1997) 'The development of father-infant relationships' in ME Lamb (ed), The Role of the Father in Child Development 3rd edn (New York, Wiley) 104–20, 332–42.

Lamb, ME (1999) 'Non-custodial fathers and their impact on the children of divorce' in RA Thompson and PR Amato (eds), The Post-divorce Family: Research and Policy Issues (Thousand Oaks, CA, Sage) 105–25.

Lamb, ME (2002a) 'Infant-father attachments and their impact on child Development' in CS Tamis-LeMonda and N Cabrera (eds), *Handbook of Father Involvement: Multidisciplinary Perspectives* (Mahwah, NJ, Erlbaum) 93–117.

Lamb, ME (2002b) 'Placing children's interests first: Developmentally appropriate parenting plans' *The Virginia Journal of Social Policy and the Law* 10, 98–119.

Lamb, ME, Bornstein, MH and Teti, DM (2002) *Development in Infancy* 4th edn (Mahwah, NJ, Erlbaum).

Lamb, ME and Kelly, JB (2001) 'Using the empirical literature to guide the development of parenting plans for young children: A rejoinder to Solomon and Biringen' *Family Courts Review* 39, 365–71.

Lamb, ME and Lewis, C (2004) 'The development and significance of father-child relationships in two-parent families' in ME Lamb (ed), *The Role of the Father in Child Development* 4th edn (Hoboken, NJ, John Wiley & Sons) 272–306.

Lamb, ME and Lewis, C (2005) 'The role of parent-child relationships in child Development' in MH Bornstein and ME Lamb (eds), *Developmental Science: An Advanced Textbook* 5th edn (Mahwah, NJ, Erlbaum) 429–68.

Lamb, ME, Sternberg, KJ and Thompson, RA (1997) 'The effects of divorce and custody arrangements on children's behavior, development, and adjustment' *Family and Conciliation Courts Review* 35, 393–404.

Lamb, ME, Thompson, RA, Gardner, WP and Charnov, EL (1985) *Infant-mother Attachment* (Hillsdale, NJ, Erlbaum).

Maccoby, EE and Mnookin, RH (1992) *Dividing the Child: Social and Legal Dilemmas of Custody* (Cambridge, MA, Harvard University Press).

McLanahan, SS (1999) 'Father absence and the welfare of children' in EM Hetherington (ed), *Coping with Divorce, Single Parenting, and Remarriage* (Mahwah, NJ, Erlbaum) 117–46.

McLanahan, SS and Sandefur, G (1994) *Growing up with a Single Parent: what Hurts, what Helps* (Cambridge, MA, Harvard University Press).

McLanahan, SS and Teitler, J (1999) 'The consequences of father absence' in ME Lamb (ed), *Parenting and Child Development in 'Nontraditional' Families* (Mahwah, NJ, Erlbaum) 83–102.

Nord, C, Brimhall, D and West, J (1997) 'Fathers' involvement in their children's schools' National Center for Education Statistics, US Department of Education, Washington, DC 20208-5574.

Parke, R (1996) *Fatherhood* (Cambridge, MA, Harvard University Press).

McNeal, C and Amato, PR (1998) 'Parents' marital violence: Long-term consequences for children' *Journal of Family Issues* 19, 123–39.

Pedro-Carroll, J, Nakhnikian, E and Montes, G (2001) 'Assisting children through transition: Helping parents protect their children from the toxic effects of ongoing conflict in the aftermath of divorce' *Family Court Review* 39, 377–92.

Pleck, JH and Masciadrelli, B (2004) 'Paternal involvement: Levels, sources, and consequences' in ME Lamb (ed), *The Role of the Father in Child Development* 4th edn (Hoboken, NJ, Wiley) 222–71.

Pruett, MK, Insabella, GM and Gustafson, K (2005) 'The Collaborative Divorce Project: A court-based intervention for separating parents with young children' *Family Court Review* 43, 38–51.

Robertson, J and Robertson, J (1971) 'Young children in brief separation: A fresh look' *Psychoanalytic Study of the Child* 26, 264–315.

Simons, RL and Associates (1996) *Understanding Differences between Divorced and Intact Families* (Thousand Oaks, CA, Sage Publications).

Simons, RL, Lin, KH, Gordon, LC, Conger, RD and Lorenz, FO (1999) 'Explaining the higher incidence of adjustment problems among children of divorce compared with those in two-parent families' *Journal of Marriage and the Family* 61, 1020–33.

Solomon, J and Biringen, Z (2001) 'Another look at the developmental research: Commentary on Kelly and Lamb's "Using child development research to make appropriate custody and access decisions for young children"' *Family Courts Review* 39, 355–64.

Solomon, J and George, C (1999a) 'The development of attachment in separated and divorced families: Effects of overnight visitation, parent, and couple variables' *Attachment and Human Development* 1, 2–33.

Solomon, J and George, C (1999b) 'The effects of overnight visitation in divorced and separated families: A longitudinal follow-up' in J Solomon and C George (eds), *Attachment Disorganization* (New York, Guilford) 243–64.

Sternberg, KJ (1997) 'Fathers, the missing parents in research on family violence' in ME Lamb (ed), The Role of the Father in Child Development 3rd edn (New York, Wiley) 284–308, 392–97.

Sternberg, KJ, Baradaran, LP, Abbott, CB, Lamb, ME and Guterman, E (2006) 'Type of violence, age, and gender differences in the effects of family violence on children's behavior problems: A mega-analysis' *Developmental Review* 26, 89–112.

Sternberg, KJ and Lamb, ME (1999) 'Violent families' in ME Lamb (ed), *Parenting and Child Development in 'Nontraditional' Families* (Mahwah, NJ, Erlbaum) 305–25.

Sternberg, KJ, Lamb, ME and Dawud-Noursi, S (1998) 'Understanding domestic violence and its effects: Making sense of divergent reports and perspectives' in GW Holden, R Geffner and EW Jouriles (eds), *Children Exposed to Family Violence* (Washington, DC, American Psychological Association) 121–56.

Sullivan, MJ (2004) 'Ethical, legal, and professional practice issues involved in acting as a psychologist parent coordinator in child custody cases' *Family Court Review* 42, 576.

Thompson, RA (in press) 'Early sociopersonality development' in W Damon, RA Lerner and N Eisenberg (eds), *Handbook of Child Development vol 3. Social, emotional, and personality development* 6th edn (Hoboken, NJ, Wiley).

Thompson, RA and Laible, DJ (1999) 'Noncustodial parents' in ME Lamb (ed), *Parenting and Child Development in 'Nontraditional' Families* (Mahwah, NJ, Erlbaum) 103–23.

Trinder, L and Lamb, ME (2005) 'Measuring up? The relationship between correlates of children's adjustment and both family law and policy in England' *Louisiana Law Review* 65, 1509–37.

Van lJzendoorn, MH and DeWolff, MS (1997) 'In search of the absent father—Meta-analyses of infant-father attachment: A rejoinder to our discussants' *Child Development* 68, 604–09.

Warshak, RA (2000) 'Blanket restrictions: Overnight contact between parents and young children' *Family and Conciliation Courts Review* 38, 422–45.

Woodward, L, Fergusson, D and Belsky, J (2000) 'Timing of parental separation and attachment to parents in adolescence: Results of a prospective study from birth to age 16' *Journal of Marriage and the Family* 62, 162–74.

Wolfe, DA, Crooks, CV, Lee, V, McIntyre-Smith, A and Jaffe, PG (2003) 'The effects of children's exposure to domestic violence: A meta-analysis and critique' *Clinical Child and Family Psychology Review* 6, 171–87.

Yarrow, LJ (1963) 'Research in dimensions of early maternal care' *Merrill-Palmer Quarterly* 9, 101–14.

Yarrow, LJ and Goodwin, M (1973) 'The immediate impact of separation: Reactions of infants to a change in mother figures' in LJ Stone, HT Smith and LB Murphy (eds), *The Competent Infant* (New York, Basic Books) 1032–40.

2

Why Some Children see their Father and Others do not; Questions Arising from a Pilot Study

LAURA CARDIA-VONÈCHE AND BENOIT BASTARD

INTRODUCTION

THE RELATIONSHIP CHILDREN have with the parent they do not live with after a separation or a divorce has recently aroused much interest and debate. In countries where statistics are available, the data suggests that there may be a substantial risk that the bond between a child and a non-resident parent—mainly the father—will fade after the parents' separation. In France, Villeneuve-Gokalp's[1] study shows that a third of such children (32 per cent) have no contact with their fathers when they do not share the same home. Among her sample, 42 per cent see their fathers regularly and the remaining 28 per cent irregularly. In recent years the figures have not changed except that those children who see their fathers regularly tend to see them more than they would have done in the past, leading one to believe that fathers today are more involved in rearing and educating their offspring.

How can this diversity of situations and the constant nature of the data be explained when there is increasing consensus that children should be able to maintain ties[2] with both parents, and co-parenthood should be combined with respect for children's rights?

One explanation often proposed suggests that the child–parent bond after a divorce or separation depends on the quality of the parents' relationship. If conflict persists after divorce, the chances a child will have of going freely from one parent to another will diminish and perhaps disappear completely. However, a common understanding concerning the children will allow both parents to have free access to their offspring, and to accept the responsibility for their upbringing in a shared way. Another

---

[1] C Villeneuve-Gokalp, 'La double famille des enfants de parents séparés' (1999) *Population* 1, 9–36.
[2] Convention on the Rights of the Child, UNO Assembly resolution 44/25 of 20 November 1989.

explanation has also been put forward according to which the possibility of maintaining close bonds after separation depends on the previous emotional investment of the 'non-resident' parents—fathers, in nearly 90 per cent of the situations—towards their children during the union. From this point of view, a father who was very involved in domestic and educational tasks is more likely to preserve a close tie with his children than one who remained distant and was not committed. Indeed how can one imagine that the latter could discover fatherhood at the time of separation?

Such explanations are certainly enlightening, but do they account for the reality? In this chapter, we propose another viewpoint according to which the previous assumptions can be related to a more general interpretation associated with the characteristics of the way a family functions. Indeed, we would like to underline the fact that the observations made on the continuity or the rupture of bonds in a post-divorce situation can be linked to the way in which the couples organised their relationship, and the sharing of domestic and parental roles throughout their union. To support this viewpoint, we will use the results of an exploratory investigation into family relationships after separation which began in 2000 and was carried out over a three-year period. This investigation concerns exclusively single-parent families headed by a woman, of whom there were 29 in the study. Qualitative interviews were carried out some years ago, offering the opportunity to gather data on family life before and after separation, focusing on child rearing and the specific role each parent carried out held with respect to this task.[3] The different cases encountered will be presented below. Later we will return to the analysis of the parameters that determine whether a child sees his father or not.

WHAT ARE FATHER–CHILD RELATIONSHIPS MADE UP OF AFTER SEPARATION?

The data assembled presents diverse situations which illustrate the general trends mentioned above: certain children see their fathers regularly, while others only see them occasionally, or never.

Children who see their Fathers Regularly

In one kind of situation (n = 6), the children see their father regularly. In this group, both parents have constantly been concerned about limiting their conflict so that their children would be kept out of it. They decided

[3] B Bastard, L Cardia-Vonèche, M-A Mazoyer (with S Ruspoli and S Voiturin), *Monoparentalité et santé. Les conséquences de la rupture familiale sur la prise en charge de la santé dans la famille* (Paris, CSO, 1999). See also: B Bastard, L Cardia-Vonèche, 'Ruptures conjugales et prise en charge de la santé dans la famille' (**1999**) *Cahiers de démographie et de sociologie médicales* no 2–3, 231–51.

together, and to their mutual satisfaction, on how the children could go from one parent's home to the other. In consequence they are organised from a practical point of view, trying to live close enough to each other so that their offspring can attend one school and keep their circle of friends. Moreover, some of these parents share some activities both together with their children, such as birthdays or religious holidays. More generally, these parents are particularly concerned about their children's psychological well-being. This can be seen in their attentiveness to their children's difficulties and unhappiness resulting from the separation, and their appeals to specialists for help.

Whether the separation is the consequence of a common decision or has taken place on the request of one of the spouses, the relationship between the children and the parent with whom they do not reside persists and includes both extended families. In certain cases, the fact that the father takes care of the children while they are in his house often, according to the mothers, represents greater personal investment than when the parents were together.

The example of Blandine illustrates this well. In this case, the split brought harmony back to the ex-spouses. It allowed them to become 'good friends'. The father is very close to his children and Blandine is on good terms with him. Blandine said:

> He's a person who is very close to his children, and I'm on good terms with him. We sometimes have lunch together just for the pleasure of being together. I still see his family who are still very attached to my children. No conflicts about money or drama ... I assume that the more my children see their father, the happier they will be. There are no problems. For the kids, we both wanted to continue being their parents.

Blandine believes that, since their separation, the father spends more time with the children than before. He is better organised and every fortnight he has them over for the entire weekend:

> The time they spend together is of a much better quality than before, so much so that our older child has discovered his dad since our break-up.

Family holidays are often spent together, and some vacation periods too. The fact that the father has a new partner has not upset relations which are described as "courteous".

Discontinuous Parent–child Relationships

The situation is completely different in other cases, comprising half of our sample (n = 17). In these situations the children see their fathers irregularly. Some of them regret it and are much affected by it, according to the mothers, while others are very angry with their fathers and are very reluctant to retain any bond with them. In our presentation below we will differentiate between cases where ties persist but are chaotic and those where meetings are rare.

Chaotic Relations

In the first set of situations encounters take place, but not regularly. The mothers who were interviewed regretted this state of affairs and hoped or encouraged the fathers in certain cases to be with their children more often. The mothers, however, are disappointed or angry with the situation. The conflict between the ex-spouses has not been overcome but continues concerning the subject of sharing parental responsibilities.

Let us look at the cases of Nadège and Camille. For these two mothers, it is very important that the father maintains ties with his children. Camille, who says she is still 'angry' with her ex-husband, does not allow herself to express this feeling in order to preserve some contact between her teenage children and their father. Their relationship is difficult. Occasionally they speak to each other and then stop communicating. When Camille is particularly angry with the father, he stops exercising his right of access. Consequently the father–child relationship is also difficult. Camille said:

> Their father has a hard time accepting his role as a father outside of the family structure. With our eldest this is reflected in a major conflict: they haven't met in months. With our second child things are going better and I must say that it's thanks to my initiative. Whenever possible I tried to bring the father back into the game. It wasn't for myself but because I thought it was essential that a fourteen year old boy should have him as a model. (Camille)

Camille is counscious of how important teenager–father relationships are, and she went to a lawyer for advice on how to reinstate the father in his parental role in spite of the grudge she held against him. A registered letter to the father unblocked the situation: he immediately got in touch and the children were delighted to see him again after four months.

In order to maintain a bond between their offspring and their ex-partners, some mothers accept the fathers' requests and give up trying to establish regular visits such as those set up by the post-separation agreements. Nadège and Camille are very flexible and are organised around their ex-spouses' needs. Visits take place according to the fathers' availability and not according to the arrangements made at divorce:

> It's never regular! No rhythm is imposed by the arrangement. Their father does see and take care of them—but he doesn't really know how to—according to the schedule that was laid down, because that would be out of the question for him. I'd say he was an 'impulsive' father. A father who is certainly very fond of his sons, who theoretically would like to take care of them, but he is constantly burdened by his own activities and by the spokes the boys put in his wheels.

They are older now and don't respond in the same way to a father who wasn't always present. (Camille)

Nadège also thinks that it is important for a father to be there for his children. As their relationship is good, she is willing to accept his 'fluctuating' access:

He's got rights of access every other weekend and half of all holidays but he's never done that. He only takes them when he fancies it. The kids don't complain anyway. When they do meet, it turns out alright. I wanted him to see them as he liked. For example he'll phone my son and say 'Wednesday I'll come and pick you up after school'. He'll go fetch him, take him out for lunch and drive him home. (Nadège)

According to these two mothers, the presence of a father figure is very important for a child's development. They regret the lack of the fathers' involvement, reproach them for being absent from educational tasks and for showing little interest in their children's development:

I'd have liked him to take better care of them regarding school, and in other ways. Play with them more. For me separation hasn't changed much because I was in the habit of taking all the decisions alone anyway. Concerning school, I was the one who made decisions. He didn't get too involved in those things. What I always reproached him for was that he never really took enough care of his kids, in my opinion. (Nadège)

Despite these grievances they all say they try to transmit a positive father figure to their children and try to involve him in their education. Nadège insisted that her ex-husband should share their daughter's school fees. She managed to persuade him to send her to a private school and to cover part of the costs. She has done the same for her son:

My daughter is 19 and has had chaotic schooling. She has flunked her senior year before graduation. We put her in a private school. Last year our son went to Germany so I asked my husband to pay for half of the trip because it wasn't included in the alimony. Every time I ask he says yes. There are no problems. (Nadège)

Camille thinks the father of her children does not fulfil an authoritarian role when it is necessary. She thinks he is a bit of 'a hippy' himself. When she informed him of some trouble her elder son had got into, he neither worried about 'scolding nor about paying for repairs'.

Fathers who are Nearly Non-existent

In a large number of these families fathers are in practice absent from their children's lives. They sometimes reappear after months of silence, keep up a relationship with their offspring for a while and then vanish again. Such is Garance's case. The relation between her children and their father has got worse as a result of the separation. During the marriage, he had taken part in domestic life and was 'very kind' to the children. He took the separation his wife had wanted badly and was very destabilised by it, involving his children in the ensuing conflict, a fact for which Garance reproaches him bitterly, because the children suffered from it a great deal. Finding a new partner who is very jealous of the children has not helped and visits have become scarce and shorter.

Adja's case also reflects this kind of scenario. The father hasn't kept in touch. He left before the birth of their third child whom he has never seen. He was also absent from the burial of one of his daughters who died in the meanwhile. However, immediately after the separation, even though he lived abroad, he would phone at regular intervals, once a week for a while, but then not phone for a month. He still says he would like to return but Adja does not trust him on this. During the marriage, this man scarcely took care of the children, hardly helped around the house and only paid for part of the household expenses. When he departed he left the family with unpaid rent and large electricity bills. Relations with him have been very difficult for the past three years. Nevertheless Adja says she tries to maintain a positive father figure:

> He doesn't speak to the kids, I tell them about him. Men don't care ... He says he'll come ... I don't know when ...

She insists on the fact that her children are very attached to their father: every time the phone rings, the youngest thinks that it is his dad who is calling him. The child who has died also often used to ask for him:

> The kids talk a lot about him, but I don't know ... Sometimes he asks for forgiveness, but I don't trust him.

Adja mentions that she 'doesn't even want to speak to him on the phone', however she does not want to divorce, as it would risk upsetting the relations between the children and their father, even though she would receive more alimony if she formalised their separation:

> If I do go through with divorce procedures and he comes, it will cause more problems. That's why I've refused ...

No Relationship between the Children and their Fathers

For the final group in the sample, the father–child relationship has become completely non-existent. Either geographical distance prevents contact or the conflict between the parents is so violent that it has severed all father–child bonds. In three cases the mother initiated the separation and at the same time decided to leave the father's country of residence.

Lola maintained some contact, by phone and mail, with her African partner who remained in Dakar after she decided to return to France. Because of the distance the child has not seen his father since the separation. Lola occasionally speaks to her ex on the phone but her son is not included in these contacts. Lola does not want her son to be in touch with his father and so makes him into just 'a father in a photograph'. She does wonder what consequences this absence will have in the future. She is conscious that the separation has caused some suffering for the child, and this has been signalled by his school and has led to the need for professional help. Whatever her fears may be, she still wants to maintain an image of the estranged father in her son's eyes. This has led her to limit her relations with new partners. A man with whom she had a relationship did get involved with her son, which she appreciated at the time, but she now considers this to be completely out of the question for her. Nevertheless, while she refuses a surrogate father, Lola complains that she has to face all the educational tasks on her own.

WHICH HYPOTHESES EXPLAIN THE MAINTENANCE OF PARENT-CHILD RELATIONSHIPS AFTER SEPARATION?

The analysis of these situations leads us to ask which factors determine whether a father–child relationship will persist after parental separation. Above, we put forward the hypothesis that the way the child goes from one parent to the other would depend on the state of the parents relationship at the time of separation and afterwards. This hypothesis is challenged, however, in our sample, when we look at mothers who are in extreme conflict with their ex-partners but who do not exclude the latter from their children's lives. Some mothers would like to facilitate the father–child relationship even though they are very angry with him, criticise him and are very dissatisfied with the way the visits take place. Others wish to keep open the possibility for their children to rekindle a relationship with their fathers, even if it may be sporadic, and want to avoid a legal separation from their partner even when they no longer want to speak to him, even on the phone.

The other hypothesis we put forward, stating that the quality of the post-separation bonds depends on a father's involvement in the domestic and educational tasks during marriage, is also challenged. In the case of Garance, we noticed that the father had been very involved in family life. Nevertheless, the break-up of the couple was accompanied by a father–child separation. On the other hand, we have observed situations, such as Blandine's, in which the father was rather distant during marriage but then found a paternal role after separation. To explain these results we must therefore seek other reasons linked to the way in which the couple was organised prior to splitting up. We refer to the perspective of typology[4] analysis applied to family behaviour. These typologies take into account two important dimensions in the organisation of a family: on the one hand the relationship families have with their environment, and on the other the relationship the members of a household have with each other. This second axis is particularly important in accounting for the way in which child–parent relationships work out after separation

This dimension demonstrates the way in which subjects mark out their personal spaces and express their wishes. What space is left to 'self' or to 'us' in the functioning of a couple or family? Analyses carried out from this perspective have led to the identification of two modes, associative and osmotic (closely-knit). In the associative role priority is given to the 'self'. Personal values and beliefs are not necessarily shared. Family activities—leisure time or visits to relatives for example—do not necessarily include every member. Contrarily in osmotic families the accent is put on the 'us', on the assimilation and interdependence of each individual, on adhering to family beliefs and on enhancing activities partaken together. Using these typologies, we can reinterpret the data on post-separation parent–child relationships.

In the case of families which function in an associative mode, family roles are not predetermined by the status imposed upon each member, but are attributed by the couple themselves. The father's role, whether he plays an important domestic role or not, is the result of a negotiation by the parents. In reorganising family daily life after separation, his role is not questioned. He redefines his presence and his participation in the children's upbringing taking into account his own timetable and his spouse's opinion.

Practical and financial conditions may be re-discussed at any time. The fact that the father does not share the same home as the mother and children does not prevent him from participating in important family events such as birthdays or celebrations. In the associative mode, conjugality and parenthood are distinct, so that conflicts concerning the spouses do not interfere with the parental relationship. The data from our study confirms this analysis for the group which maintains father–child relationships which have a continuity in relation to how they were before separation.

According to the mothers we interviewed, any necessary reorganisation had been negotiated and discussed previously. The fathers remained as present as before separation. The mothers encouraged their involvement and favoured sharing parental tasks in order to reduce their own burden.

---

[4] J Kellerhals, R Lévy and E Widmer, *Mesure et démesure du couple* (Payot and Rivages, 2004).

We noticed that these parents were sensitive to the feelings of their children for whom separation, even if it had gone smoothly, remained painful. These women were well adapted to the separation, economically autonomous and maintaining certain ties with their former spouses. However, the upbringing and the maintenance of bonds with the father were dependent on negotiations between the parents.

Relationships between fathers and their offspring which are irregular or non-existent, differ from those described before. These situations lead us to ask which characteristics explain the rupture or deterioration of ties between fathers and children. We find it helpful to refer to paradigms from the perspective of typology analysis applied to family functioning and to others which derive from a broader anthropological perspective, concerning migrant women from societies in which there is a clear allocation of gender roles.

A large number of the families who did not maintain constant ties, function in the osmotic mode. These families are characterised by the couple's investment in ideals of faithfulness and long lasting relationships. In these situations, father, mother and child form an osmotic whole, in which each member finds an identity and family status. In this mode, the spouses (or parents) are in the habit of sharing everything, of submitting everything they do or think to the approval of the other member of the nucleus.

We might expect such entities, in which an individual's life makes sense vis-à-vis the spouse's, and where one looks out onto the world through one's partner's eyes, to be unable to maintain ties beyond separation. Their unity is broken by the departure of one of the spouses and the members of the nucleus are particularly affected by the split. The participation of a non-resident parent within the nucleus is inconceivable. Nothing other than total adherence to a collective involving all aspects of life is acceptable. The split affects the identity of each member and creates tension between them in such a way that maintaining father–child relationships is jeopardised. Therefore father–child relationships are difficult and discontinuous because of the parents' split. Several women in the sample continued to complain about the lack of commitment shown by the fathers after separation in the same way they had done during the marriage.

There is another group of families in which ties were non-existent or interrupted who differ from those described above. For them, analysis using the concept of 'fusion' is not appropriate. These are families in which, unlike in contemporary family models (associative or osmotic), an institutional allocation of family roles takes place. This is the case for families from the Magreb and African countries. In the societies to which these families are attached and which we might call 'holistic', collective interests prevail over individual ones and a person's identity is determined by the role assigned by the group. The criteria used for choosing a husband are based more on his potential capacity for founding and rearing a family than on personal affinities, and on matrimonial strategies favorable to the group.[5] The sharing of household chores leaves women in charge of the domestic sphere. In these situations, women find the main meaning of their lives in the role assigned to them as mothers. Before and after separation, they structure their lives around their children. Their personal desires are left aside. One woman says 'I give my life to my children'.

Male domination is normal and accepted as such by women. In the context of immigration in which communitarian regulation is weakened, this may lead to certain excesses of male power. Having accepted attachment of their personal goals to the upbringing of their children, these women have understandably a high degree of tolerance towards their husbands' behaviour, and separation only takes place on the man's initiative or because of a situation which has become intolerable for the children themselves.

During marriage, the father is scarcely present in family life, and these women experience his departure as an opportunity to regain a certain harmony in everyday life with their children. But because of the lack of alimony from the husband, separation is also the source of great difficulties from a financial point of view, as well as from a sentimental one.

In these families father–child relations are often distant. Due to his traditional role, the father often took few responsibilities towards his children during the marriage. Father–child relations are more institutional than emotional and the father represents a distant model of authority just as he was before separation. Mothers often try to preserve a space for the father. Some even attempt to act as a mediator in their ex-husband's relation with their children but this is either prevented by the children, in situations where they fear the father's violent behaviour, or by the fathers themselves when they do not respond to their children's demands.

CONCLUSION

This analysis has led us to shed the illusion, generated by the presentation of the data, of a continuum from ideal situations where children would circulate from one parent to the other in harmony, to a complete break in relations, with intermediary solutions and occasional contact somewhere in the middle. In actual fact, the differences in the frequency of contact is rooted in the ways the families functioned before the split and which endure afterwards. It would therefore be wrong to believe that the differences we noted simply reflect the good or bad terms the parents were on during the separation. The possibility of maintaining contact between child and

---

[5] See, P Bourdieu and M von Allmen, 'Les rapports de parenté comme rapports de production symbolique. Stratégies matrimoniales en Algérie' (1985) *Actes de la recherche en sciences sociales* no 59, 49–60.

non-resident parent depends on the mode in which the family functions, which includes or excludes the opportunity to make space for the parent who has departed. They are therefore situations which are structurally different, and which function in different ways.

These observations can be extended to comment on how couples organise father–child relations after separation and to actions which can be undertaken when father–child relations seem threatened. Knowing that current criteria regarding the handling of separations insist strongly on joint care of the children and their circulating from one parent to the other, we can imagine that divorcing couples attached to an associative mode will have the appropriate resources and competences to meet the demands of this familial organisation. Their way of being a couple permits dissociating conjugal and parental relations. But what of solutions that are set up when the risk of a break in non-resident parent and child relations appears? What can we expect from measures, in particular those which refer to the reasons we mentioned above—ie conflicts between the parents or the father's uncommitted attitude? Interventions aimed at improving the parental relationship, such as family mediation, may be useful. But we find it hard to imagine that they will convince parents who functioned in an osmotic mode to engage in negotiation and thus change their vision of marriage and remain on viable terms even after separation. Similarly, regarding osmotic families, preventive measures which aim at involving the fathers in their offspring's upbringing cannot guarantee the maintenance of these bonds.

These remarks underline just how hard it is to imagine and apply co-parenthood, the expected norm, for many couples who are attached to an osmotic mode. In these cases, father–child separations are inevitable and lead necessarily to the weakening and disappearance of these ties.

Finally, regarding couples who correspond to an institutional and traditional perspective as mentioned above, we can only say that the norm concerning sharing roles is not relevant for them. How could it be of any use to persuade them to adopt such norms? The realisation that many children never or rarely see their fathers must lead to an acceptance that this is due to the different ways in which a family can function. The father's mode of attachment to his child depends on how the family operates. Instead of wanting to install a father–child relation at all costs, even when it is weakened or inexistent, it is paramount that other forms of support for the children in question should be found.

3

From Marriage to Parenthood: Rethinking Parenthood in Times of Reproductive Innovation

MALGORZATA FUSZARA AND JACEK KURCZEWSKI

INTRODUCTION

IT IS INTRIGUING that despite all the traditional secrets and recent biotechnological experimentation, marriage still seems to be linked with parenthood to such an extent that the standard current Encyclopedia of Social and Cultural Anthropology,[1] though ending with a call for 'rethinking the universality and durability of marriage'[2] under the heading of 'Marriage'[3] does not even include a separate entry on 'Parenthood'. But while 'marriage' has different meanings in different religions and cultures, it is hardly ever equated with the biological facts of sex, and 'parenthood' assumes a different status reflecting the biological genetic relationship. Marriage is a relationship which is usually made public, while 'true' parenthood has always been problematic, as this information in itself could destroy the marriage. We suggest therefore that it is 'parenthood' which needs 'rethinking', especially at a time when we are confronted by impressive attempts by thousands of people who having asserted their idiosyncratic interpretations of marriage are laboriously trying to reconstruct—and rethink—the broken meaning of parenthood in order to fit their new forms of relationships. We wish to review the variety of strange 'parenthoods' before discussing in detail the obviously complicated construction of lesbian parenthood.

---

[1] Edited by A Barnard and J Spencer, Routledge, London and New York, first published 1996, reprinted 2003.
[2] *Ibid.*
[3] Francoise Zonabend, 'Marriage' 350–52.

AMOR INCONDICIONAL

The technological revolution in reproduction has undermined the biological objectivity which had been taken for granted for centuries. If the mother is the person who gave birth to the child, she is no longer necessarily the same person who produced the eggs. The complex relationships which can develop have recently been exemplified in the case of Tina Cade which has been called by the media in Almodovarian style the 'Case of Amor Incondicional'.

In December 2004 55-year-old Tina Cade gave birth to her own grandchildren—two boys and a girl—by Caesarean section at Bon Secours St Mary's Hospital. She served as a surrogate for her oldest daughter, Camille Hammond, and Hammond's husband, Jason. Hammond and her husband, both doctors at Johns Hopkins University in Baltimore, had tried for four years to become pregnant. Cade approached the couple with the idea of carrying their child and began hormone treatment to turn back her biological clock—she had already entered the menopause—and prepare her for pregnancy. Months later, Cade underwent in-vitro fertilisation and three embryos were implanted.

She told *The Early Show* co-anchor Gretchen Carlson, 'It's meant everything! It's been—it's been kind of on hold for two years now, trying to make this dream come true. And before, it was a fantasy. Right up until the point that they told me they had delivered the children, the babies. But it's not a fantasy now. I've got three lovely grandchildren who I have yet to see!'

'I was a caring incubator and that's how I saw myself', Cade, who is director of multicultural affairs at the University of Richmond, said: 'Just to love them. Unconditional love. That conquers so many hurdles and challenges'.[4]

This case is only one of many that has attracted media attention in recent years, but it is a compelling example of the new attitude that has developed around traditional bonds and roles. The surrogate mother presents her action as arising from love, another dimension of maternal care. In terms of the biology, the case is in fact less surprising as no new genetic link had been established, and the child is born of the grandmother's womb within the same blood line. The complexity is related to the family's normative generational structure. If the duties of mothers are thought to be different from those of grandmothers, than the division is blurred. But the difference might have been related to the physical resources related to age and not to the position in the inter-generational chain as such. In old tribal societies the concept of 'classificatory motherhood' had to be introduced, as each child had not only its biological mother, but her sisters and

---

[4] *El Pais* of 31 December 2004, CBS and Associated Press.

cousins of the same generation. This form of motherhood often included breastfeeding, especially within the polygynous home.

VARIETIES OF PARENTHOOD

Three different concepts of parenthood are relevant here. Genetic parenthood, in which the transmission of genetic material takes place between individual X and Y in the process of giving life to Z. The concept of genetic parenthood strictly speaking is a recent development, for though the concept of blood lines was widespread in some societies such as the Trobrianders, the male biological role had been neglected .The only certain biological fact is that of motherhood, while paternity is subject to cultural variation. Furthermore, it is only recently that it has become scientificically possible to check the genetic link between persons other than mother and her child. And, at the same time, genetic engineering has given rise to a second more complex form of genetic parenthood, in which original material may be divided among two or more genitors, and the biological certainty of motherhood has been undermined by the development of reproductive technologies that divide even this aspect between more than one mother (see *Cade*).

All these developments have put pressure on the legal definition of parenthood. Courts are dealing with more and more cases in which it is important to decide who is the parent. Establishing parenthood is now no longer obvious in the case of mother and requires the extralegal technicality of DNA measurements.

When dealing with difficult cases the courts have always looked into the social relations of the parties. The facts of having sex, providing food and shelter, and upbringing have always been considered and set against other social relations under which paternal rights and duties are derived from legal relationships, above all marriage and acknowledged kinship bonds. This complex set of considerations leads to the construction of social parenthood which may be, but need not be, identical with genetic parenthood. If we consider the case of a woman who raises a child with her husband but the newborn infant had been exchanged for another infant in the hospital by a careless nurse. Such things happen, and in fictional stories have always attracted an audience.

EXCURSION INTO COMPARATIVE ANTHROPOLOGY OF FAMILY LAW

Bronisław Malinowski stresses biological 'needs', physiological as well as psychological around which cultural apparatus develop including individual sanctions and duties. Mutual satisfaction of sexual needs is universal in a marriage. The positive aspect of this duty is not a burden for those involved, as Malinowski aptly observes (if we exclude marital rape) unlike its negative side which is the prohibition of sex outside the marriage. In a classical Petrazyckian way Malinowski focuses on the normative bond of a reciprocal, imperative—attributive nature, pointing to the demanding duty of marital loyalty. Then he adds the paternal or maternal proclivities which form the biological focus of further normative and cultural institutions. Malinowski's stress on the biological 'facts of life' as against ethnographical concern with rituals and local theories seems to be based on his discovery of Trobrianders' ignorance about physiological paternity. In *Crime and Custom in a Savage Society*[5] he points to the strength of the emotional bond that develops between the husband of the mother and the boy born to the woman. Clearly, knowledge of physiological fatherhood was irrelevant in this case. The important factor was the strength of affective attachment developed by the 'fathering' father in the process of bringing up the child, who would then be legally abandoned for the sake of the man's nephews. In matrilineal society where there is ignorance of the physiology of reproduction, every parenthood is of a 'social' character and an 'illicit' affective bond like the one described by Malinowski in the case of the paramount chief of Omarakana is based on no other ground than that of actual upbringing. But this bond is, as Malinowski observes, accompanied by the belief that the father, strictly speaking the mother's husband and lord of household is not 'physiologically neutral' but that he 'physically shapes the outer features and character of the child by his permanent co-presence'.[6] Strictly speaking we are dealing with a specific Trobriand theory about the physiological role of the father, a deeply 'cultural' interpretation of some striking resemblances that may be observed between father and child who are unaware of either the old physiology or the new genetics.

Malinowski is, of course, wrong to conclude from the Trobriand case that this supports the 'natural', 'physiological' and 'fundamental' character of paternity. Nothing in nature prevents the innocent Trobriand husband from assuming a fatherly bond with a newborn child, warmly welcomed after a 12-month absence from home. In another paragraph he says that in no society is marriage other than an individual personal contract between one woman and one man. Here the 'individual' is opposed to the 'collective', in contrast to the 'cultural anthropology' developed later by Levi-Strauss; Malinowski wants to make clear that it is not groups who enter into a contract but the marriage ritual that sanctions the personal union of two individuals. The word 'free' does not, however, appear in this context

---

[5] Kegan Paul, London, 1926.
[6] Bronisław Malinowski, *The sexual life of savages in north-western Melanesia: and ethnographic account of courtship, marriage and family life among the natives of the Trobriand Islands* (New York, Liveright, 1926).

and rightly so as marriage contracts, oral or written, explicit or implicit, are not always made between freely contracting individuals. 'Individuality' in this context means the individuality of the parties who marry, but not their exclusive rights to contract. 'Individuality' does not mean that the child born to a married woman is born to her partner. A sentence from the EE Evans-Pritchard's study of Nuer family law exemplifies the complex state of affairs that can surround the issue As in many African societies in order to legalise the offspring of a union as children of the mother's partner, the union had to be solemnised with the relevant ceremonies and transfer of cattle from the bridegroom's kin to those of the bride. 'Bridewealth pay-ments may therefore be viewed as a technique for creating and maintaining new social relationships between persons for whom there are no pre-existing patterns of behaviour. They are one of the many ways in which gifts and payments are used in primitive societies. Bridewealth may thus be thought of as providing a kind of social scaffolding, a temporary structure of behav-ioural patterns, which enables the union to be built up. It ceases to be of any great significance once the new family is firmly established after the birth of the second child'.[7]

The Nuer are a wonderful example of the main theme of Malinowski's writing, namely 'social' or 'cultural' fatherhood. He observed that there is a moral obligation on the part of the surviving younger sibling to marry a woman 'in the name' of the deceased, if the latter died unmarried or mar-ried and childless, so that his name can be passed onto the further genera-tion. Such a failure—not only among the Nuer—would be actual death, rather than the mere death of body. We can see here how the notion of 'individuality' may be misleading. It is the 'individual' who suffers in after-life if his name has not been passed on, but the 'name' in itself that must be continued from individual to individual. Like the naive Trobrianders the physiologically more advanced Nuer take less account of genetics but regard 'social genealogy' as more important. As good pastoralists they know that a male is needed to procreate a child, but this procreative link is irrelevant in terms of their culture. To calm the deceased sibling's soul they need to marry for him and procreate for him a new being to embody the name. As Nuer are rigidly logical in their reasoning they do not exclude women from the same process, if a barren woman dies her closest young kin should marry for her AS A HUSBAND to father her child who will bear her name. Apart from the fact that this implies gender neutrality of names, not only is the deceased sister's paternity fictitious, but the same might be said of the substitute paternity performed by, for example, her younger brother. After all, Nuer have a fear that supernatural plagues will fall on close siblings committing incest so, 'It seems that he must not cohabit with

[7] EE Evans-Pritchard, *Kinship and Marriage Among the Nuer* (Oxford, Clarendon, 1991) 96.

the wife himself, because in these circumstances "your wife is like your sister", but must arrange for a stranger, perhaps a Dinka, to cohabit with her in the hut he builds for her in his homestead'.[8]

All this is made possible because paternity is a legally established fact, or better still, constructed by appropriate rituals and the transfer of bride-wealth. Whoever sends the cattle, is the father says Nuer law and the final beauty of the legal logic involved is made clear when we learn that it is not uncommon for a solitary barren woman to marry another woman AS THE HUSBAND and to hire the Dinka compensated materially for his procreative labour to produce the offspring to be recognised as the she-husband's if she has sent the bridewealth cattle expected by the law. '[... I]f she is rich she may marry several wives. She is their legal husband and can demand damages if they have relations with men without her consent. She is also the father of their children, and on the marriages of their daughters she receives "the cattle of the father", and her brothers and sisters receive the other cattle which go to the father's side in the distribution of bridewealth. Her children are called after her, as though she were a man, and I was told that they address her as "father". She administers her home and herd as a man would do, being treated by her wives and children with the deference they would show to a male husband and father'.[9] More recent studies provide the example of the legal claim for paternity on part of the girlfriend of the mother who happened to have sexual intercourse with a male before 'rubbing against her friend'.

As for men-only unions, we have information from Kwakiutl, a nation of warriors on another side of the globe and in another environment. Here as Boas[10] recorded, the importance of the name was also great and in order not to lose the rights linked with it the daughterless father had to marry his son as a daughter to a willing pretender, all due to the complicated pattern of succession through the women. What would be more ingenious in case of the barren man than that he may marry his leg or hand to the young man in order to put the marital exchange in motion.

Striking as this may seem, these cases suggest that it is not the procreation of the offspring which lies at the core of the marriage, but the legitimisation of the children who as a result of the marriage count as offspring.

WHAT IS A PARENT?

The question 'What is a parent?' therefore did not originate within the contemporary European or American court, but has been persistently

---

[8] *Ibid*, at 112.
[9] *Ibid*, at 109.
[10] F Boas, *The Social Organization and Secret Societies of the Kwakiutl Indians* (National Museum, Washington, 1897).

asked within legal anthropology, where various ingenious family rules have been studied. This offers us a perspective on the European present day reality where various patterns are encountered, even in an apparently orthodox country such as predominantly Roman Catholic Poland. Here, parental power had been considered as unitary in its scope for centuries. In the patrilinear monogamous systems dominant in Europe parental power was paternal power, though mitigated by the facts of maternal dependency and marital stability. This form was inculcated in Roman law, and Canon law, and summarised in the Code of Napoleon. Serial monogamy resulting first from mortality, and later from divorce has complicated the system. In addition, we now have a heterogeneity of legal traditions brought by the new Europeans from the Indian sub-continent, the West Indies, Africa, the Far East, and the near East. This had been dealt with by the reintroduction of the personal status law, though subject to the general limits of European laws. A third, recent influence derives from the sexual revolution that started in the 1960s, with the invention of contraceptive pills which allowed sexual mobility and relaxed moral standards. Thus, the state today through the courts is facing an exuberant variety of family models that requires reconsideration of the basic legal concept of parenthood. It should be observed, however, that most of the changes are changes in perception and interpretation, as polygamy, foster parenting, single parenting and homosexuality have played a part of European family life for centuries. The traditional non-European legal systems remain a rich source of both concepts and solutions.

The first of these changes is the de-genderisation of the parental role, best illustrated by single parenting by both men and women. With the emphasis always being put on the mother, it is no surprise that most people still find it difficult to accept the 'mothering' by a male, but the acknowledged father in this role is met with compassion and pity that may make him socially discriminated against, though in an unusual way. With social expectations of the male lifestyle still differing from those of the woman, male parents tend to get 'excluded' or perhaps 'excluded themselves' from 'normal' social life.

The extended family was the dominant pattern in traditional Europe, but seemed to die out towards the end of the industrial era. Its vestiges in eastern and southern Europe are considered to be symptoms of backwardness. However, the issue comes to the fore as the demography of Europe changes, and the population ages and the birthrate falls. Under the communist regime with scarcity of goods and services, Polish society developed extended family networks to help with survival, and included above all, obligations of mutual support that extended beyond the nuclear family to distant relatives and further generations. Such recreated extended family links tended also to include people who are not related but are 'close friends'.[11] The combined social resources helped lonely people to survive, and people with children to be able to work.

These processes make for the further 'de-parenting' of parenthood. It is rare for non-parents to assume the whole package of parental activities. But in our field of research we encountered, for example children being left with the grandparents by the parent(s) who have moved abroad to work, in the context of high unemployment.

We have observed the dis-connecting of parental rights and duties. A rich pattern of real life situations can be presented. Retirement is a signal that more parental duties are to be taken up by the retired grandparent(s) who care for the child. Among childless relatives, the ambiguous role of the aunt needs to be considered. And in Roman Catholic cultures the godparents also assume some material obligations. Cross-gendering is eased by marketisation (ready food and disposable nappies, while traditional 'paternal' duties such as discipline and household subsistence are 'de-gendered' through the elimination of uni-centered power in family relations and growing gender equalisationion in the labour market. The patterns which developed in times of scarcity may prove functional under the conditions of job scarcity and the end of the state as the 'substitute parent'.

Three concomitant changes in the legal culture of European societies recognise:

(1) institutionalisation of the non-gendered role of 'parent' who needs not to be genetrix or genitor of the child;
(2) pluralisation and extension of parental duties within a network of support with division of work in time and/or in kind;
(3) growing regulation of fertilisation and other biological aspects of procreation.

THE MALE IN THE MATERNAL ROLE

In contemporary young (opposite sex) families with higher education we note a new relationship between the father and child and a different role for the father. The father now frequently performs activities once considered typically maternal. The formation of a role for the father that differs from that of previous generations begins before the child's birth. As our interviews show,[12] future fathers attend childbirth education classes (which

[11] Cf M Fuszara and J Kurczewski, 'Family Values, Friendship Values: Opposition or Continuity?' in M Maclean (ed), *Family Law and Family Values* (Oxford, Hart Publishing, 2005) 45–58.
[12] Three interviews with fathers made in 2004. In their families mothers are going every day to work, fathers stay with child at home.

was not possible for their parents' generation), where they learn the role they may play during childbirth and in caring for the newborn: '"I think I certainly wanted to be there during delivery, and that requires attendance at childbirth education classes. (...) There were ten couples there, women with their husbands and each of them wanted to be at the delivery, 10 out of 10'.

As we learn from these interviews, in these classes pressure is often exerted on the future parents that the father along with the mother, rather than the older generation, should take care of the child.

'Grandmas beat it' is the harshest phrase cited by surveyed childbirth education class participants. During the classes, future parents are persuaded not to hand over care to grandmothers, which was and frequently continues to be the custom in Poland. This is justified mainly by the changes in childcare practice that have occurred between the generations of present mothers and their mothers (eg, in feeding 'upon request'), but also the role that the modern father should play in the life of the child. Currently, it is increasingly common for the mother to return to her job after the birth while the father cares for the newborn. For the less educated, this may occur only as a result of unemployment. However, for those with higher education, this may be a conscious choice by the child's parents. Recently, a book has become quite popular in Poland, initially written as an internet blog by a father caring for his son; describing the child's development, their conversations and experiences. Such situations also occur among persons with a high public profile, whose experience has been described in popular periodicals. For example, a couple of athletes, who after the birth of their child, the father suspended his career and cared for the daughter while the mother returned to sport. Such a model may be found among today's 20–30 year-olds in large cities. The following daily timetable, once typical only for mothers, may be found among fathers caring for small children: '(Wake up) 6.20 am, I make breakfast for my wife, my son and me. At 7.30 am, my wife leaves for work and I basically spend the whole day with my son; depending on the time of year, amount of work, she comes home late, I spend the whole day with my son. The rhythm of my day is adapted to the child, basically. Obviously, he's less active in the morning, he wakes up, he'll eat something or other, whine, later we'll eat breakfast then go for a walk. We come home, eat lunch. In the meantime, obviously I wash the dishes. Frankie plays by himself, I read to him ... I read to him a lot and he really likes that, being read to ... .(...) lunch, and then we go out, depending on the time of year, actually in the winter, we play at home and wait for mom to get back from work. She gets back around 6.30 pm, 8.00 pm at the latest, if she's in Warsaw. Today, she's on a business trip, so she'll be back after 9'.

In interviews, fathers caring for small children describe the joy of accompanying the child in its development, observing and helping. 'I think

I can say I find fulfilment in this somehow. I find reserves of paternal love that I want to bestow on Frank', said one of the respondents caring for a small child while the wife works. Because such a situation is still unusual, people living in this way encounter various reactions from their environment: 'Here, the opinions are split. I've even heard very negative reactions. They feel I should work and Justyna should be with Frank morning until night. Others feel the child should be with a nanny and we should both work. Others still feel that if [caring for the child–ed.] does not bother me, then why not ...' Though such a situation continues to be the exception, it is occurring increasingly frequently. What's more, because the current generation of grandfathers are much older than their wives, there are cases where the retired grandfather helps the father to care for a small child (eg takes the child for walks, baby-sits when the father has to run errands), while the mother and grandmother work, thus executing a model that only recently was not heard of at all.

Fathers play a maternal role in male single parent families too. Małgorzata Malińska studied 31 cases of male single parents in Poznań in 1994.[13] Of those, 21 were employed, but despite wide variation in income, only five considered their financial situation to be good. This negative assessment results from the fact that single parenting precludes taking extra jobs, which is the most popular way of improving one's economic position. Single fathers rarely receive regular alimony from mothers of the child.

The effect of single male parenting is a limitation of social life due to lack of time. 'Coming back from a job one should take care of the kids, help them in their homework, clean the house, do laundry. Soon it is night. Where is the time for leisure?' (asks a 42-year-old divorced father raising two children aged 7 and 9). Some continue to do 'housework' at the weekend as well, though others go out and meet their parents (the grandparents of children). Often these fathers claim that what they do is a continuation of the unequal share of parental duties during the marriage with their wives being absent at home, though sometimes it's clear that the assumption of full parental responsibility was a shock, especially for widowers. But even a 40-year-old divorcee who is raising three daughters aged 8, 14 and 16 years acknowledges the shock as he 'didn't know anything about laundry, cooking. I needed to learn when I was left alone. A female neighbour helped me as she wrote down recipes and showed me how to cook. At the beginning I didn't know how to organise the time. I was standing in the kitchen on watch, if I left immediately something got burnt. Now I know, all work is well planned'. Contacts are limited

---

[13] Małgorzata Malińska, "Funkcjonowanie samotnych ojców w rodzinie" [Functioning of Single Fathers in Family], unpublished MA thesis tutored by Anna Michalska, Chair in Sociology of Family, Adam Mickiewicz University, Poznań, 1994.

to the closest family and old friends. Fathers also complain about the exaggerated sympathy they encounter as they contradict the traditional concept of female/male parental responsibility. This lowers the likelihood of forming a new relationship. The majority of those interviewed felt themselves emotionally handicapped by the lack of a female partner. 'One is missing someone close to oneself', 'I miss having someone to talk to about troubles and pleasures'. 'The worst time is the late evening when the kids are asleep and home is quiet and empty'. Nevertheless, most were not planning a new union, giving the welfare of the children as the reason. 'Kids are the reason. One should look for a woman who would love them, care for them as for her own. Where can one find such woman?' 'One should now think of the kids. Nobody can ensure that the woman will be good to kids, and I do not want to take a risk'. 'It could develop in various ways with a new wife. In the beginning she will say that kids are not an obstacle and later she will complain'. The decision to make a new union is often postponed until the children are older.

WHO IS ALLOWED TO BE A PARENT? CHILDREN IN HOMOSEXUAL RELATIONSHIPS

Just as in other countries, there is an ongoing debate in Poland about the legal registration of homosexual partnerships. Some draft legislation applies to both heterosexual as well as homosexual relationships, while others concern only the latter. As in other states, the issue of adoption by homosexual couples engenders great controversy. In the Bill recently approved by the Senate, such couples would not have the right to adopt a child but would have the right to jointly rear one of the partner's children. Pursuhttp://www.admin.ox.ac.uk/fp/wd62-036.shtmant to art. 7 of the bill:

> 'A partner shall jointly care for the person and property of the minor child remaining under the sole custody of the other partner.
>
> In the event of a threat to the health or life of the minor child described in item 1, the partner without parenting rights shall take all actions required by the minor child's welfare. He or she should forthwith notify the other partner regarding actions taken.
>
> The partner described in item 2 shall be entitled to represent the child described in item 1 in ongoing matters of daily life in the event the partner possessing sole custody is temporarily incapacitated from performing legal acts on the minor child's behalf.
>
> The family court may limit the right described in item 3 should the minor child's welfare so require'.[14]

---

[14] Senate bill, draft No 548, 2004.

The Bill also provided for a certain alimony obligation. It provided for the same alimony as is due to a stepchild from the spouse of a biological parent.

The draft was submitted by a group of senators. Discussion regarding the draft Bill brought opposition from rightist parties based on their support for the heterosexual family model, but representatives of leftist groupings also made hostile comments:

> I am a member of the Polish left and due its nature; I want to be a democrat, socially utilitarian, just and modern. I would like everyone to live happily in Poland and across the entire world, the Poles in Poland, foreigners, believers, atheists, and finally those in traditional marriages and those with other preferences.
>
> The bill under discussion should be close to my heart, but unfortunately it is not. I cannot back this bill. The obstacle is the traditional, strong, sound, effective child rearing in a Polish family. A family that is based on strong ties with grandparents, parents, children and grandchildren. The traditional Polish family is to me the greatest of treasures and in my opinion, is, or, to speak more honestly, should be Poland's greatest national treasure. And it is solely for this reason that today, I say that I am not yet ready to legally approve single gender unions. I simply have not been prepared to define a union, as one other than a union between persons of different genders. Speaking frankly, I am simply not ready.[15]

Two views clashed in discussion of the draft bill. Even though they were in conflict, both were justified by reference to the 'child's welfare', indicating once again what a broad and amorphous category that is. Opponents of adoption maintain that a child must be taught the model of a 'typical' family, one that consists of people who, from the biological perspective, can have a child, ie a woman and man. But single sex union adoption supporters indicate, that in addition to the diversity of family models in today's world, our culture has always accepted the recurrent model of two persons of the same gender rearing a child. This is especially so for two women, such as a mother and grandmother, sisters or a mother assisted by other women, implying that this model is not new. Nevertheless, homo-sexual women raising children speak of their fear of 'coming out' (which is occurring with increasing frequency), as this is often associated with negative consequences–loss of a job, social ostracism in their small-town community, etc. 'I've only told three members of my family that I'm a lesbian. My husband has no idea because he would forbid me to see my son. Kamil asks no questions at all. I've been thinking about what I will tell him. I once took him to a lake with a friend. He was six then and asked

---

[15] Senate of the Republic of Poland minutes of 14.09.2004, Senator Tadeusz Rzemykowski, Alliance of Democratic Left.

"Mom, why are there only girls here?" I explained that all the daddies are at work. Ania officially plays the role of a "hetero." At work they think she's divorced'.[16]

That is the most frequent situation, though an increasing number of events such as pride parades, support groups, internet pages advising on how to become a mother through insemination may help resolve the problems of people who want to become single mothers by choice, including mothers remaining in homosexual relationships. It is difficult to estimate if the passing of the bill would contribute to a change in attitudes. It is unlikely we will have an opportunity to find that out. Though the Left was in government until Autumn 2005 the bill was not passed. As the new parliament is far more rightist the bill is unlikely to pass at all.

The draft legislation on domestic partnerships was rejected by the Sejm. We were therefore interested in how homosexual persons cope with jointly raising children—those from prior, heterosexual relationships and those born during homosexual relationships. Due to rejection of the draft legislation, Polish law does not regulate such situations. In order to check what happens in practice, we conducted interviews with lesbians jointly raising children. The surveys turned out to be very difficult, largely due to a reluctance to talk about private matters, as well as fears of spreading too much information about this subject. We had the impression that the respondents are afraid of publicising the problem and do not know what the consequences could be of public discussion. In practice, such situations are regulated in a flexible manner, by private agreements, shaped by the parties themselves.

In the end five interviews were conducted with lesbian mothers (one was an expectant mother at the time of the interview). With one exception, all the children came from prior heterosexual marriages. We were especially interested in how they get along in the complex parental arrangement in these relationships. What is the relationship between the biological fathers and the children and how do they get along? How are relationships shaped between the biological mother's partner and the children they are jointly raising? What is the relationship of the sperm donor with the future mother and plans for future relations with the child? Do they believe that official regulation—a legal act on domestic partnerships—would change their situation and how would this affect them?

Relations with the Biological Father

In all cases the mother had custody after the divorce, and in one case childcare was divided between both biological parents. In nearly all

---

[16] I Michalewicz, This article was published in November 2003 in 'Stolica', a weekly supplement to the *Życie Warszawy* daily.

cases we studied the relations of children with their biological parents were very good. In no case did the lesbian relationship of the mother of a child lead to conflict with the former husband–biological father of the child: 'there is good and rather frequent contact, regular, the boys are with me four days, with Krzysztof three and this arrangement is very open, Krzysztof knows perfectly well whom I live with. and vice-versa, I know what is going on in his life'. 'I was a wife, I terribly wanted to have a child, my husband was and is a very good and kind person, we always talked about this, that if I were with a woman, he would understand and he always loved the children (...). He has an exceptional degree of empathy and I know that he would be a good father and I value him greatly, sure there was also a time when I was happy with him in the sense of the relationship, we remain in contact daily (...) we have known each other 23 years, I think hardly a day goes by when we don't talk on the phone, he is really an outstanding person—friend (...) (my daughter—MF) has a wonderful relationship with him'.

The only exception is the case of a divorced mother who after many years of affiliation left the Jehovah Witnesses while her husband remained. For several years her daughter lived with the mother, and knew of the mother's sexual orientation though she also maintained relations with her father. Several years later, as an adult, she chose to join the religious community and this led to the end of contact between the mother and daughter. Nevertheless, the respondent emphasised that this resulted from her withdrawal from the religious community and not due to her sexual orientation.

It should be added that the first of the cases cited above also points to the value of private understandings, and even [Leon] Petrazyckian 'unofficial law' rather than official law. In Poland, according to a decision of the Supreme Court which objected to joint parental custody whereby the child would live for a while with the mother and for a while with the father–in practice courts rule for joint parental rights while the child lives with the mother. The Supreme Court assumed that the child should have a uniform educational environment and for this reason should live with one of the parents after the divorce. In practice though, it turned out that people independently shape their relations in a manner in which they deem right, not attaching significant weight to the court decisions.

Nevertheless, it has to be said that the interviews were conducted entirely with women who were educated, self-reliant, financially independent, and very conscious of their rights and choices. In other situations, relations would certainly not work out so free of conflict—because frequently relations between divorced parents are not conflict free, and being lesbian may complicate the mother's situation. Press reports on this topic, though infrequent, demonstrate this.

Relations of Children with the Mother's Partner

As we have already pointed out, all the children came from marriages, hence the mothers' partners were someone 'new' to the children. Obviously, the manner of working out relations depends on the child's age, and their ability to understand the situation. Partners normally put in a lot of effort for the children to accept them, and for mothers this is frequently the primary criteria determining whether they can live together: 'on my side there was a declaration that I really wanted the boys to choose me as well, I mean I didn't want to impose anything on them and place them in such a situation where I suddenly show up, and we are living together (...) we went for a walk and we talked about nothing important and at a certain point I asked what it would be like if I visited more often? (...) he said—super, super, great. Then I asked what it would be like if I came to live with you at some point? That would be even better, it would be wonderful (...) the next day (...) he went to my old apartment, where I lived to help pack my bags, move out, he was very committed, it was also very charming, very heartwarming, it was also friendship from the very start, and so mutual'.

In this model and rather conflict free situation, the rights of both caretakers of the children seem to be almost equal. The biological mother said: 'what does it mean to raise children? In terms of issues of a technical nature this means: to feed, launder, clean the room—we do this together depending on which of us has time, a convenient situation. To me the issue of upbringing is a much more fundamental issue, that is talking, closeness and so on ... I think the first few days showed that she was accepted immediately, unconditionally and in a rather wonderful manner and suddenly it turned out that I cannot say I am raising the boys alone, we are raising them together, just as in good marriages, isn't it?'

Despite such partnership relations, the biological mother is granted greater authority in deciding important matters concerning the children: 'nevertheless, more important issues, significant decisions are taken by the mother aren't they? Well, if there are issues associated with the school, meetings, etc in a natural manner and I also think from the viewpoint of social acceptance it is more beneficial for the mother to take care of these, besides I also think that it is good for children to address their mother in such a natural manner'.

The respondent's reference to 'social acceptance' may have an impact on how the child perceives this situation. Even though the model of raising children by two or more women has been accepted culturally for ages, the respondents mention situations in which the surroundings 'signal' to the child that their situation is atypical. Questions that preschool teachers blurt out, 'your *auntie* has come for you again?' is only one way children are asked to doubt their situation.

Acceptance of the partner by a much older child is also important for mothers, fully understanding what the relationships of mothers with their partners is based on. This is how one presented what was the very important reaction of her daughter to the fact of her mother's new love: 'Firstly, I like (her mother's new partner). Secondly, I am in a relationship with Jaś, so I understand just how important and special the relationship is and I was hoping that you would encounter this in life at some point'.

Choosing the Father of the Future Child

One of the couples that we interviewed was expecting a child. The primary question in this situation is the choice of the biological father. After reviewing various possibilities and arguments in favor and against, in the light of lack of trust in sperm banks, 'social considerations', as the respondents defined this, again turned out to have decisive significance in making a choice in this matter: 'there is the social issue, this means that we made sure that the child could at some point say who his/her father is, or somehow identify him socially, that's to say we didn't mean the father to function with the child as a father, rather that he be identifiable, that he could be shown the photo, told what his name is'.

It was also important for the situation to be understandable to the children of the second partner and 'equally' for all the children: 'there is one more reason—my children, I didn't want them to get confused due to the fact that she is pregnant and who knows with whom, right? So they could feel (...) this is what the family looks like, that their father exists and there is a new child who also has a father somewhere, we were also concerned about this". We were both concerned to prevent such situations where they say: we have a father and you don't, because sometimes children can be unpleasant and cruel'. It was also pointed out that even in these very open and unconventional relationships the mother made reference to this, for the children to have an concept that the 'family looks like this' and that a biological father—man—is not completely absent.

They got help in this situation—hence biological paternity—from a gay friend. No one hides the fact that the situation is unusual for everyone and no one is certain of their future reactions: 'He was probably afraid of this, that he does not know how he will react, he doesn't know if he will change and want to have contact with the child and we won't allow this. In turn, we were also afraid to some extent that he might lose it and want to take the child'. In this situation flexibility and adapting solutions to the specific stage seems to be the best solution–as the second partner stated: 'we agreed to flexibly react to the current stage, that means the role of a friend in the house and he will remain such, for certain we won't prevent contacts and so forth'. How does the expectant mother sum up the current solution: 'we established that depending on how the situation develops, while the child is little then between us and when the child gets older then also between us, because the chemistry between people plays out differently, no? Hence we will react to that flexibly somehow and that was everything we were able to establish, on the other hand that much'.

The second of the partners adds: 'We reached the conclusion that other things cannot be fixed, because this is not credible ...'

So it was established that while the child is young the female partners will decide on the relationship with the biological father, when slightly older—the child along with the biological father. Nevertheless, it should be stressed that only private agreements, unofficial law, shaped by the parties alone, regulate everything here. Official laws were directly 'evaded' by the parties (though in the light of official law of course such agreements have no binding force). It was established that the child's mother will not give the father's name: 'I won't give (the father's name, we don't have any claims, he doesn't have any claims and from what we found out, we have a year to demand a paternity order, after a year this is not possible; on the other hand he is the kind of person for whom such legal determinations are really irrelevant, to for him reality is most important ...'

Opinions of the Draft Legislation

We asked respondents for their opinion on the domestic partnership law and the possibility for homosexual couples to adopt children. All the respondents believed that the legislation should be passed in order to create the possibility of concluding relationships: 'I think that people should have the power to conclude various kinds of contracts with each other, associated with inheritance of property, granting them rights and duties, if they want this, this possibility should exist, I don't understand why only heterosexual persons can do this (...) this should apply to any relationship'; 'if the legislation on domestic partnerships was not just a dead end, so that it would have specific legislative, insurance solutions, then obviously yes and why not? So we could jointly settle taxes, if we could manage our policies, later, then of course yes'.

On the other hand responses to the question concerning the adoption of children were considerably more varied. Some respondents clearly supported this possibility: 'I also believe the right to adopt children should exist (...) I can as a single mother, but if I wrote a domestic partnership contract then not? Where is the logic in this?' This same respondent stressed that the state does not intervene in single motherhood; it is the exclusive and private matter of the woman: 'the state does not delve into whether I get drunk and end up pregnant, whether I am a sufficiently responsible person to do this and give birth to a child? No one asks this question, then why does the state ask this question in another situation, after all this is my body and if I want to get pregnant I will get pregnant when I want and in any manner'.

Thus, intervention in motherhood in the case of homosexual couples would be a 'negative distinction' of these situations in comparison to any other way of 'becoming a mother'. As other respondents point out, women are in a privileged position, single motherhood is something known socially, accepted and obvious: 'In terms of society, generally the matter is settled for us, I am a divorcee–an ideal situation, no one asks me anything, you know this is not a problem. I have the definite impression of the privilege of our situation ...'

Socially, the situation for men is different and such a solution gives rise to doubts among some women respondents: 'if we lived on an uninhabited island and then let all the lesbians and gays adopt children (...) though to speak the truth sometimes I ask myself the question, if I were a man in the current situation that I am facing would I decide to have a child that has two fathers ... because two mothers is still easier'.

Who is Family?

We also asked these respondents the question of who they count as family. This question, very current in terms of the various transformations families are undergoing, has an additional justification in their case—this is a question of whether their biological family accepts their homosexual relationships sufficiently for their partners and their children's partners to be part of the circle of their own family. Respondents emphasise though, that this applies not only to homosexual relationships: 'our difficulties happen equally in male—female situations (...) relationships, they are nothing strange. The problem for me is this, that my mother does not really accept my relationship (...) due to the boys (sons of my partner), (...) she likes my partner a lot, they get along well, though without the boys, she has not yet gotten to know the boys and I think that she doesn't feel very comfortable, (...) her problem is that she doesn't know how to find a role for herself, once she told my older sister that Magda's kids already have grandmother, even two grandmothers, why bother with a third'. In the estimation of the respondents the problem is not so much sexual or even the problem of 'drawing' children into an atypical situation, but a problem that could be defined as an 'uncertain investment', even more uncertain in that it doesn't provide any official entitlements:

'I think that for her the problem is that I am living with a woman and somehow I will provide for the family—*not my own* ... (...) I am raising the two sons of somebody else, working and will have to lay out money and here you know ... (smiles). And they're not my family and they will one day remind me that I am really not one of them'. The respondents rather frequently point out that currently the biological family has much less importance, that if not for 'blood ties' they would probably never meet them, since they have different interests: ' it imposes this on us, that the family is of blood ties, but … I always had different feelings, because I always had very loose ties with my family'. The fact that the 'biological family' is frequently not the closest circle of people does not mean that the respondents do not have obligations to them. In some cases these obligations also mean protecting parents from knowledge about their own lifestyles: 'yes, parents as well, are also family, a family that deserves something and that increasingly requires care due to their age and also not to harm them, for example to speak to them about my own relations and emotions would harm them'.

The respondents completely agreed on this, that their friends are closest to them and due to this closeness they name them family: 'friends are family (…) I believe that people close in spirit are closer than family'; 'I always felt closer to friends than to persons I am related to by blood'; 'I think that our friends are the persons closest to us'. One of the respondents put particular emphasis on the fact that a family is those persons with whom you build a future and for this reason she defines as family the person with whom she created a home open to many women, though in most cases without sexual ties. She also includes the friend with whom she is building 'plans for old age' as family (who is not and never was her sexual partner): 'in a certain sense my friend is also family. For our old age we want to buy and run a pension house and we have joint retirement plans and I have a relationship to her like family, like a sister that I want to retire with and we will spend this time together, isn't this family?'

State or Private Regulation?

Undoubtedly, in Poland the period of communism made it difficult to accept the interference of the state in private life. Respondents stressed the fact that free, autonomous choices dominate in the private sphere. They emphasise that regardless of legal regulation they 'will do what they want'. They are creating many rules in their private relations, surely more functional than rigid legal regulations. Nevertheless, the lack of state intervention also has another side to it—it means that certain phenomenon lack legal regulations and the inability to register domestic partnerships is certainly seen as a manifestation of this. Even if the respondents are unsure if they would like to make use of them, such a possibility would legitimise their life choices. For this reason, the dispute in this matter is important in Poland largely in the symbolic sphere.

Nevertheless, legal regulations also have other consequences—they are a kind of limitation to flexible, private solutions building unofficial, ad hoc created law. Specific regulation would not permit flexible decisions in many cases—for example, in the case of contact with the future biological father with the child, and as respondents point out—responsible people are unable to foresee all their future decisions—hence the importance of leaving everything to a 'later decision', to the flexible shaping of their relations. In this situation the lack of regulation also has its good side, especially when 'coming out' would be socially difficult for many couples. In Poland it is not the only example of a situation where the lack of strict legal regulations seems to be a benefit. Cases of transsexualism appear similar. A change of sex, together with surgery, is possible and has been possible for decades, though weakly regulated. This 'gap' opens up the possibility for flexible shaping of situations, decision-making freedom adapted each time to individual cases. This seems to confirm the thesis that in the most private cases, the lack of legal regulations seems better than an excess.

PROSPECTS

Nuer and similar traditional family laws provide excellent examples of the flexibility that allows for practical solutions to practical needs. In a society that considers the child valuable this makes possible metaphysical as well practical continuity for individuals. No child is wasted, and every adult is provided with the possibility of having a child. Family legal regimes developed in the West have for centuries excluded some from the chain of reproduction by focusing on the physiological concept of parenthood symbolised as 'transmission of blood', whether this is the sperm, eggs or blood. The physiological theory of parenthood 'by blood' co-existed with others. The Christian doctrine of Divine creation considering not procreation but God's parenthood is referred to daily by millions of believers. If the relationship between teacher and pupil is personal it may result in intellectual parenthood and the transmission of tradition through generations. As for property, the line of succession has been almost always subject to the arbitrary whims of testators. So what are prospects for parenthood in the new age?

The *Cade* case and other similar cases may bring about the widening of the notion of motherhood across the generations, especially if the improvement in the health service, prolongation of age and reproductive age are considered. The 'grand age' divide might thus—as so many other dividing lines in post-modernity—be crossed over, not absolutely, of course, but without the dramatic passage of menopause leaving a whole generation of mothers above the child. We also have the new line of experiment recently opened up by linking two mothers for the one child. The child of many mothers is a genetic reality. 'Classificatory motherhood' will embrace plural motherhood in all senses of the word. However, all these changes may well be considered within previous human experience. If we think of the distinction between male and female roles in parenting, the old Roman maxim that *Mater certa est* is going into disuse. The conclusion is that both mother and father are uncertain which may escalate legal conflicts, but need not undermine parental feelings and attitudes. Even if genes are not passed through the parents, the sense of transmission remains if its metaphysical meaning continues. The conclusion reached by Malinowski seems to be appropriate here when he says that the anthropologist despite the variety of family patterns observes the persistence of the institution of parenthood while it is understood as the 'personal bond based upon socially conceived procreation'.[17] In this sense the new developments fit the old institution.

But that would be too optimistic as a conclusion. In speaking about de-genderisation one encounters two different situations. One is when the gender of the role incumbent is irrelevant as to who will play the given role, but there remains a set of at least two—conveniently called mother and father—different roles to play. In the traditional Nuer family a woman may play the role of the father, and when she does—at least according to EE Evans-Pritchard, she is addressed as such. This is by no means related to sexual activity. The Nuer she-father may have sex with a Dinka domestic or neighbour like her wife does in order to get pregnant. Paternity and maternity are different and complementary. Sex and parenthood are divorced but sex difference, or rather the gender difference, remains as the basic distinction within the family. The defence of the conservative family and marriage model in that case may be expressed in the concern: 'can a woman perform the tasks of the father?' As to the opposite question 'can a man perform the duties of the mother?' the well-intentioned Polish single fathers offer an affirmative answer. The fact is, however, that the latter unintended experiment deals with another meaning of non-gendered parenthood. Of course, the single man as both father and mother or the single woman as both are not uncommon in the European social landscape though always found defective on the presumption of the duality of the parenthood. The lesbians we interviewed, however, provide a new challenge as they abolish maternity reducing it to technicalities in the same way as paternity. If two women are parenting a child claiming no difference in their gender roles (homosexuality in the strongest sense of the word) instead of 'playing' husband and wife the distinction between father and mother is abolished as well. In such a family parenthood is fully de-gendered and generalised. New reproductive technologies made this possible, though not necessary; and they may support socially-gendered parenthood as undifferentiated parenthood as well. Now one may, however, still express a doubt as to whether the biological fact of gender sexual differences will be overcame in such a total way, or whether maternity and paternity will continue though in new combinations and new roles.

---

[17] Cf A Giddens, *The Transformation of Intmacy: Sexuality, Love and Eroticism in Modern Societies* (Cambridge, Polity Press 1992); M Fuszara and J Kurczewski in M Maclean (ed), *Family Law and Family Values*; M Bienko (Not Biełko as erroneously in M Fuszara and J Kurczewski), P Malzenska, *Marital Friendship* (Warsaw, Zak, 2001).

Recently (November 2005) a leading Polish newspaper *Rzeczpospolita* presented two competing views on marriage and family; the more open and permissive attitude was expressed by a German, while the Polish opponent ironically suggested that the he might end up nursing a child acquired through a lottery. Taking into consideration the falling birthrate in Polish and other central European societies, one might really suspect that child rearing will soon become such a rare experience that to distribute its value fairly a lottery will have to be used. On the other hand, human reproduction has always been linked with chance. Genetic transmission until now was hidden behind appearances. The end of humanity will not come when people stop marrying, not even if they cease to be interested in heterosexual sex, but when they cease to be interested in child rearing. On the other hand, these calamities seem fortunately far from being a realistic forecast. It is rather that marriage becomes a post-material bond of friendship[17] and thus perhaps a more intimate pure relationship possibly divorced from sex which is increasingly separate from procreation. Undoing formerly close relations is the problem, not the disappearance of any of these. Adoption, adultery and promiscuity have long worked towards making genetic reproduction only one of many links between parents and children, and the new reproductive technology only widens the scope of these paths for the future.

Part 2

The Conflicts Associated with Post-separation Parenting

4

The Parenting Contest: Problems of Ongoing Conflict over Children

VANESSA MAY AND CAROL SMART

INTRODUCTION

PRIOR TO THE introduction of the Children Act 1989 (England and Wales) there was a great deal of concern over the extent to which legal procedures and legal terminology promoted an adversarial attitude between parents and contributed to hostility at the time of divorce or separation. The architects of the Children Act hoped that by affirming the paramountcy of the welfare principle and promoting a policy of negotiation between parents coupled with non-intervention by the courts, the legislation would go some way to defuse conflict between divorcing parents. The Act was essentially based on the aspiration that a renewed emphasis on the welfare of the child would deflect parents away from (backwards looking) hostility towards a joint (future oriented) parenting project. In refusing to dwell on the past the new ethos also hoped to move parents on in emotional terms, rather than allowing bad feelings to dominate the divorce process. The Act also abolished the legal terms 'custody' and 'access', which were seen to cause a sense of inequality or of winners and losers among parents. These demonstrably inappropriate terms were replaced by the concepts of 'residence' and 'contact', and the new term 'parental responsibility' was introduced to deflect emphasis away from the idea of parental rights over children. The courts were also encouraged to work on the basis that an agreement achieved voluntarily between parents was better than a situation where the judge had to impose an order on the parents (known as the 'no order' principle) (Dewar, 2000) and thus courts hoped to steer (some would say pressure) parents towards an agreement (Davis and Pearce, 1999c). All these measures, taken together, were meant to emphasise a sense of 'shared' parenting after divorce or separation and to impress on separated and divorced parents that they should desist from continued conflict over children's matters because of the harm caused to children. Furthermore, with the implementation of the Child Support Act 1991 and the setting up of the Child Support Agency, child support issues were separated from the judicial management of divorce, separation, matrimonial property, residence and contact. Although this reform was driven by different principles and developed separately from the Children Act, it was also hoped that in turning child support into an essentially bureaucratic issue, separate from personal and/or emotional issues, the opportunities for conflict would be reduced.

More recently still, with the realisation that conflict between parents seems not to have abated, it has been felt that it would help parents to overcome their conflicts if they could be directed towards their children's needs and anguish more clearly. So an increasing emphasis has been placed on the voice of the child, in addition to the more conventional welfare of the child principle. So more information is being made available to parents about children's experiences of divorce, and greater consideration is being given to involving the voices of children (if not actual children) in mediation and court processes.

The laudable goals of the Children Act 1989 have not, however, been fully met and there is increasing frustration with parents who seem, from the courts' perspective, unable to act in accordance with the best interests of their children. In response to this the British Government produced a Green Paper entitled *Parental separation: Children's Needs and Parents' Responsibilities* (2004) in which new reforms were aired. These, once again, aimed to tackle the issue of conflict between separated and divorced parents through the introduction of new measures. These included the introduction of 'parenting plans', a restructuring of the legal aid system, the use of in-court conciliation, the launch of the Family Resolutions Pilot Project, changing the role of CAFCASS away from passive report writing towards more active problem-solving, better monitoring and enforcement of contact orders, and a wider use of Family Assistance Orders.

It was in this context that we undertook a study of residence and contact disputes in court (Smart et al, 2003; Smart et al, 2005) in order to explore the question why some parents seem to find it impossible to 'move on' from their conflict despite pressures to do so from the new child centred ethos, the legal profession and the courts. In this chapter we highlight first the complex array of issues underlying residence and contact disputes before looking at possible reasons why, in some cases, conflict fails to abate. We argue that there are a number of levels that need to be addressed when seeking to understand these conflicts and we also acknowledge that it may be impossible to 'resolve' conflict where the issues have become deeply embedded in the parental or post-divorce identities of the parties involved. We also question the modern divorce ethos which presumes that rational, well-adjusted parents will (or should) 'move on' from the emotional pain of divorce. This is because we found that the injuries of divorce are rarely in the past but are, for some couples at least, constantly refreshed in the present because the original problem was either never resolved or because new problems arise as circumstances change.

THE STUDY

The data for this study were gathered from three county courts in England which were selected on the basis of their different catchment areas. This offered us a reasonable geographical spread as well as a variety of different cultural localities. We conducted the study in three stages. The first stage consisted of an overview of a random sample of residence and contact disputes brought to the three county courts in the year 2000. At this stage, we were interested in gaining an understanding of the types of dispute brought to court, and of how the courts dealt with them in general. In the second stage, we conducted a closer analysis of a subsample of these files to get a more detailed picture of the court process and the arguments put forward by the various parties. Court files provide limited information on these disputes however, and so we felt it was important to supplement this with data on how the individual parents involved in these court processes perceived their experiences. To this end, the final stage of the study consisted of interviews with 61 mothers and fathers who had been involved in these disputes. The findings of this chapter draw on all three stages, but the main argument presented here is based on data from the interviews with the parents. All the interview quotes have been anonymised to protect the identity of our interviewees.

ISSUES FUELLING DISPUTES OVER RESIDENCE AND CONTACT

In Smart and May (2004) we reported on findings which indicated that disputes over residence and contact tend to involve a complex array of issues. Putting this briefly, we found that the disputes presented as being about children's welfare, but these issues were often enmeshed in parental disputes and arose from the problems of the relationship rather than relating independently to the children (assuming that this is feasible anyway). In addition to these presenting concerns over children's welfare, there were three main issues that parents brought to court: financial disputes; the aftermath of broken trust; and the problem of adjusting to new partners.

Financial Disputes

In accord with many other studies (Maclean and Eekelaar, 1997; Lewis et al, 2002: 29, 39–40; Bradshaw et al, 1999; Trinder et al, 2002: 33; Herring, 2003: 95–96; Davis, Wikeley and Young, 1998; Barton, 1998 and Smart's Preface to *Fathers' Rights Activsm and Law Reform*, Collier and Sheldon eds, 2006), we found that the parents in our sample felt that child support and contact were interconnected issues. Typically, residential parents (most often mothers) claimed that the contact parent (most often fathers) showed their lack of commitment to the children by failing to pay child support, and thus they were deemed to have forfeited their right to contact. This feeling, it appears, runs very deep because financial support appears to be taken as a proxy for love. Thus, culturally speaking the 'good' father is still predominantly envisaged as a good provider while the converse, the poor provider, is seen as a poor excuse for a father:

> Susan: Yes, basically he went from paying two hundred and eighty odd pounds a month maintenance to twenty two pounds something a month maintenance and then he did not have to pay any maintenance at all after that. After about two or three months I thought 'Well if he is not paying maintenance, when I know that he has got money, when I knew that he had got money and he was not paying maintenance', I thought, 'Well right, he won't have the pleasure of seeing his son'. (Residential mother, contact dispute)

Many parents worked with the moral calculation that the father who is economically supportive shows himself to be sufficiently decent to merit contact. It is taken as a sign of trustworthiness and good character. The father who does not do his duty by his children is seen to be an unworthy figure in their lives and when the courts appear to 'overlook' this deep character flaw it is often found to be quite offensive to everyday morality:

> Ellen: I cannot get a penny and I feel that that is another issue that really the court should pick up and sort out. And I feel most disgruntled that time and time again the issue of maintenance was brought up very, very vaguely and just wiped under the carpet. (Residential mother, contact dispute)

These parents' views may be out of step with current ideas about the wisdom of separating issues of financial support from issues of contact, yet they hold fast to a moral code in which it is the father's obligation to support his children and, through this economic support, to demonstrate both love and responsibility, while it is the mother's obligation to facilitate the father—child bond or relationship as long as he behaves as fathers 'should'.

The belief that paying child support is a moral duty appears to receive wide support in England and Wales. An Omnibus Survey in 2004 reported that 81 per cent of the respondents thought that fathers should pay child support (Peacey and Rainford, 2004: 14). Sixty-seven per cent of the respondents went further and asserted that a father should pay the same amount of support to his first family regardless of whether he had subsequent children (Peacey and Rainford, 2004, 15). In other words a commitment to the duty that fathers should provide economic support for their (first) children runs deep. This finding is relevant to our smaller qualitative study because it puts in context the strength of feeling that parents express when a father fails to support his children, or when a father is supporting his children yet cannot have contact. We found that the bureaucratic disaggregation of financial support from emotional support was not something that many parents could readily grasp because it simply ran counter to their ethical code. For the parents it was a combined moral obligation, not a disaggregated bureaucratic one.[1]

The Aftermath of Broken Trust

Another set of issues that could be uppermost in parents' minds was to do with broken trust, broken vows, and how to come to terms with what was perceived to be bad faith on the part of a former spouse. This meant that although parents often knew that they 'should' be focusing on their children, they were actually preoccupied with blame and recrimination. Trinder et al (2002: 38) also found that the way in which the emotions connected with a relationship breakdown were managed by parents affected the quality and quantity of contact. The parents in our sample, for example, could use details of past infidelity against the other parent. In these cases, it seemed as though the dispute was actually about the failed relationship between the parents, and this acrimony spilled over into matters of contact and residence. Thus, some parents might have agreed contact, but the arrangements kept breaking down because of their continued bitterness rather than for reasons to do with the best interests of the child.

In the interviews some parents went further and would make a link between bad behaviour and suitability to parent. This is what Day Sclater (1999: 172) has identified as a part of the divorce process, namely looking back at the past to make sense of and reinterpret events. And James (2003: 136–37) argues that it is perhaps too much to expect that parents should not do this. In our sample, such revisiting of the past could mean that the parent who had left the marriage was seen as having less of a claim to the children:

> Richard: In fact I do think if you commit adultery you should forfeit the right for everything.
> *Interviewer: Children included?*
> Richard: Yes because you have broken, you have broken a contract really haven't you? I mean anything in life if you break a contract you have broke it haven't

---

[1] Although the Children Act 1989 treats these issues as separate, it is actually confusing for parents that the Child Support Agency, when calculating child support payments, *does* take the amount of contact into consideration.

you, because what is the point of having that, what is that marriage licence for? You know surely it is a contract for something isn't it? (Contact father, residence dispute)

According to this view the party who was 'morally culpable' or 'to blame' for the relationship breakdown should not benefit from their behaviour. Such views are not supported by the Children Act 1989, but interestingly they would not have been incongruous with legal policy before the Divorce Reform Act 1969. In our sample it was mainly fathers who held these views and they were quite clear that they were the innocent parties and that justice lay in punishing the guilty. This meant that 'losing' the residence of their children added insult to injury and that these fathers could not 'get over' their anger at all easily.

Adjusting to New Partners

The third issue raised by many of the parents as central to the conflict was that of new partners. Even quite good arrangements that might have existed between divorced parents could be disrupted when one of them re-partnered (Simpson et al, 1995: 17, 30–31; Trinder et al, 2002: 32; Bradshaw et al, 1999: 110–111; Smart and Neale, 1999). This theme of new partners igniting or being the root cause of a dispute also emerged from our interview data. We got the impression from many of the accounts that arrangements might have been running relatively smoothly until one of the parents re-partnered, which then caused problems for contact with the children.

> Steven: And obviously the more, I explained to my ex-wife, the more I got settled, which she was quite happy with, which she put in her initial statement to the court, that obviously the access would increase as time went on. And she did not have a problem with it. After six months she then started a relationship with someone she knew and I knew in the past and it deteriorated to the point were we had to go to court. (Contact father, contact dispute)

In other cases, it was the contact parent's new partner who gave rise to problems with contact. In these cases non-residential parents often saw the emergence of new hostility as the result of jealous and/or spiteful behaviour on the part of the residential parents; behaviour that they believed was against the interests of the children. Residential parents, however, spoke of their worry about their children being brought up by or being 'taken over' by a potential rival parent (cf Trinder et al, 2002: 32). In some of the interviews we conducted it was clear that the arrival of a new partner could signal 'real' problems as, for example, in the case of a father we interviewed who admitted that his children's mother had stopped contact because his second wife had been an alcoholic. In this case, once his second marriage ended, his first wife allowed staying contact with their children to be resumed. So the fears that parents may have about new 'step' parents can be well founded and speak deeply to issues of who they feel they can trust to look after their children.

Conflict Refreshed

Parents who appear to be unable to be civil to one another years after a divorce are often seen as in need of psychological help. This is because divorce is seen as a rupture which, although acknowledged as being very painful, is an adverse life event that can and should be left behind as time starts to heal the wounds. However, in the relatively new context of contemporary divorce, parents are expected to remain in contact with one another, and even to continue to parent jointly. This means that there are constant opportunities for conflicts (and pain) to be refreshed. A residential mother whose standard of living is depressed and who receives very little child support may find it hard to 'get over' the fact that her ex-husband collects the children in a new BMW. The following quote from Ellen shows how a sense of injustice may be continually refreshed:

> Ellen: When Wes left me I was penniless, I feel very disgruntled that the court would not in any way pick up any maintenance issues, 'Oh we will just leave that to the CSA'. I am still waiting for the CSA to sort it out and it is four years down the line. I feel very disgruntled about that because my ex-husband has a three hundred acre farm in [X]shire, he has a 4 × 4 Shogun, she has a Nissan Patrol, they have race horses, they have just bought a brand new tractor. (Residential mother, contact dispute)

Equally, if a former spouse has a series of new relationships and expects the children to treat each one in the same way as a parent—regardless of their affinity towards the children—then the conflict is not necessarily an 'old' one based on jealousy, but a new one based on concern for the children. If a parent suspects a new partner of abusive or inappropriate behaviour this is also not experienced as something to be 'got over':

> Norman: Then I heard that Ashley had been hit. I was walking past the school and Ashley said 'Dad, dad, dad'. And of course I got over to her 'What is up darling?' 'Lee hit me'. Well it's like rocket fuel that is someone has hit your kid.
> *Interviewer: That is your ex-wife's boyfriend?*
> Norman: Yes, so I calmed down, 'Fine, Ashley, leave it with me'. I got in the car straight down to Social Services, told them, [X], 'Right' he said, 'I will look into it'. (Contact father, residence dispute)

These parents considered their *current* circumstances as a problem, not their past circumstances. They were not necessarily in conflict because of unresolved emotions about the divorce[2] but because of new issues thrown up in the course of the new relationship they were forging with an ex-spouse. Unfortunately for these parents, many of the issues that they believed to be central to their dispute were not considered to be significant by the court if they did not directly impinge on the welfare of the children. The court's wish to disaggregate these issues (to avoid unnecessarily dwelling on difficult issues) was considered by many parents to be unethical, or at least uncaring. In cases such as these, simply trying to deflect the conflict or hoping that it could be resolved by a few hours' of mediation is an unrealistic expectation. We argue that in order to tackle and perhaps resolve their conflicts, these parents may require an alternative or additional arena to the courts[3] where they can at least voice their hurt and feel as though they are listened to, if not work through their conflict. This, however, is not the primary task of the courts, nor can they be expected to shoulder it within present legal and institutional constraints. However, some of the parents who expect the courts to work within the same moral framework and with the same ethical principles as they themselves do, will perhaps perpetually be dissatisfied with the courts and feel they have suffered an injustice that they are unwilling to accept. A father like Jeffrey (below) for example simply operated with a set of values or ideas that are at complete variance with empirical reality:

> Jeffrey: The simple truth was as the judge said in his own words 'It is normal for the children to live with their mother so that is where they will live'. Frankly I think that is a load of rubbish. It is not normal for the children to live with their mother. It is normal for the children to live with their father; that is the normal thing. The family follows the father, where the father has work the family goes with the father. That is the normal, that is normality, however I lost the children who were forced to go back home. (Contact father, residence dispute; the children live in another town and have staying contact over the holidays)

PERSONAL INVESTMENTS IN CONFLICT

Above we have provided an overview of the kinds of dispute that are brought to court by parents. These often involved difficult emotions and deep-seated issues for parents, which partly explain why some parents were unable to focus solely on the issue of children's welfare, or to 'move on' from a dispute by forgetting past ills and focusing on future co-operation

---

[2] Although it is quite possible that 'old' and 'new' emotions can combine in these circumstances and certainly that 'new'conflicts may themselves resurrect old feelings and old reactions.

[3] In cases of failure to pay child support, of course, it is not a matter of counselling but one of improving the service to residential parents through the Child Support Agency.

with their former spouse. However, we argue that this alone does not explain why some parents remain locked in conflict for years, while other parents, who on the face of it enter the legal system with similar disputes, manage to resolve these relatively speedily with the help of the courts. So the issue we now move on to discuss is an even more profound aspect of these disputes and is one that is tied in with these parents' perception of themselves as moral beings. This issue we have termed the 'parenting contest'.

We propose that the prolonged nature of some disputes can partly be explained by the at times significant personal investments that these parents placed in the conflict itself. For some parents the outcome of the court case was tied in with their identity as a moral person and as a 'good' parent. In addition, many parents approached their court case with an adversarial stance, believing that the outcome should be one of a 'winner' and a 'loser' (notwithstanding the Children Act's attempt to do away with the idea of one parent winning and the other parent losing). The combined effect of these two tendencies was that for many parents the prospect of losing their case was too dire to contemplate. The consequences of such a loss would have been too overwhelming for their sense of self and sense of worth as a parent.

In this sense these conflicts were not solely about the issues under dispute, but also about personal qualities. These things often overlap of course but we feel there is an important nuance to be grasped here which helps us understand what is going on for some of these parents. Losing an argument over an 'issue' may be significant for anyone in a dispute, but appearing to lose the 'parenting contest' means that a parent is required to redefine him or herself as an inadequate person—or to accept that the courts have defined them as less adequate than the other parent. Those parents who set the stakes of their conflict in this way inevitably had problems dealing with what they then saw as a 'failure' if they did not 'win' residence or a larger portion of contact.

That there was a 'parenting contest' going on for some parents became apparent in our interviews from the manner in which the interviewees tended to construct themselves as the 'good' parent who was in the right and whose case was based on the best interests of the children, while the other parent was constructed as a 'bad' parent who had been in the wrong and whose main motivation in the dispute was pettiness or revenge. Thus many of the interviewees tried to convince the interviewer that the other parent was a completely inadequate parent who could not know, or was not interested in, the children's best interests, while also presenting themselves as the parent with superior parenting capabilities and a better/closer relationship with the children (cf Bradshaw et al, 1999: 119; Day Sclater and Kaganas, 2003: 158). Thus Sandra below is already anticipating that if her children fall into difficulties as they grow up it will be because of their father. She does not understand the situation as one involving interactions between both parents and the children:

> Sandra: They are just going to grow up to be … well hopefully the way I bring them up, they are not going to be like their dad. But what they have seen and how he has behaved I would not be surprised if they went totally off the rails, you know, if I didn't try and guide them, that is just how I feel. (Residential mother, contact dispute)

When discussing and comparing the two parents' abilities to care for their children, the interviewees tended to focus on three central elements: caring for the children's material needs; caring for the children's emotional needs; and providing the children with a suitable environment in which to grow up. Parents engaged in a contest with one another were keen to suggest that the standards of their care were superior to those of their former spouse. Many voiced fears for their children's well-being through neglect or abuse by the other parent:

> Norman: Apart from the children are scruffy, Ashley has always got nits in her hair. When she comes round here the first thing I do is give her a bath because she stinks of urine and all sorts of things, because the environment she is living in now, is like, it is very difficult to say. (Contact father, residence dispute)

In their efforts to construct their own parenting as superior, the parents provided an insight into their own relationship with their children. Norman, for example, seems unaware that his reaction to his daughter may be emotionally harmful—even if it seems sensible in terms of personal hygiene. Parents like Norman insisted that they had a more loving relationship and deeper emotional connection with their children than the other parent did. Equally, Gina below sought opportunities to prove her superiority:

> Gina: I have asked them, I don't question them, but you try to establish the kind of relationship that he has with them and there has been time when I have said, I mean I go up to Scot and Otto every night, I give them a kiss and a hug and we have a cuddle and a laugh and I go 'I love you' and they go 'I love you too mum, I love you loads'. And I will say to Scot 'So does dad come and tuck you up and say he loves you?' You know kind of bringing that subject [up] and I say 'He never says he loves you?' and he goes 'No' and I have never seen him hug or kiss those boys, at the front door he just goes 'See you lads'. It is bizarre. (Residential mother)

In this extract it is possible to see the ways in which Gina subtly disparages the children's father and seeks to demonstrate to them (and to herself and the interviewer) that she is the better parent.

A third building block in the construction of the 'good parent' emerged in the passages where the parents talked about how they were able and willing to provide a better example for their children by encouraging them to achieve their fullest potential and by setting a good example and boundaries:

> Tariq: You know it was just continuous you know just basically trying her best to make me give up on my children instead of looking it as well you know everything is stable now and the children are getting [on]. And the children start, you know, my boy just went straight out in school and he is in the top classes now. Amazing—from a withdrawn little child, you can see the photo there, he is withdrawn. Now you look at him, they have totally changed, you know they are happy, they are content and that is what makes you realise that I have done the right thing. Do you know what I mean? And when I wake up in a morning and I see the smile and I think to myself 'Thank god I did the right thing'. (Residential father, residence dispute)

Of course, we cannot have an opinion on whether Tariq was a 'better parent' or not, nor whether his children were thriving more with him than they would have done with their mother. Rather the point is that this quotation reveals how important it is for this father to have (and to show) evidence of his superior parenting abilities. Other fathers too were so convinced that they were better parents that they simply could not comprehend why the courts did not see their case in the same light:

> Nadeem: I was not expecting that kind of response, or reaction to what I had done for my children. ... I kept saying to myself I am not doing anything wrong. I am the father of these children; I have every right to stand up for their rights because they are too young to stand up for themselves. And therefore I expect the authorities, the judges, everybody to listen to me. (Contact father, residence dispute which has become a contact dispute, no contact)

Despite the aims of the Children Act 1989, it can be argued that the legal process nonetheless sustains (even if it does not approve of) an adversarial approach to disputes. As King (2000: 542) argues because the courts make 'legal' decisions, it means that one parent must be found to be right and the other 'wrong'. This contributes to the sense of losing that we have found in our interviews. Because residence and contact disputes are resolved on the basis of children's welfare, the parents seemed to think that the 'winner' of the case had been seen by the court as the 'good' parent, while the 'loser' had been branded a 'bad' parent. The parents often alluded to such issues by viewing the court's decision in terms of quality of parenting. Although Sharon in the quotation below did not feel she lost the parenting contest, her summary of the decision making process makes it clear that she thought that the courts were weighing up the qualities and capabilities of each parent and measuring them against each other:

> Sharon: So sort of things are viewed on both sides, we were both found to be equally good parents, there was no real sort of bad view taken on the fact that we

lived in a flat without a garden. The fact that he has got a detached house with a garden in a village location. The only recommendation would be for Michelle not to change schools. Which, by which time we were living here, that was the downfall of things not going quite how we wanted them to go. ... They could find nothing wrong with either parent. We were both equally capable on the parenting skills that they like to term it as. (Contact mother, residence dispute)

The parents who felt they had 'lost' evinced surprise at the ease with which the other parent had been able to 'dupe' the court into believing that they were capable parents:

Russell: The way she was going on in court, making packs and packs of lies up and I used to sit there and I just could not believe that she used to come out with it and the thing that really disgusted me in the court was, she used to say all these things in court and tell packs of lies and when the court welfare officer was assigned to the case, when it was found out not to be true it did not seem to make any difference. And it absolutely disgusted me that she was just being given this ticket to just tell lies and so what if you were found out that it is a lie, so what. And then this just gave her more of an incentive to go and tell more and more lies and that I could not come to terms with that all. (Contact father, contact dispute)

While the parents who believed they had 'won' seemed to feel no small degree of vindication:

Interviewer: *Did you feel you got to say your piece? You said the barrister was questioning your skills as a mum?*
Julianne: Yes, yes I got this inner strength from somewhere I don't know where it came from and I still say this to this day, I honestly don't know where it came from. ... And this inner strength just came from nowhere and this barrister was, you know, really trying to rip me to pieces and I stuck up for myself and I thought yes, I came out of there and when the judge said 'Residence will remain the same', I could not help it, I sort of went 'Yes! I have done it again'.

These interviews thus give an insight into why these conflicts can become so entrenched, namely because the parents have so much invested in the conflict including their own identity and reputation as a 'good' parent. It is therefore perhaps understandable that parents who find themselves in this position may find 'losing' a hard pill to swallow and will continue to make their case and fight their corner because to not do so would mean conceding to an evaluation as a 'bad' parent.

It is also worth considering that a parent who adopts this approach and who has gone to court has probably kept close friends and family informed of their intentions and so can find it even more difficult to back down because of the 'loss of face' that would be involved. They would have to admit to family and friends to having been wrong or appear to be accepting a situation that is not in the best interests of their children. This would not only go against their own sense of being a 'good' parent but would make it 'public' that they are judged to be unsatisfactory parents.

The Management of Emotions

The focus on the unreasonableness of parents who take their conflicts to court or who cannot come to a resolution masks another set of issues we uncovered in our interviews. This is the problem of managing other people's emotions when a parent's own emotional state may be precarious. In particular parents have to manage the difficult emotions of their children and they have to be able to interpret them in order to know how to respond. Research on children's own reports on their emotional responses to contact reveals that they may feel ambivalence, a sense of bereavement and loss at transition times, a sense of guilt about leaving a parent, and also a sense of disappointment with one or both parents (Smart et al, 2001). We found that the manner in which parents 'read' and manage these difficult and sometime conflicting emotions could become part of the ongoing conflict between parents. So, if a child returns from a visit visibly upset, the residential parent may interpret this as meaning the visit is harmful to the child. Or if a child cries on leaving the residential parent it may be interpreted as meaning the child does not want to go with the contact parent. Of course, these interpretations may be 'correct', however it is also possible that some parents may 'over-interpret' their children's feelings and see them as extensions of their own emotions. In the quotation below, Susan is reflexive about her son's reactions and she does not take his upset to be a lever in a battle to reduce contact:

> Susan: I know there is going to be times when Nicholas does not want to go to his dad's, there is something going on here that he wants to stay for. Or there is going to be times that he does not want to come home from his dad's. And I know that and I expect that, I am anticipating it; but it has not happened very often. He went through a really, really clingy stage when he was about three or four but it did not last long. But I can remember his dad stood at the door saying 'Come on Nicholas you are coming to daddy's'. 'I don't want to go'. But I don't think it was long after his brother was born, so maybe he felt a bit left out of it when he went, I don't know. (Residential mother, contact dispute)

It is easy to see how another parent might draw a different conclusion to this situation, namely that her child was behaving in this manner because he preferred to be with his mother. Equally it is possible to see that the father might think the mother encouraged this 'clinginess' in order to exclude him. These are excruciatingly difficult situations and they pose difficult emotional dilemmas that parents have to deal with without any professional help or support. It is understandable that, in the context of lack of trust, problems with money and new partners, such issues can contribute to a prolonging of hostilities between the parents. The parenting contest can be refreshed when children exhibit what could be interpreted as preferences, which in turn can be interpreted by parents as proof that they indeed are the 'better' parent, thus perhaps re-igniting the original reasons for dispute. The quotation from Hafiz below seems, in the light of this, to be a classic example of igniting the fuse of renewed and destructive conflict:

> Hafiz: In the early days when I used to have contact I would sort of bring him home and then when it was time for me to take him back he would not want to go back to the mother. I had to actually convince him 'Look let's go there and ask mum whether he could still stay an extra couple of days' and he would actually cry really, really cry and he would not want to go back. (Contact father, contact dispute)

CONCLUSIONS

In this chapter, we have discussed the ways in which conflicts over residence and contact are composed of various strands some of which may not be directly concerned with the children's best interests, we have pointed out that it is difficult to 'get over' disputes which are constantly refreshed, and indicated how difficult it can be for parents to manage and interpret the emotions of others, especially their children. In addition, we have argued that some parents construct their disputes as a parenting contest between the 'good' and the 'bad' parent resulting in a 'winner' and a 'loser' scenario where the stakes are extremely high. All these factors combined mean that in some cases parents may find it virtually impossible to back down from their stance, especially if they continue to believe that their arguments represent the best interests of the children.

It is not surprising therefore that some cases are difficult to resolve nor is it surprising that the legal system itself and family law professionals become despairing of how to settle these most entrenched conflicts. Responses to these conflicts have, in debates, swung from the punitive (imprisonment or removal of the child) to semi-therapeutic (provision of more mediation or more Family Assistance Orders) and in some cases these may be either appropriate or helpful. But the problem is that family courts have neither the resources nor the knowledge to find out or know exactly which of the available 'remedies' is likely to be suited to a particular family. As Lamb has argued (see chapter one in this book) the courts know that in some cases of conflicted contact the damage to the child of insisting on contact outweighs the benefits of sustaining a relationship—yet no one knows when this point is reached in any particular case. Notwithstanding this, courts are, we suggest, moving inexorably towards the micro-management of family life because of the political pressures on them to sort out post-separation parental conflict. Yet, even assuming that this drift towards an intensified governance of individual families was acceptable, the courts do not have the appropriate knowledge and tools to succeed in this goal. This is producing a kind of modern folly in which family courts are being increasingly set up as if they can and should solve complex human relationship problems. When they fail, as our research suggests they are likely to, they will be required to produce a greater intensification of effort and so the cycle will repeat itself. The question that therefore perhaps requires greater attention is whether, if the aims of family policy are to protect and promote the well-being of children, this is ultimately the best use of scarce resources.

REFERENCES

Barton, C (1998) 'Third time lucky for child support? The 1998 Green Paper' *Family Law* 28, 668–72.

Bradshaw, J, Stimson, C, Skinner, C and Williams, J (1999) *Absent Fathers?* (London, Routledge).

Davis, G and Pearce, J (1999c) 'A view from the trenches—Practice and procedure in section 8 applications' *Family Law* 29, 457–66.

Davis, G, Wikeley, N and Young, R (with Barron, J and Bedward, J (1998) Child Support in Action (Oxford, Hart Publishing).

Day Sclater, S (1999) *Divorce: A Psychosocial Study* (Aldershot, Ashgate).

Day Sclater, S and Kaganas, F (2003) 'Contact: Mothers, welfare and rights' in A Bainham, B Lindley, M Richards and L Trinder (eds), *Children and their Families: Contact, Rights and Welfare* (Oxford, Hart Publishing).

Dewar, J (2000) 'The family and its discontents' *International Journal of Law, Policy and the Family* 14, 59–85.

Herring, J (2003) 'Connecting contact: Contact in a private law setting' in A Bainham, B Lindley, M Richards, and L Trinder (eds), *Children and their Families: Contact, Rights and Welfare* (Oxford, Hart Publishing).

James, A (2003) 'Squaring the circle—the social, legal and welfare organisation of contact' in A Bainham, B Lindley, M Richards, and L Trinder (eds), *Children and their Families: Contact, Rights and Welfare* (Oxford, Hart Publishing).

King, M (2000) 'Future uncertainty as a challenge to law's programmes: The dilemma of parental disputes' *Modern Law Review* 63, 523–43.

Lewis, C, Papacosta, A and Warin, J (2002) *Cohabitation, Separation and Fatherhood* (York, Joseph Rowntree Foundation).

Maclean, M and Eekelaar, J (1997) *The Parental Obligation: A Study of Parenthood across Households* (Oxford, Hart Publishing).

Parental Separation: Children's Needs and Parents' Responsibilities (2004) Government Green Paper, Cm 6273 (London, The Stationery Office).

Parental Separation: Children's Needs and Parents' Responsibilities—Next Steps (2004) Government Report of the responses to consultation and agenda for action, Cm 6452 (London, The Stationery Office).

Peacey, V and Rainford, L (2004) *Attitudes towards child support and knowledge of the Child Support Agency, 2004* (Research Report No 226) (London, Corporate Document Services/Department for Work and Pensions).

Simpson, B, McCarthy, P and Walker, J (1995) 'Being there: Fathers after divorce' (Relate Centre for Family Studies, University of Newcastle upon Tyne).

Smart, C, May, V, Wade, A, and Furniss, C (2003) *Residence and contact disputes in court,* vol 1 (Research Series No 6/03) (London, Department for Constitutional Affairs).

Smart, C, and May, V (2004) 'Why can't they agree? The underlying complexity of contact and residence disputes' *Journal of Social Welfare and Family Law* 26, 347–60.

Smart, C, May, V, Wade, A and Furniss, C (2005) *Residence and contact disputes in court,* vol 2 (Research Series No 4/05) (London, Department for Constitutional Affairs).

Smart, C, and Neale, B (1999) *Family Fragments?* (Cambridge, Polity Press).

Smart, C, Neale, B, Wade, A (2001) *The Changing Experience of Childhood: Families and Divorce* (Cambridge, Polity Press).

Smart, C (2006) 'Preface' in R Collier and S Sheldon (eds), *Father's Rights, Activism and Law Reform* (Oxford, Hart Publishing).

Trinder, L, Beek, M, and Connolly, J (2002) *Making contact: How parents and children negotiate and experience contact after divorce* (York, Joseph Rowntree Foundation).

5

Dangerous Dads and Malicious Mothers: The Relevance of Gender to Contact Disputes

LIZ TRINDER

INTRODUCTION

PROFOUND CHANGES IN the pattern of family life over recent decades have been accompanied by considerable rethinking of social norms about family relationships, rights and obligations, particularly following family reordering. Some of the drivers or influences on the development of new social norms are ideas about the importance (or otherwise) of the blood tie, generational status, culture and relationship quality (see, for example, Bainham et al, 1999; Bainham et al, 2003). In this chapter, however, I focus on the role gender plays in debates about post-divorce or post-separation parenting, particularly in relation to disputes about contact.

Over recent years the debate about post-divorce or separation parenting in both the UK and elsewhere has become increasingly split, even polarised, on gendered lines. Child residence/contact has developed as a key site for what has been described as a 'gender war' (eg Bala, 1999). Pressure groups, generally representing either mothers or fathers, have been extremely active in attempting to shape public opinion on residence/contact issues as well as seeking to influence policy and practice within and surrounding the family justice system. In the UK fathers' rights groups such as Fathers 4 Justice were particularly prominent until disbanding in January 2006 after media reports of their plans to kidnap the son of Prime Minister Tony Blair, but groups representing mothers such as Women's Aid have also been very active in the area. In this chapter I first explore two opposing constructions of the problem of contact offered by the two sides: the malicious mother and dangerous dad narratives. I then track the influence of each narrative on policy within the family justice system. I then draw on a recent empirical study to explore the extent to which these constructions do in fact reflect the concerns of mothers and fathers involved in legal disputes about contact. The findings suggest that gender does shape some aspects of post-divorce parenting and some parents do employ gendered themes, including the dangerous dad and malicious mother narratives. In other respects, however, gender also obscures the common problems and conflicts of parents involved in disputes about contact.

THE LEGAL FRAMEWORK: FROM PATERNAL RIGHTS TO GENDER NEUTRALITY

In England, as in other Western jurisdictions, gender has waxed and waned as a critical or at least visible determinant of parental rights and responsibilities following divorce. Prior to the Custody of Infants Act 1839 all legal rights over legitimate children were vested in fathers (Bainham, 2005). The rights of mothers were slowly developed over the course of the nineteenth century with the Guardianship of Infants Act 1886 extending the discretionary powers of the court to award mothers custody of children up to the age of 21 (Smart, 1989; Bainham, 2005). Mothers only acquired statutory equality with fathers in custody disputes with the Guardianship of Infants Act in 1925. It is worth noting, however, that this move also reflected a shift away from parental rights (whether those of fathers or mothers) and towards parental duties towards children and child welfare as the 'first and paramount consideration' (Smart, 1989; Day Sclater et al, 1999).

Since 1925 the legislative framework governing arrangements for post-separation or divorced parenting has been avowedly gender-neutral. The current legal framework provided by the Children Act 1989 makes no specific reference to parental gender and instead the concept of parental responsibility applies equally to mothers and fathers. The one exception to this, the lack of automatic parental responsibility for unmarried fathers in the original legislation, has been partially remedied so that since 2003, unmarried fathers jointly registering a child's birth also have PR automatically.[1] Otherwise the Children Act 1989 avoids articulating specific guidelines about post-separation parenting. There is no presumption of contact with non-resident parents, though such a presumption or assumption was established (and continues) in case law and local court practice (Bailey-Harris, 2001). Nor does the Act specify rules to guide the determination of contact or residence, such as the 'friendly parent' or 'primary caretaker' rules. Instead the Act requires that the child's welfare should be the paramount consideration in court decision-making (s 1(1)), with courts required to consider a 'welfare checklist'.

---

[1] Adoption and Children Act 2002, s 111. The change was informed by research finding significant numbers of unmarried fathers were unaware of their lack of legal status (Pickford, 1999). Unmarried fathers who have not jointly registered the birth, or did so prior to 2003, can register a Parental Responsibility Agreement (PRA) with the mothers' consent, or apply to the court for a Parental Responsibility Order if the mother refuses her consent. Courts seldom refuse to grant PR to genetic fathers.

PARENTING IN PRACTICE

Although the legal framework is apparently gender-neutral, family and parental practices remain highly gendered. Over the last decade father involvement in child care in intact families has increased, but still remains significantly lower than for mothers, even in dual-earner families (see Lamb and Lewis, 2004; O'Brien and Shemilt, 2003; Barrett, 2004).

The pattern of residence and involvement post-separation is also clearly differentiated on gender lines. In the 2001 census 91 per cent of children in lone or single parent families were living with their mothers, a figure that is very similar in other Commonwealth jurisdictions (Pryor and Rogers, 2001). It is worth noting that under English law it is up to parents to make decisions about residence and contact following separation or divorce with the courts available only if parents cannot reach agreement. In practice only about 10 per cent of families turn to the courts for assistance in reaching decisions (Blackwell and Dawe, 2003). Thus the predominance of mother-resident parents generally reflects parental rather than professional decision-making or, in some cases, a process of drift into non-decision-making. Of course, the gender-neutral language of 'parenthood' in the Children Act 1989 did not aspire to shift patterns of primary caretaking.

The result, however, is that post-separation parenting has a strongly gendered character with a high degree of overlap between the categories of resident/non-resident parent and mother/father. This is equally true for parents who approach or have used the courts as for parents who agree arrangements privately. In our study reported below, for example, 89 per cent of parents who were approaching the court with a dispute about contact for the first time were in resident mother/non-resident father arrangements.

PRESSURE GROUPS AND POLICE

The gendered reality of post-divorce parenting has contributed to the development in England of pressure groups largely representing either mothers or fathers. In broad terms, groups representing fathers have emphasised the importance of fathers to children post-separation but argued that resident mothers all too often seek to exclude fathers from their children's lives, while family courts fail to address this or actively reinforce anti-father biases (see, for example, the oral and written evidence provided by Families Need Fathers, Planetary Alliance for Fathers in Exile and Shared Parenting Information Group to the Joint Committee on the Draft Children (Contact) and Adoption Bill (HC, 2005). In contrast, groups representing mothers have campaigned on issues of mother and child safety post-separation, particularly in the context of domestic violence, and have sought to enhance protective measures within the family justice system (see, for example, the oral and written evidence provided by Women's Aid and Refuge to the Joint Committee on the Draft Children (Contact) and Adoption Bill (HC, 2005). In effect the two sets of pressure groups are presenting diametrically opposed narratives of the post-separation problem, of either malicious mothers or dangerous dads, although both sides are united in their criticism of the family justice system.

The pattern of two opposing sets of gender-based advocacy groups (and using similar narratives) is evident in a wide range of Western jurisdictions. Coltrane and Hickman (1992) analysing the position in the US and Rhoades and Boyd (2004) comparing Australia and Canada, have also highlighted the dual narratives adopted by lobby groups. The analysis of Coltrane and Hickman (1992) is particularly useful in identifying the rhetorical tactics used by pressure groups to press their cases, including the use of horror stories. As Coltrane and Hickman (1992: 416) put it 'In dramatic fashion, these horror stories typically portrayed a morally righteous victim and a heartless ex-spouse. In one version, fathers were helpless victims of vindictive and bitter ex-wives. In another, fathers were unfeeling brutes who abandoned worthy wives and children, or worse, twisted psychopaths who physically or sexually abused their children to get back at their ex-wives'.

Interestingly, both Coltrane and Hickman (1992) and Rhoades and Boyd (2004) have identified how effective pressure groups have been in campaigning to change policy. The influence of pressure groups is also clearly detectable in the development of policy in England. Both sides of the debate have attracted, successively, considerable attention within the media and within the family justice system. The linking of contact and domestic violence came to prominence first, with concerns about whether what appeared to be presumptions about contact putting women and children at risk (eg Hester and Pearson, 1993; Hester and Radford, 1996). In 1999, a report from the influential Advisory Board on Family Law (Children Act Sub-Committee) called for greater awareness of domestic violence, proposing new guidelines for identification, and more effective management of risk, but ruling out a presumption that there should be no contact when domestic violence had occurred as campaigners had wished. In a leading judgment, the Court of Appeal echoed the report's conclusions.[2]

The implications of these earlier campaigns are gradually being worked through into the system. In 2002 the Children Act 1989 was amended to require that courts consider the impact on a child of simply witnessing domestic violence when making decisions about contact or residence.[3]

---

[2] *Re L* (Contact: Domestic Violence), *Re V* (Contact: Domestic Violence), *Re M* (Contact: Domestic Violence), *Re H* (Contact: Domestic Violence) [2000] 2 FLR 334. The Court of Appeal drew heavily on a specially commissioned report by two eminent child psychiatrists (Sturge and Glaser, 2000).

[3] Adoption and Children Act 2002, s 120.

More recently the standard application form for a residence or contact order has been revised, giving both applicant and respondent an opportunity to detail any allegations of harm. It is unclear at this stage exactly how the courts will deal with this new information not least because approximately 50 per cent of contact/residence cases involve allegations of harm (Buchanan et al, 2001; Smart et al, 2003; Trinder et al, 2005) while there remains a strong presumption of contact operating within the family courts (Bailey-Harris, 2001). The options available to the courts to assist with the management of risk remain underdeveloped. 'Supported' or low-vigilance contact centres have developed rapidly over the last decade but there remain very few 'supervised' or higher vigilance centres, so higher risk cases can be referred inappropriately to supported contact centres (Aris et al, 2002).

More recently, however, it is the concerns of father's rights groups that have both dominated the media and appear to have the stronger influence on the direction of policy. A range of groups have argued for a statutory presumption of contact, a presumption of a minimum quantum of contact or a 50/50 division of time, and stronger enforcement measures for contact orders (eg Geldof, 2003) all set within a perception of obstructive or gate keeping mothers/resident parents.

In an even-handed, although not necessarily the most integrated fashion, the Children Act Sub-Committee followed its report on domestic violence with a second report, *Making Contact Work* (2002). The report recommended a range of services for families not seeking court intervention, acknowledged that court involvement could make conflict worse, and called for a wider range of enforcement options. A number of High Court judges also entered the fray, highlighting problems of delay, lack of judicial continuity and problems with enforcement.[4]

In response to widespread popular interest in contact and increasing criticism of the family justice system from a range of quarters, the Government responded by issuing a consultation paper on contact, 'Children's Needs and Parents' Responsibilities', in 2004 (DCA, 2004a), followed by a consultation response (Secretary of State, 2005) and a Children (Contact) and Adoption Bill in 2005.[5] The approach is one that gives a little to each

---

[4] The Father v The Mother and O by CAFCASS Legal [2003] EWHC 3031 (Fam); A Father (Mr A) v A Mother (Mrs A) [2004] EWHC 142 (Fam); F v M [2004] EWHC 727 (Fam)—Munby para 4: 'Those who are critical of our family justice system may well see this case as exemplifying everything that is wrong with the system. I can understand such a view. The melancholy truth is that this case illustrates all too uncomfortably the failings of the system. ... Responsible voices are raised in condemnation of our system. We need to take note. We need to act. And we need to act now'.

[5] The Consultation Paper and Government Response are available at: http://www.dfes.gov.uk/childrensneeds/. The bill is available at: http://www.publications.parliament.uk/pa/pabills.htm

constituency without offering radical reform, and, perhaps most crucially, is largely resource neutral. There is not, for example, any scheme for parent information programmes of the type included in the Family Law Act, nor an expansion of support services for children despite a dearth of such services (Hawthorne et al, 2003). In many ways, the Government's approach involved familiar themes, minimising conflict by improving parental access to services that might help them reach agreement without going to court, encouraging mediation (although mandatory mediation was ruled out) and piloting a legal advice phone line and a collaborative law model.

The Government's chief focus, however, was on the 10 per cent of families who go to court. Despite strong pressure from fathers' rights groups, a statutory presumption of contact for contested cases was ruled out, as were presumptions of a minimum quantum of contact or 50/50 shared care, in order to maintain the Children Act 1989 welfare principle, which requires the court in making any decision about the care or upbringing of a child to give paramount consideration to the best interests of that child. Instead there is (another) new procedure designed to ensure continuous case management and avoidance of unnecessary delay (President of the Family Division, 2005). Long-standing efforts to facilitate parental agreement without contested hearings are also continued with plans to extend in-court conciliation, a brief method of dispute resolution on court premises, to all courts.

Alongside the 'support' measures are new powers in enforcement cases, which currently comprise about 15 per cent of contact applications (DCA, 2004b). The new 'get tough' options include community service of 40–200 hours, curfews (including electronic tagging), or ordering compensation when breaches of a contact order have financial consequences, although for the contact parent only. Whether or not these measures will facilitate high quality contact is unclear, but it is disconcerting that the draft bill merely directs the court to take account of a child's welfare in exercising these powers, rather than making the child's welfare the paramount consideration as in all other private law matters. Equally, while the court must take into account 'reasonable excuses' for non-compliance it is not required to first consider the continued appropriateness of the original order before exercising its enforcement powers.

In many respects therefore the dominant messages or stock narratives of the advocacy groups, of dangerous dads and malicious mothers have been incorporated into policy. The dominant message appears to be that the family justice system is geared towards treating cases as either about risk or about enforcement. In the next section I will turn to the accounts of mothers and fathers involved in contested applications to examine whether this binary division is adequate or relevant. Do the stances of advocacy groups and policy-makers reflect the concerns and issues raised by 'mainstream' courts users?

THE EVALUATION OF IN-COURT CONCILIATION
RESEARCH STUDY

The author with colleagues was commissioned by the Department for Constitutional Affairs in London to evaluate a number of local schemes whereby conciliation in contact disputes was offered in the court setting (Trinder et al, 2005). The in-court conciliation study was designed to explore the effectiveness of court-based 'mediation' or dispute resolution schemes. However, the study also provides a useful insight into the experiences and perspectives of 'typical' or bread and butter contact cases in the county courts. The sample consists of data from 250 parents (50 per cent mothers, 54.8 per cent resident parents, 51.2 per cent respondents) recruited in three different court areas at first directions appointments and interviewed very shortly afterwards. The response rate was 67 per cent of all parents attending first directions appointments. The study was funded by the Department for Constitutional Affairs.

The majority, 64 per cent of parents, had not previously been to court, and only 8 per cent could be described as perpetual litigants with multiple applications. Parents had been separated for two years on average, although for many parents problems with arrangements had surfaced relatively quickly, on average eight months from separation.

The pattern of contact was highly variable. A quarter of parents reported that there had been no direct contact for at least six months prior to the application, while 4 out of 10 reported that contact had broken down just before, and often prompting, the application to court. The actual amount of contact varied substantially across the sample, from no, or very limited, contact in a contact centre to actual or close to 50/50 shared care arrangements. Just over half (57 per cent) of parents reported that contact had included some overnight stays. The average amount of contact was 64 hours per month (median 17) prior to the application, dropping to an average 55 hours (median 10) when the application was made as a result of the increase in cases where contact had broken down. There were no significant differences between resident and non-resident parents in the reports of the amount of contact occurring.

PARENTAL PERSPECTIVES ON CONTACT PROBLEMS

We measured the nature and extent of contact problems by presenting all parents, resident and non-resident, mothers and fathers, with the same list of potential contact problems[6] and asked whether the problem had

---

[6] The items are listed in Table 1. The list of contact problems items was adapted from Wolchik et al (1996). In that study, however, different lists (and issues) were presented to resident and non-resident parents, precluding comparisons.

occurred, and with what frequency, in the three months leading up the court application. The results highlight both strong similarities and differences in the perspectives of men and women.

The first point to make is that both mothers and fathers reported a wide range of problems relating to contact. Very few parents reported problems with just one or two contact-related issues. Instead parents were facing a wide range of difficulties, with an average of 7 out of a maximum 14 issues. Interestingly there was no significant difference between the number of problems reported by mothers and fathers, with respective means of 6.6 and 6.1 (p = .173).

The responses to specific issues also reflect clearly gendered responses with significant differences between the perceptions of resident and non-resident parents on many issues. However, this is far from being the whole picture. On some key issues what was more striking is how similar both groups of parents were in their perceptions and reactions.

Looking at the differences first, there is some evidence of the malicious mother and dangerous dad narratives evident in the responses. Fathers were indeed significantly more likely than mothers to report problems related to the blocking of contact, that is that their ex-partner lacked commitment to contact, that their ex-partner had threatened to end contact and that their ex-partner had attempted to control or interfere with their relationship with the children (Table 1). In contrast mothers were significantly more likely than fathers to raise concerns about violence, with more than half of mothers reporting that a fear of violence made it more difficult to sort out contact problems.[7]

Although the data therefore do offer support for the dangerous dad and malicious mother narratives, the picture is considerably more complex. There are at least five other sets of problems that parents frequently raise: commitment and reliability, child reactions, parenting quality and competence, third parties/new partners and the relationship between money and contact. Furthermore, these do not necessarily run on predictable gendered lines.

On the first issue, of commitment to contact and reliability, mothers and fathers were equally likely to accuse the other of unreliability, indeed a majority of both groups did so. Similarly, although there was a significant difference between mothers and fathers in terms of reports of a lack of commitment to contact, it is worth noting that a majority of mothers did consider that fathers were not sufficiently committed to contact.

---

[7] Nearly half (49.2%) of women cited domestic violence or emotional abuse as a reason for the separation, compared with 15% of men. Nearly a quarter (22.4%) of women reported that there had been an injunction at some stage.

Table 1. Contact problems ever occurring in the three months prior to the court application, by resident or non-resident parent (percentages)

	Overall (n = 250)	Mothers (n = 125)	Fathers (n = 125)	p^{8*}
Ex not committed enough to contact	76.1	66.1	86.2	.000*
Threat to stop (having) contact by ex	43.5	18.7	68.3	.000*
Threat to stop (having) contact by self	26.4	45.9	7.3	.000*
Ex not sticking to arrangements	68.1	64.8	71.6	.367
Self not sticking to arrangements	33.3	38.1	28.4	.184
Children upset, unsettled or difficult when coming or going	64.1	76.9	51.0	.000*
Children not wanting to go for contact or return home	56.7	63.8	49.5	[.052]
Ex not enough attention, supervision or discipline	63.7	64.4	63.1	.968
Ex too harsh in discipline or might physically harm children	43.3	47.6	38.8	.255
Ex spoiling the children	37.2	48.2	29.1	.025*
Ex tries to control your activities/what you do with children	57.9	48.1	67.6	.007*
Children see people you don't want them to see	51.2	51.5	51.0	1.00
Conflicts over money make contact more difficult	52.2	56.0	48.4	.282
Fear of violence makes it more difficult to sort out problems with ex	43.4	58.4	28.2	.000*

There was a clear gender difference in terms of children's reactions to contact, with mothers significantly more likely than fathers to report that children were upset by transitions or were refusing contact. However, again although there is a significant difference, these issues were also a concern for half of the fathers. Equally, child safety has hitherto been considered in public debates only in relation to dangerous dads. The message from our data is that both mothers and fathers have extensive concerns about the parenting quality of the other, with no significant differences between the two groups on lax or inattentive parenting or harsh or potentially abusive parenting.

---

[8] Chi square test. Items where there is a significant difference between groups at <.05 level are denoted with an asterisk.

Finally, around half of the sample reported problems on the two remaining items reflecting inter-parental 'conflict' items; that is, the presence of third parties and conflicts over money impacting on contact.

In sum our representative sample of parents involved in bread and butter contested contact cases both supported and challenged the dominant narratives of dangerousness and gate-keeping. There were clear gender differences running in the predicted direction with reports from fathers of maternal blocking of contact and from mothers of a fear of violence. Beyond that, however, the two monoliths begin to break down with multiple problems reported by both sets of parents spanning lack of reliability, child reactions to transitions, parenting competence/quality, third parties/new partners and financial conflicts. On some issues there were significant gender differences—attempts to control the other's parenting was one–but to focus just on the statistical difference draws attention away from the fact that this issue was also a problem for half of all mothers. Dangerousness and gate keeping is therefore just one part of the story or one of the stories that could be told. Alongside those issues are a wide range of other forgotten or excluded issues reflecting mutual conflict and mistrust, including reliability, money and quality of parenting, that do not fit easily within bipolar gendered narratives.

Although these findings do not fit with the positions of advocacy groups or the broad drift of policy in England, they are fairly consistent with other research studies. The work of Smart and May (chapter four in this volume and Smart et al, 2005) has also identified the range of issues including parenting quality, money and new partners that parents of both genders raise as part of the 'parenting contest', even if the court does not regard all of these as legitimate or relevant issues. Recent work from Australia has also identified the complexity of issues. Rhoades (2002), for example, analysing enforcement cases, found very few examples of the stock story of the 'no contact mother'. Instead her analysis of the court files identified a wide range of issues broadly similar to the concerns of our parents, including (non-resident) parenting capacity, substance abuse, new partners and mutual hostility. Rodgers et al (2004) have also flagged up the issue of mental health issues and personality disorder as a significant contributor to entrenched cases, an issue that so far has not been discussed or investigated in a UK context.

Before moving on, one question that we have not yet explored is whether the 'gender' differences we have identified so far are indeed about gender or whether they reflect situational differences between resident and non-resident parents. In our study there were simply too few resident father/ non-resident mother arrangements to conduct separate analyses. Other work on non-resident mothers (eg Kielty, 2005) suggests that in some respects the experience of post-divorce parenting is defined by both situation and gender with non-resident mothers experiencing similar issues as non-resident fathers while also facing additional challenges as a result of societal and internalised expectations of the 'good mother'. Gender then seems to be a significant part of the story, but far from the entirety.

MAKING SENSE OF THE DEBATE

The empirical evidence from parents involved in contested contact cases provides only partial support for a bifurcated gender-based dangerousness versus gatekeeping approach. When parents themselves are asked what the issues are, or when family justice professionals assess the situation, the problems presented are much messier and complex and not solely distinguishable on gender grounds. Why then do the two gender narratives appear to have been so influential in terms of shaping the public debate and, to some extent, the policy response?

Part of the attraction of the two competing gender narratives is that they present clear and distinguishable opposites in a form that is potentially amenable to the binary approach of the law (King and Piper, 1995). Rather than dealing with messy conflicts with multiple causes, manifestations and consequences, it is simpler to construct problems as either about gatekeeping mothers or dangerous dads. This analysis is highly consistent with Dewar and Parker's (2000) analysis of the shift in English family law away from a post-war functionalist era characterised by discretion and individualised outcomes to the current complex era where, by contrast, rights, rules and general principles have become more salient. In this context, more straightforward accounts such as the gate keeping mother or dangerous father lend themselves more easily to rule-based decision-making.

The alternative is much more messy. Moving beyond a binary gendered analysis to focus on mutual conflicts on a wide range of issues will require a considerable shift in approach in the UK. As yet there are no comprehensive programmes or interventions in the UK to help parents resolve, manage or contain conflict or support children directly (Hunt, chapter eleven this volume) despite the unambiguous message from developmental research that the critical factor for children's adjustment is interparental conflict (Lamb, chapter one this volume). Nor is there what looks like the more comprehensive range of services to address risk, work on conflict or support children that are developing in Germany (Mueller-Johnson, chapter seven this volume) or Australia (Sheehan, Dewan and Carson, and Fehlberg and Hunter chapters nine and ten in this volume; Moloney, 2005).

CONCLUSION

In a highly useful analysis Morgan (1996) mapped out the different ways in which family and gender interconnect, construct and modify each other. Morgan's analysis highlights how significant gender is in understanding family processes, and by extension, post-separation families and family law. However, his recognition that gender can obscure family, resulting in Morgan's terms in an 'over-gendered conception of the family' is of particular relevance here. Gender is indeed an important and profound shaper of family life and does strongly influence parental perceptions or experiences of contact disputes. However, in other respects the highly gendered debate initiated and fuelled by pressure groups does not reflect the full range of issues and concerns raised by parents in dispute about contact. That is not to say that risks posed by fathers or gate keeping by mothers do not exist but it is clear from parents themselves that it is far from the whole story and has deflected attention from the cross-gender issues of mutual parental conflict, mistrust and hostility. It is to be hoped that future policy developments in the UK are able to focus more clearly on finding some solutions to addressing these conflicts.

REFERENCES

Advisory Board on Family Law (Children Act Sub-Committee) (2001) *Making Contact Work: A Report to the Lord Chancellor on the Facilitation of Arrangements for Contact Between Children and their Non-Residential Parents and the Enforcement of Court Orders for Contact. A Report to the Lord Chancellor* (London, Lord Chancellor's Department).

Advisory Board on Family Law (Children Act Sub-Committee) (1999) *Contact Between Children and Violent Parents* (London, Lord Chancellor's Department).

Aris, A, Harrison, C and Humphreys, C (2002) *Safety And Child Contact* (London, Department for Constitutional Affairs).

Bailey-Harris, R (2001) 'Contact—challenging conventional wisdom?' 13 *Child and Family Law Quarterly* 361–70.

Bainham, A (2005) *Children: The Modern Law* 3rd edn (Bristol, Jordan Publishing).

Bainham, A, Day Sclater, S and Richards, M (eds) (1999) *What is a Parent? A Socio-Legal Analysis* (Oxford, Hart Publishing).

Bainham, A, Lindley, B, Richards, M and Trinder, L (eds) (2003) *Children and Their Families: Contact, Rights and Welfare* (Oxford, Hart Publishing).

Bala, N (1999) 'Report From Canada's Gender War Zone: Reforming the Child related Provisions of the Divorce Act' 16 *Canadian Journal of Family Law* 163.

Barrett, H (2004) *UK Family Trends 1994-2004* (London, National Family and Parenting Institute).

Blackwell, A and Dawe, F (2003) *Non–Resident Parental Contact. Final Report* (London, Office for National Statistics).

Buchanan, A, Hunt, J, Bretherton, H and Bream, V (2001) *Families in Conflict: The Family Court Welfare Service: the perspectives of children and parents* (Bristol, The Policy Press).

Coltrane, S and Hickman, N (1992) 'The Rhetoric of Rights and Needs: Moral Discourse in the Reform of Child Custody and Child Support Laws' 39 *Social Problems* 400.

Day Sclater, S, Bainham, A and Richards, M (1999) 'Introduction' in A Bainham, S Day Sclater and M Richards (eds), *What is a Parent? A Socio-Legal Analysis* (Oxford, Hart Publishing) 1–22.

Day Sclater, S and Yates, C (1999) 'The psycho-politics of post-divorce parenting' in A Bainham, S Day Sclater and M Richards (eds), *What is a Parent? A Socio-Legal Analysis* (Oxford, Hart Publishing).

Department for Constitutional Affairs, Department for Education and Skills and the Department for Trade and Industry (2004a) *Parental Separation: Children's Needs and Parents' Responsibilities* Cm 6273 (London, The Stationery Office).

Department for Constitutional Affairs, Department for Education and Skills and the Department for Trade and Industry (2004b) *Parental Separation: Children's Needs and Parents' Responsibilities, Supporting evidence for consultation paper* (London, The Stationery Office).

Dewar, J and Parker, S (2000) 'English Family Law since World War II: From Status to Chaos' in S Katz, J Eekelaar and M Maclean (eds), *Cross Currents: Family Law and Policy in the US and England* (Oxford, Oxford University Press).

Geldof, B (2003) 'The Real Love that Dare not Speak its Name' in A Bainham, B Lindley, M Richards and L Trinder (eds), *Children and their Families: Contact, Rights and Welfare* (Oxford, Hart Publishing).

Hawthorne, J, Jessop, J, Pryor, J and Richards, M (2003) *Supporting children through family change: A review of interventions and services for children of divorcing and separating parents* (York, Joseph Rowntree Foundation).

Hester, M and Pearson, C (1993) 'Domestic violence, mediation and child contact arrangements: issues from current research' 3 *Family Mediation* 3.

Hester, M and Radford, L (1996) *Domestic Violence and Child Contact Arrangements in England and Denmark* (Bristol, The Policy Press).

House of Commons/House of Lords Joint Committee on the Draft Children (Contact) and Adoption Bill (2005) *Draft Children (Contact) and Adoption Bill. Volume II: Evidence* HC 400-II, HL Paper 100-II (London, The Stationery Office).

Kielty, S (2005) 'Mothers are non-resident parents too: A consideration of Mother's Perspectives on Non-Residential Parenthood' 27 *Journal of Social Welfare and Family Law* 1.

King, M and Piper, C (1995) *How the Law Thinks About Children* 2nd edn (Aldershot, Arena).

Lamb, ME and Lewis, C (2004) 'The Development and Significance of Father–Child Relationships in Two-parent Families' in ME Lamb (ed), *The Role of the Father in Child Development* 4th edn (Chichester, Wiley).

Moloney, L (2005) 'Government's Response to the Family Law Maze: The Family Relationship Centres Proposal' 11 *Journal of Family Studies* 11.

Morgan, D (1996) *Family Connections* (Cambridge, Polity Press).

O'Brien, M and Shemilt, I (2003) *Working Fathers: Earning and Caring* (London, Equal Opportunities Commission).

Pickford, R (1999) *Fathers, Marriage and the Law* (London, Joseph Rowntree Foundation).

President of the Family Division (2005) *The Private Law Programme* (London, Department for Constitutional Affairs) http://www.dca.gov.uk/pubs/profguide. htm

Pryor, J and Rodgers, B (2001) *Children in Changing Families: Life after Parental Separation* (Oxford, Blackwell).

Rhoades, H (2002) 'The "No Contact Mother"' *International Journal of Law, Policy and the Family* 16.

Rhoades, H and Boyd, S (2004) 'Reforming Custody Laws: A Comparative Study' 18 *International Journal of Law, Policy and the Family* 119.

Rodgers, B, Smyth B and Robinson, E (2004) 'Mental health and the Family Law system' 10 *Journal of Family Studies* 50.

Smart, C (1989) 'Power and the Politics of Child Custody' in C Smart and S Sevenhuijsen (eds), *Child Custody and the Politics of Gender* (London, Routledge).

Smart, C, May, V, Wade, A and Furniss, C (2003) *Residence and contact disputes in Court* vol 1 (Research Series 6/03) (London, Department for Constitutional Affairs).

Smart, C, May, V, Wade, A and Furniss, C (2003) *Residence and contact disputes in Court* vol 2 (Research Series 4/05) (London, Department for Constitutional Affairs).

Smart, C and Neale, B (1997) 'Arguments against virtue—must contact be enforced?' 27 *Family Law* 332.

Sturge, C and Glaser, D (2000) Contact and Domestic Violence—The Experts' Court Report' 30 *Family Law* 615.

Trinder, L, Connolly, J, Kellett, J, Notley, C and Swift, L (2005) *Making Contact Happen or Making Contact Work? The Process and Outcomes Of In-Court Conciliation* (London, Department for Constitutional Affairs).

Wolchik, S, Fenaughty, A and Braver, S (1996) 'Residential And Nonresidential Parents' Perspectives On Visitation Problems' 45 *Family Relations* 230.

6

Legal Discourse and Gender Neutrality in Child Custody Reform in Spain

AGURTZANE GORIENA LEKUE

THE EGALITARIAN JURIDICAL CONSTRUCTION OF FAMILY

T HE SOCIAL AND political changes[1] and the new Constitution of 1975 have been followed by a wave of legislative reform which has transformed regulation in the area of family relationships in the last thirty years, and particularly so in the field of civil family law.[2] The main reforms have, on the one hand, established equality between the rights of wives and husbands in 1975,[3] including equal rights to decide on the economic regime for the marriage and abolishing any reference to a husband's authority and the wife's need for permission to act. By means of article 66 of the Civil Code 'husband and wife are equal in rights and duties'. By this article and articles 67 and 70 the traditional marital state in which the husband had authority over all the members of the family, including the wife, was abolished.[4] There was also a need to promote civil and economic equality between the rights of spouses, and to protect the rights of children. The Civil Code reformed family regulation in 1981, regarding,[5] marriage, separation and divorce. The new rules implementing the constitutional

---

[1] See I Alberdi, *Informe sobre la situación de la familia en España* (Ministerio de Asuntos Sociales, Madrid, 1995).

[2] T Piconto Novales, 'Sociología Jurídica de la familia: cambio legislativo y políticas sociales' in *Derecho y Sociedad* AAVV (Valencia, Tirant lo Blanch, 1998) 660.

[3] By 14/1975 Law, 2 May (BOE 107, 5 May) which reformed the Civil Code.

[4] As Mazzotta shows in her paper, the family law reform made in Italy in 1975, represents the substitution of 'institutional' family and the increasing recognition of individual rights, in detriment of the family unit. Oñati Workshop on 'Contact between children and separated parents' 15 and 16 September 2005.

[5] In 1981 there were two different laws: 11/1981 Law, 13 May (BOE 119, 19 May), reforms the Civil Code in matters of filiation, parental authority (patria potestas) and the economic system inside marriage; and 30/1981 Law, 7 July (BOE 172, 20 July) reforms the Civil Code regulation of marriage and establishes the procedure in cases of separation, divorce and nullity.

principles of equality between spouses, and between children[6] born within or outside marriage, established equality between spouses in rights and duties, legalising a symmetrical order between these in order to guarantee the protection of children. Joint parental authority was settled in article 154 of the Civil Code replacing the exclusive parental authority of the father, and it is conceptualised as a right and a duty. Another legal reform took place in 1990, applying the principle of non-discrimination,[7] eliminating the legal provision that attributed custody of children under seven years old to the mother. The last important reform has been the Juridical Protection of Minors Law,[8] which changed both the Civil Code and the Procedural Code, in 1996. This reform has provided for integral protection of the minor and the best interest of the child, according to the new philosophy of the United Nations Convention on Children's Rights of 30 November 1989. In particular, Spanish law now recognises 'the right to be heard' in any judicial or administrative process affecting the child.

FORMAL EQUALITY BUT REAL INEQUALITY

Nevertheless, the formal equality recognised in law is not accompanied by effective realisation of the equality principle during a couple relationship.

Child Care during Marriage or Living Together

Twenty-four years after this legal equality provision, in reality women's position in the couple relationship has changed little. Studies about internal relationships within families show that in spite of the redefinition of the roles of spouses—characterised mainly by a more egalitarian redistribution of domestic tasks compared with the traditional Spanish family—the change only reflects attitudes and general opinions among Spanish people, not reflected behaviour.[9] The de-genderisation of parental roles is more symbolic than real while the couple is together. In the same sense, male participation in child care—exceptions apart—has not changed in a qualitative way. In Spain different facts reveal that equal participation by fathers in child care—physical, emotional and educational—does not exist, and in the great majority of families, this care is provided mainly or exclusively by mothers.

---

[6] Arts 14 and 32 of the Spanish Constitution.
[7] 11/1990 Law, 15 October (BOE 250, 18 October 1990) reforms the Civil Code, in application of no discrimination with regard to sex.
[8] 1/1996 Organic Law, 15 January (BOE 15, 17 January) reforms the Civil Code and Civil Procedural Code on Juridical Protection of the Minor.
[9] V Informe Sociológico de la Fundación Foessa, 1995, at 150–51, quoted by T Piconto Novales, above n 2, at 665.

For example, taking the January 2005 figures, women made up 58.88 per cent of the unemployed in the 25–54 age group and men only 41.12 per cent. Of those in part-time jobs, 70.21 per cent are women and 29.79 per cent men. Of those leaving work because of family responsibilities, 96.38 per cent are women and only 3.62 per cent men. Maternity leave was taken by 239,858 in 2003, while paternity leave was taken by 3,762.[10] So, the data confirms that it is mothers who mainly take responsibility for the care of their children—as well as elderly dependent people. Nevertheless, the pathological phases of the couple relationship—represented by separations and divorce—demonstrate still more that spouses are *equal* in respect of economic patrimony[11] and *different* in respect of care responsibilities.

Child Custody Agreements or Decisions

Judicial data show us the same conclusion. In fact, in separation and divorce processes, mothers demand custody in 98 per cent of cases. The percentage of mother custody in consensual separations is 95 per cent and here we must take into account that parents negotiate and arrive at an agreement. If we analyse the contentious processes, we can see that in 80/85 per cent of cases there is no discussion about the issue of custody, because fathers do not claim this.[12] These data coincide with that given in 2.1 and demonstrate, on the one hand, a real inequality between women and men in child care, while on the other, this is not a problem for the majority of Spanish fathers.

Despite pre-judgments and social stereotypes—that sometimes influence decisions about custody[13]—most decisions give custody to the mother in consensual separations and divorces because the parties decide in an autonomous way; and with regard to contentious separations and divorces—in the 15–20 per cent where custody is claimed by both parents—because it is mothers who take the responsibility for child care whether they work outside home or not. It is because the mother's presence—as Amato says—guarantees a continuity with the preceding way of life for the child

---

[10] These data are taken from the dossier 'Women in ciphers' from the Institute of Woman and form the INE (National Statistic Institute).

[11] About this assertion we could also make some considerations, but this is not the subject of the chapter.

[12] It is important to know that in the contentious processes, women relate violence within family in 64 per cent of cases, and in 92 per cent of judicial demands they ask for urgent provisional measures, because in two of three judicial contentious separations there are physical and/or psychical aggressions. The increasing rate of deaths of women because familiar violence ratifies these facts.

[13] As Supreme Court Sentence 22 May 1999; La Coruña Province Court 6 September 2002; Valencia Province Court 28 October 2002, in which tender year's doctrine is followed to decide on the custody.

or children. The primary caretaker principle is applied very often in the jurisprudence.

THE LEGAL CONSTRUCTION OF THE BEST INTERESTS OF THE CHILD

As we have already seen, Spanish family law is based on two main principles: the 'equality principle' between both parents which underlies the couple relationship and 'the best interest of the child principle'. Following other recent family law,[14] a new interpretation of both principles has been made to prescribe joint physical custody[15]—joint legal custody had already been incorporated with the 1981 law reform, prescribing shared authority to make all major decisions concerning the children. Let us analyse critically how parental authority has been interpreted and applied by jurisprudence.

Shared Parental Authority in the Interests of the Child

The recognition of a general principle of parental authority implies a generalisation without any assurance that the familiar environment is suitable for its implementation. We need to remember that the Civil Code does not specify the requirements or conditions needed to maintain joint parental authority, and it has been argued that the interests of the child is the generic criterion that a judge must bear in mind when making a decision in this field.[16] A realistic view of family conflict shows that if parents agree to share parental authority, it would be of benefit to the child, but this ideal situation is very difficult to achieve in a conflicted family.[17] Some authors recognise that far from supporting good relationships, this kind of parental authority is instead a source of disputes and problems that damage the interest of the child.[18] In the same way, different authors are aware that the system cannot work without a minimum of understanding between the couple,[19] and agreement between the parents is extremely important in order to succeed in this joint exercise. They assert that an initial disagreement will probably increase the difficulties that shared parental authority brings

---

[14] In France, the new 2002–305 Law, about parental authority, has supposed a kind of joint physical custody system.

[15] By 15/2005 Law, 8 July, reforms the Civil Code in the matter of child custody, providing the judge with the possibility of stating joint physical custody.

[16] *Seisdedos Muiño*, 335.

[17] M Lopez Alarcon, separación y divorcio: cuestiones particulares (1982) *Revista Jurídica española La Ley* 2.

[18] E Fosar Benlloch, *Estudios de Derecho de Familia II* (Barcelona, Bosch, 1982); R Garcia Varela, *La Ley de Divorcio: experiencias de su aplicación* (Madrid, Colex, 1982).

[19] *Ibid*, at 335.

in separation, divorce and nullity cases, to the detriment of the child. But they recognise that everything depends on the judicial valuation of that interest in each case, which gives occasion for discretionary decisions. Maybe for that reason, the Spanish legislator in 1981 did not prescribe shared authority between parents after a separation or a divorce. Instead, the legislator established individual authority for the non-judicial separation and divorce cases as well as for unmarried separation cases.[20] But for married couples, some authors think that article 92.4 must be applied, instead of article 156.5, because the former is specially indicated for judicial separations, divorces and nullity cases. This article prescribes that the measures the judge can take can be either giving the whole or partial exercise of the parental authority to one parent. Starting from this article, a group of authors think the shared model to be a possibility.[21] Other authors consider that a broad interpretation of article 156 must be made, so that it can be applied not only to de facto separations and to unmarried couples, but to married couple separation, divorce and nullity cases.[22] Notwithstanding the legal provision of article 156.5, some authors, making a restrictive interpretation, have interpreted it to mean that if the judge makes no order on this issue, the exercise of parental authority remains shared, just as it was during the marriage. They have interpreted article 92.4 settling for joint exercise of parental authority, for the cases of married parents, and the individual parental authority expressly settled in article 156.5 for the cases of unmarried parents. And, in the same sense, jurisprudence[23] has interpreted that if

[20] Art 156.5 of the Civil Code which prescribes: ' If parents live separately, parental authority will be exercised by the parent with whom the child lives ...'

[21] De Los Mozos and Herrero Garcia, *Matrimonio y Divorcio; comentariosal nuevo Título IV del Libro I del Código Civil*, coordinados por Lacruz Berdejo (Madrid, Civitas, 1982); E Fosar Benlloch, *Estudios de Derecho de Familia II* (Barcelona, Bosch, 1982); R Garcia Varela, *La Ley de Divorcio: experiencias de su aplicación* (Madrid, Colex, 1982); M Lopez Alarcon "Efectos de las sentencias de nulidad, separación y divorcio: cuestiones generales" (1982) *Revista Jurídica española La Ley* 2 ; Lopez and Lopez, 'Comentario al artículo 90 del Código Civil' en VVAA *Comentarios al nuevo Título IV del Libro I del Código Civil* coordinados por Lacruz Berdejo (Madrid, Civitas, 1982) Zanon Masdeu, El divorcio en españa, *Ley de 7 de julio de 1981*(Barcelona, Ed Acervo, 1981).

[22] Bayod Lopez, *El supuesto de hecho del párrafo 5 del artículo 156 CC: Qué casos son subsumibles en esta disposición?* RCDI, 1991, 939; Bercovitz Roriguez-Cano, *Comentario al artículo 156* in AAVV. Comentarios a las reformas del Derecho de Familia, 1984, 1069; De Prada Gonzalez, *Notas sobre la patria potestad en las reforma del Código*, RDN, 1981, abril-junio, 343; Diez-Picazo and Gullon, *Notas sobre la reforma del Código Civil en materia de patria potestad*, ADC, 1982, P Fosar Benlloch, *Estudios de Derecho de Familia* Tomo II, (Barcelona, Bosch, 1982) 318; Fuente Noriega, *La patria potestad compartida en el Código Civil español* (Montecorvo, Madrid, 1986). Lopez and Lopez, 'Comentario al artículo 90 del Código Civil' in VVAA *Comentarios al nuevo Título IV del Libro I del Código Civil* coordinados por Lacruz Berdejo, (Madrid, Civitas, 1982); Roca Trias, *Comentario al artículo 92* in AAVV, Comentarios a las reformas del Derecho de Familia, 1984, and in AAVV, Comentario del Código Civil, Ministerio de Justicia, 1991, 390; Sancho Rebullida in Lacruz Berdejo et al, *Elementos de Derecho Civil IV, Derecho de Familia* (Barcelona, Bosch, 1990).

[23] SAT La Coruña 30th mai 1988, RGD 1898, 2550.

no other provision is made by parents themselves, shared parental authority must be settled, because this is the default model ordered by family law. So, we can see that the doctrine and the jurisprudence—not the legislator— have identified the interest of the child with joint parental authority and have encouraged the use of this formulation in a large number of cases. But this conception lacks reality, because if in an intact family the exercise of joint authority is very often artificial, we cannot imagine how the exercise of shared parental authority will create union between parents. Parents who have a good relationship will continue to have it after separation or divorce. On the contrary, the application of this model in a conflict ambiance will make the situation worse, and this is not at all in the interest of the child, whose welfare depends on harmony between the parents.

This interpretation has also been criticised by some authors,[24] because first of all, according to a broad interpretation of article 156.5, the Code establishes two different systems: an automatic one—individual parental authority for non-judicial separation cases—because in these cases there is no judicial intervention, and so they need a way to give this position effect *ex lege*. On the other hand, for judicial separation, divorce and nullity cases, in which judicial intervention is necessary, the legislator considers it better for the judge to sort out the situation, offering different possibilities according to the special circumstances of the case.[25]

Therefore, the basis of the reasoning may be questionable. The reasoning is the following: a child is happy in a united family; in this type of family, parental authority is shared by both parents; so, to preserve the welfare of the children, shared exercise of the parental authority should be the general case. To complete the reasoning, we must admit that it is because the parental authority is shared between both parents that the child is happy in a legitimate united family. Then, if shared parental authority is extended to the disunited family, the child will be as happy as in the united family. This idea is reinforced because it attributes to the UN Convention on the Rights of the Children the wish to impose the sharing of parental authority in order to implement the right of the child to be brought up by both parents.[26]

But we are critical of this statement because the basis is not correct for several reasons. First of all, there is variability in the concept of the 'interest of the child', admitting different meanings, which can vary depending on the person who interprets, the relations between the person to whom it is applied, and the moment in time. This is the first problem with the premise.[27] Leaving aside the different considerations taken by psychologists,

---

[24] M Garcia Pastor p.
[25] *Ibid*, at
[26] L Gareil, *L'exercise de l'autorité parentale* (2004) Librairie Generale de Droit et de Jurisprudence 231.
[27] *Ibid*, at 238.

who in general emphasise the importance of both parents—and particularly the father, usually absent in one-parent families—for the construction of the personality of the child, we suggest that the majority of authors underline the complementarity of parental roles and the parental union.[28]

From this perspective it is asserted that 'the child needs the image of a couple',[29] and moreover that, 'children need a parental couple loving each other'.[30] It is true that in Spain, the exercise of parental authority after couple breakdown has not posed a great problem in society or in the courts, and shared parental authority may be the best solution according to the children's interests in a great number of cases. But the inexactness of the premise, together with the practical difficulties in dealing with this model in conflict situations, should warn against general adoption of this model of shared parenting. This is especially serious when this is not prescribed by law. Instead, the Civil Code prescribes individual parental authority as best serving the interests of the child.[31] So we suggest that the general ignorance about this question has led to the establishment of a practice that rests on promoting legitimation of a family model after marriage.[32] The new law reform has not made any great change in order to settle parental authority. So, the considerations current now, are also susceptible to application under the new regulation.

The question must be posed in terms of parental relationships with the child, not in terms of exercising parental authority. This leads us to the second legal institution and the changes effected by the recent law reform in this area.

Joint Physical Custody as the Current Model according to the Best Interests of the Child

The new article 92.5 establishes 'that joint physical custody of children will be settled when both parents ask for it in the regulatory agreement proposal or when both arrive at an agreement in the course of the process'. This supposes a formal recognition of joint physical custody that was not present before, because the law neither prohibited nor recognised this model of custody. We can assert that before the change, this system was exceptional, because it was considered harmful for the child because it did not satisfy

---

[28] G Poussin and I Sayn, *Un seul parent dans la* famille (Paris, Centurion, 1990) 172.
[29] *Ibid*, at 208.
[30] *Ibid*, at 249 and also F De Singly, *Sociologie de la Famille contemporaine* (Nathan Université, 1993) 46.
[31] M Garcia Pastor, *La situación jurídica de los hijos cuyos padres no conviven: Aspectos personales* (Madrid, McGraw Hill, Madrid, 1987) 196–97.
[32] For a deeper study on this, see T Pitch, *Un derecho para dos. La construcción jurídica del sexo, género y sexualidad* (Madrid, Trotta, 2004).

one of the child's main needs ie, stability.[33] Nevertheless, this legal prevision does not pose a problem for jurists or social agents, in general. The argument for stability has acquired a new interpretation: now it does not mean that the child must not be moved from one household to another—of course some conditions should be required—but it is conceived as ensuring that emotional stability can be offered to the child if both parents agree and can maintain a minimum of harmony to deal with this system of caring for the child.

It is article 92.8 which poses the problem because it establishes that 'exceptionally, if the conditions required in fifth paragraph are not possible, the judge, at the request of one of the parties, with the report of Public Ministry, will be able to decide joint physical custody basing it in that it is the only way to protect suitably the interest of the child'. At this point the fathers' associations do consider that the reform goes far enough, and they claim that this kind of custody should be the general rule even if there is no agreement, and they disagree with the adverb 'exceptionally', while women's associations disagree with the possibility of this model being ordered by the judge, simply at the request of the father. The article establishes some cautions so that joint physical custody will not proceed when one parent has been accused of attacking the life, physical integrity, freedom, moral integrity or sexual freedom and indemnity of the other parent or the children living with them. Neither will such a route be followed when the judge notices circumstantial evidence of domestic violence.[34] Some authors think that the system is more restrictive now, because it is based on the request of one of the parties, and this would limit the possibilities for the judge. But, this dogmatic view of the law does not take into account inequality and power relations between sexes.[35]

The justification for the new law is the aim of reducing the consequences of a separation or divorce for all the members of the family and 'to correct a practice following the previous law of 1981 which has made it difficult after separation or divorce, for children to continue having a close relationship with both parents. The consequence of this practice has been that children have unnecessarily suffered damage that can be avoided'. These damages are not specified.

So, any measure that imposes difficulties for the relationship between a parent and his/her children must be justified with serious reasons. And has

---

[33] As it was considered in the French doctrine. See: Dorner-Dolivet, *Les nouvelles dispositions relatives à l'exercice de l'autorité parentale* (ADL, 1988) 103; Nicolas-Maguin, *A propos de la garde conjointe des enfants de parents divorcés*, D, 1983, CHr 111; for the Italian doctrine, see: Bata, *Le forme di affidamento previste nella nuova legge sul divorzio* (Corriere Giuridico, 1987) 1296–99; Grimaldi, *Affidamento congiunto e alternato della prole tra `sicologia e diritto* (DFP, 1989) 304.
[34] Established in para 7 of art 92.
[35] For a deeper analyses of power relations and gender see: Smart and Sevenhuijsen (eds), *Child Custody and the Politics of Gender* (London and New York, Routledge, 1989).

to be justified for the child's protection or the best realisation of the child's benefit or interest.

The emphasis on what is best for the child is present in the regulation, but the interpretation of the principle is left to judicial practice.[36] So, as there is no definition of this principle—it is a 'white rule' an open rule, admitting of different interpretations according to the values or the ideology of the judge, the decision as to what is best for the child in this area is decided by the judge. It is necessary to have a general definition, because a general perspective on what is best for the child does not prevent an individual perspective, as the general perspective is nothing but a starting point for an *in casu* judgement. The solution adopted in Spanish law increases the discretion of the judges,[37] which can lead us to different resolutions depending on their ideology.[38]

ASYMMETRIC RELATIONSHIPS

It is here—in separation and divorce processes—where we can see an asymmetry in the relationship between the sexes, as Collier[39] and Pitch[40] have shown: while the father has a power to control the mother's behaviour in relation to the children—'the surveillance right' derived from parental authority, the mother has no legal means to make the father respect the agreed contact arrangements. For the father, not having custody, the compromises about the children are not considered as an obligation, because there are no sanctions available to guarantee that the non-custodial parent will respect the visits or will pay alimony.[41] Instead, the mother having custody has duties. And children have rights—but it is difficult for them to demand these from their fathers.[42]

The main goal of a legal change is to introduce new norms into society, and usually it is not possible to judge either their success or failure until the moment of implementation, when law is tested as it is applied to real life situations. But many judges, lawyers, and professionals whose experience is important in this area, think that an imposed joint custody will be the

---

[36] This seems to be the system in other countries like Sweden, Norway and Finland: an obligation to consider the child's wishes, with emphasis given to the age and maturity of the child. See Ryrstedt, 'Methods to resolve disputes between separated parents—in the best interest of the child' Oñati Workshop on 'Contact between children and separated parents' 15 and 16 September 2005.

[37] See Rivero Hernandez, *El interés del menor* (Madrid, Dykinson, 2000).

[38] P Ronfani, *La famiglia e il diritto* (Roma-Bari, Laterza Editori, 1998) 158.

[39] R Collier, *Masculinity, Law and the Family* (Routledge, London, 1995).

[40] Pitch, above n 32.

[41] B Hobson, *Making Men into Fathers, Men Masculinities and the Social Politics of Fatherhood* (Cambridge, Cambridge University Press, 2002) 13: says that in Spain the policies surrounding the economic duties of fathers are weak.

[42] Pitch, above n 32.

worst outcome for both parents and children involved in conflict, if it is not agreed by both parents. Only the separated men's associations, and a few jurists, consider that conflict will diminish.

Fathers have had to accept the move from a system of authority—*patria potestas*—to a simple access right, because in most cases, mothers are awarded custody. This change has touched separated and divorced parents, so that they have formed associations and called for the development of what is called joint custody.[43] The discourse of equality of rights has distorted the reality, and legal discourse on joint custody has assumed men's discourse defending the call that children need both parents. So, the normal and normative model of family, named nuclear, prevails, composed of heterosexual and preferably married couples. If the problem is to re-equilibrate parental responsibilities after separation, the new rules insist on the obligations of the parents living with the children—mothers—that consist of increasing and intensifying the relationship between children and the parent not living with them—sually fathers—more than the obligation of the fathers to visit and meet the economic responsibilities for child support and alimony.[44] The absence of sanctions for failing to fulfil these obligations strengthens the symbolic character of the affirmation of the obligation of parents to maintain ties with their children.[45]

A vision of legal equality, underestimating the social circumstances of the persons involved in the contest and increasing one side's obligations and the other side's rights, in the name of the best interest of the child, as in this law reform, shows us that paradoxically the law has became a new form of discrimination for the party in the conflict, the one discriminated against by social circumstances, the woman, without ensuring that this will improve the quality of contact between the children and their parents.

CHANGING NEW VALUES: FATHERHOOD VERSUS FATHERING

Following Hobson, we can see some tensions between fathers, fathering and fatherhood in the more immediate context of everyday family practices.[46]

---

[43] In Spanish doctrine there are not many studies about this subject. In exchange, we can see several studies about the sentiment of injustice in French doctrine. See, eg Nerson and Rubellin-Devichi in (1984) *Rev Tr Dr Civ* 108; Mazel, 'Conflict parental et peres gardiens (1985) *JCP* 3214; Carbonnier, *Droit et passion du droit sous la V République* (Flammarion, 1996) 237; Thery, *Couple, filiation et parenté aujourd'hui*, Rapport à la Ministre de l'Emploi et de la Solidarité et au garde des Sceaux, Ministre de la Justice, Jacob, La documentation française, juin 1998, 79; as well as different discourses in the French Parliament on the occasion of the laws of 7 May 1987 and 8 January 1993.

[44] Pitch, above n 32.

[45] L Gareil, *L'exercise de l'autorité parentale* (2004) Librairie Generale de Droit et de Jurisprudence.

[46] Hobson, above n 41, at 16.

Fathers are seen in relational terms to mothers and children and as elements of social structure, fatherhood can be seen as the cultural coding of men as fathers. So it includes the rights, duties, responsibilities and statuses that are attached to fathers, as well as the discursive terrain. The term 'fathering' does not admit of an easy translation to Spanish. The distinction might signify one between 'being' and 'doing'.

Thus it is increasingly likely that a child will have the experience of one or more than one household in the course of growing up, and the resulting links between different households will vary according to the wishes and expectations of the various parties involved. Here, the recognition of biological and social/household fathers comes into play. Until now, the Spanish legal framework gave preference to biological fathers in assigning rights to care and decision making, especially as both parents have joint legal custody, which means that both are capable of making decisions about the main issues concerning the child. But as Hobson says, it is unclear how much this affects daily practices of social/household fathers who reside with children. So, there can be competing interests even between men as fathers: between social and biological fathers around fathers' rights and obligations.[47]

---

[47] *Ibid.*

Part 3

Professional Intervention

7

Enabling Contact: The Involvement of Psycho-social Professionals in Supporting Contact in Germany

KATRIN MUELLER-JOHNSON

INTRODUCTION

A S LAMB'S CHAPTER in this volume shows, there is an increasing body of evidence from child developmental research which suggests that good quality bonds with both parents are beneficial to a child's development. With divorce or separation the contact to the non-residential parent can get lost, and it is therefore an important question of how to help to maintain, or newly develop, a good quality relationship with the non-residential parent. In many countries much effort has been expended from the side of the legislature, social services and non-governmental agencies, such as charities, to support families in maintaining contact after divorce.

This chapter concentrates on recent developments of contact support in Germany. It first reviews the legal background regulating contact and contact support. It then describes the involvement of several groups of psycho-social professionals who can become involved with families along the way. Whenever possible, it draws on empirical research, yet such research in the German family law area remains sparse. Especially rigorous evaluation research on the effectiveness of legal and psycho-social interventions is still needed.

CONTACT AS THE RIGHT OF THE CHILD

Following on from the reform of German family law in 1998, both parents routinely maintain shared parental responsibility after separation and divorce. This led to an increase in the rates of joint parental responsibility from 17 per cent in 1995 to 81 per cent in 2003 (Jaeger, 2005). There is a general assumption that it is in the best interests of the child to have contact with both parents (§ 1626 section 3 sentence 1 BGB).[1] The right to post-separation and post-divorce parental contact is construed as the right of the child (§ 1684 section 1 BGB) and maintaining contact is seen as a parental obligation in the interests of the child (BVerfG NJW 1993, 2671, FamRZ 1999, 85, 86). This means that both parents are responsible for making contact work. Unlike in England and Wales, the child in Germany does not only have the statutory right to have contact with the parents, but with grandparents, siblings, step-parents and former foster parents (§ 1685 BGB).

As in other countries (see contributions in this volume) most contact arrangements are negotiated by families independently out of court. The most comprehensive prevalence data on divorce and contact available in Germany for the time after the reform of the family law in 1998 comes from a study by Proksch (2002), who surveyed a large sample of divorcing parents with a one-year follow-up, as well as judges, lawyers and Youth Welfare Service staff dealing with divorcing or divorced families. Proksch's survey (N = 4773) showed that 68 per cent of contact agreements by parents with shared parental responsibility were arrived at independently; only 18 per cent were made by court order; and 9 per cent were arrived at through mediation/counselling. For families with sole custody arrangements, 43 per cent of parents agreed contact independently, 40 per cent went to court, and 9 per cent arrived at an arrangement through mediation/counselling (Proksch, 2002).

The legal requirement to enable contact means that both parents have the obligation to refrain from doing anything that would impair the relationship of the child with the other parent or that would make their relationship more difficult to maintain (§ 1684 section 2 BGB). In particular, parents are not allowed to try to undermine the relationship between the child and other parent by exerting a negative influence on the child (Palandt, § 1684, No 12). The residential parent is also under the obligation to use influence on the child actively with a view to overcoming potential negative attitudes or anxiety that may be related to contact with the other parent (eg OLG Braunschweig, FamRZ, 1999, 195; OLG Thueringen, FamRZ 2000, 47; OLG Karlsruhe, FamRZ 1999, 242), and to help the child minimise loyalty conflicts (eg OLG Bamberg, FamRZ 1995, 428; IKG Koeln, FamRZ 1998, 961, 962). It is assumed that a parent will be able to influence a child in such a way until the child is 10 years old (OLG Hamm, FamRZ 1996, 363). Another part of this obligation is the requirement to make reasonable contact arrangements with the other parent (Buete, 2005), and for instance to co-operate with a psychological expert tasked with assessing the child and its attachment bonds to the parents for the family court if

---

[1] German Civil Code (BGB = Buergerliches Gesetzbuch).

such an assessment has been order by the court (OLG Koeln, FamRZ 1998, 1463, 1464).

The construction of contact as the right of the child also means that legally it is possible for the child (though in practice the resident parent) to sue a parent who is unwilling to engage in contact with the child to force them have contact with the child (OLG Celle, MDR 2001, 395, OLG Koeln, FamRZ 2001, 1023; 2002, 979; 2004, 52, Schwab III No. 296), although doubts have been expressed doubt about the efficacy of the attempting to enforce contact against the expressed will of the non-custodial parent (OLG Nuremberg, FamRZ 2002, 413, Palandt § 1626 No 29).

ENFORCEMENT PROVISIONS

If parents do not comply with a contact agreement, the court can order the parents to comply in future (§ 1684 section 3 sentence 2 BGB), but it is agreed that this is only useful in cases where parents are merely minded not to comply with the agreement (Buete, 2005). Where the court concludes that it is the conflicted relationship between the parents or parenting problems that underlies the non-compliance with the contact agreement or the inability to reach an agreement, it can compel the parents to contact a counselling service (Buete, 2005).

Another possibility is to order a reduction of the financial spousal support paid by the contact parent to the non-cooperating parent (Buete, 2005). This reduction in spousal support is, however, to be held separate from any financial support for the child which cannot not be reduced for this reason.

The court can also threaten coercive fines or even coercive detention to move the residential parent to hand over the child for contact visits. These fines are not retroactive for contact visits which the parent already prevented, but are only to be used prospectively, intended to stop the parent from circumventing contact again. These fines are due only in a case where the contact visit was indeed obviated by the parent. If contact did not take place because the child strictly rejects contact, the court has to find in a hearing if the child's rejection is of such intensity that the residential parent cannot prevail on the child to attend contact visits. Where the child cannot be made to change its mind, coercive fines are inapplicable.

As a matter of law, a court can also impose coercive detention (OLG Frankfurt, FamRZ 2002, 1585; OLG Dresden, FamRZ 2002, 1588). In order to do so it would typically have to threaten it first, but if the behaviour of the parent is such that it is clear that the parent will not co-operate or if there is urgency, a previous threat of pain of detention is not necessary (Buete, 2005). In practice, judges have called for caution in the imposition of coercive means because they regard them as potentially more deleterious than no contact. A survey of 809 family court and appeal court

(Oberlandesgericht) judges, conducted as part of the large evaluation study of the changes to the German family law (Proksch, 2002) showed that 34 per cent of judges had never threatened fines, 47 per cent had threatened (ie specified the amount to be paid on pain of penalty) in up to five cases, 16 per cent had done so in up to 10 cases and only 0.7 per cent of judges had done so in more than 10 cases. There is no data to show how many of the contact orders in these cases were again frustrated so that the fines became due.

Proksch (2002) reports from interviews with parents that these perceive that courts dither too long until they finally impose coercive fines. This delay is experienced as very stressful and they suggested that much persistence on the side of the contact parent is needed before such measures are imposed. A more likely outcome, they said, was that parents lost their patience with the court and gave up their quest for contact. Coercive detention is threatened only extremely rarely as a means to enforce contact. Only 1.4 per cent of judges in the above-mentioned study had threatened coercive detention, and done so in less than 5 cases each (Proksch, 2002). Again, these data did not follow up on whether renewed non-compliance with the order did indeed lead to detention. To my knowledge there are no published cases in which a parent was detained to enforce a contact order.

The court can order that the parent has to hand over the child for contact visits (Herausgabeanordnung) (§ 1632 section 1 BGB). If the parent does not co-operate force can be used against the parent (§ 33 section 2 sentence 1 FGG).[2] Force is however not admissible against the child (§ 33 section 2 sentence 2 FGG). If any of these measures are not successful the court can restrict the parental authority of the residential parent and appoint a contact guardian (Umgangspfleger) (Buete, 2005), who holds the capacity to arrange and make decisions concerning contact. Such a contact custodian can ask the residential parent to hand over the child and can also bring the police in to enforce the arrangement (§ 33 section 2 FGG). More information concerning the role of the contact guardian will be given below.

As a last resort the court can finally order a change of custody. This is only to be used in exceptional circumstances because sole parental responsibility is usually only awarded for a reason. Generally the parent with sole parental responsibility has the better relationship with the child than the non-residential parent, and there were reasons in the relationship between the non-residential parent and the child that prevented joint parental responsibility. In such families, a change of custody would, rather than

---

[2] Procedural code applicable to family law (FGG = Gesetz ueber Angelegeneheiten der freiwilligen Gerichtsbarkeit).

being a punishment for the non-cooperative residential parent, constitute a punishment of the child (BGH, FamRZ 1985, 169, 170).

When deciding on imposing enforcement measures, the benefits of contact and no contact have to be balanced, and the enforcement measures' probable effects on the child have to be taken into account. The enforcement may conflict with the child's best interest because it may put pressure on the relationship with the main carer. Furthermore, coercive means such as fines or detention do not provide a long-term solution, as they would have to be enforced separately for each missed session. It has been argued that coercive fines are also often ineffective because as due to lack of financial resources the parents involved are not able to pay those fines without a negative impact on the child (Proksch, 2002).

ENABLING PROVISIONS AND THE INVOLVEMENT OF PSYCHO-SOCIAL PROFESSIONALS IN CONTACT

Rather than on enforcement the main focus is however on enabling provisions. According to 18 section 3 SGB VIII,[3] parents and children are entitled to free advice and support concerning contact issues. There is a variety of psycho-social professions who engage with families who are conflicted about contact, ranging from the social workers in the Youth Welfare Service who try support the parents in coming to an agreement prior to court date, to counsellors who provide parenting and conflict related advice, mediators, psychologists who assess the family for the court, guardians *ad litem*, contact facilitators and finally contact guardians. The work of mediators, especially in providing in-court mediation in close partnership with the legal professionals in a given case, as for instance in the 'Kochem Model' (Kochemer Modell) is described in detail elsewhere in this volume (see Voegli, this volume). The involvement of the other professionals will be described in detail in the following pages.

Youth Welfare Service and Counselling

When a divorce is filed, the Youth Welfare Service's psycho-social service is notified automatically. In cases where the parents continue to maintain joint parental responsibility, the youth welfare service sends out a letter to the family informing them about freely available advice and counselling for separation and parenting concerns. For families where a parent files for sole parental responsibility the Youth Welfare Service makes a mandatory appointment with the family to ascertain for the court their views as to the contact arrangements. For those families filing for sole custody, about

---

[3] Code applicable to welfare law (SBG = Sozialgesetzbuch).

half the initial contacts are by letter only, 9 per cent by phone only, and in about 40 per cent of cases there is a visit by a social worker (Proksch, 2002). At this point the social worker is in a role similar to CAFCASS, the advice and support service for families using the courts in England and Wales; the social worker will then meet the parents in order to ascertain how they would like contact to be arranged. If the parents have not agreed on anything prior to the visit, the social worker also tries to facilitate an arrangement during this meeting and, finally, provides a report to court.

If at the following court hearing no agreement has been reached but the court forms the opinion that the parents may come to an agreement eventually after more mediation and/or counselling, it can suspend the case and refer the parents to the counselling/mediation service within the Youth Welfare Service (Buete, 2005). This part of the service works separately from the general psycho-social service that worked with the family prior to the court date. The rationale for this separation is to ensure confidentiality of the counselling process. In addition to services directly delivered by staff from the Youth Welfare Service there are third party providers who contract with the Youth Welfare Service and who also provide counselling and advice in separation/divorce and parenting matters free of charge. In addition to being referred to the services by the court, parents and children can also self-refer. Proksch's (2002) parent survey indicates that quite a substantial number of parents make use of these services, either during or after the separation or divorce. In 1999/2000 the rate of parents taking advantage of these services was between 35 and 40 per cent of parents with joint parental responsibility (percentage depending on which parent was asked and whether the children lived with them or not) and 28–39 per cent of parents with sole custody. The lowest rate of use was for both types of custody arrangements by fathers who lived without their children (34.9 per cent joint custody, 28.7 per cent sole custody) and the highest for mothers who lived with their children (39.4 per cent for joint custody, 39.5 per cent for sole custody). After the divorce the rates of counselling/advice ranged for shared custody families from 16 per cent for fathers without children to 25 per cent for mothers with children, and for families with sole custody, from 17 per cent for fathers without children to 29 per cent for mothers with children (Proksch, 2002).

Most counselling arrangements were relatively brief, ranging from 1–3 sessions in total, but between 5 and 10 per cent of parents out of the total sample attended more than 10 sessions. As to be expected, during the time of the divorce these sessions addressed to about two-thirds concerns that were relationship and divorce related and to about one third parenting issues. After divorce, counselling sessions concerned mainly parenting-related issues, and less conflict-related issues or mediation. Mediation was generally not common in the Proksch (2002) data and many parents reported that they did not know about it.

Parents are generally satisfied with the counselling and advice provided by the Youth Welfare Services. A recent survey investigated retrospective satisfaction of families who were known to the Youth Welfare Service for separation or divorce in 2000–01 (N = 201) (Buchholz-Graf and Sgolik, 2004). These were mostly parents with joint parental responsibility (only 40 per cent had filed for sole custody). A total of 66 per cent of families had received counselling or advice from the Youth Welfare Service. Of the parents with shared parental responsibility, 43 per cent contacted the Welfare Service for information or counselling sessions. Most parents, those with joint custody and those with sole custody, said that they found the counselling/advice important (69 per cent and 74 per cent respectively). The majority said that they would do it again (68 per cent and 63 per cent, respectively) and that they would recommend such sessions to others (71 per cent and 63 per cent respectively).

In cases in which families self-refer to counselling there has usually been a long history of problems and failed attempts to make contact work informally, eg with assistance of other family members for hand-over. It can frequently be seen as a last straw for very highly conflicted families.

Psychological Expert Assessment

It has been estimated that psychological expert assessments are ordered in between 3 per cent and 10 per cent of all family law cases (Balloff, 2003). Unfortunately there are no empirical data on the percentage of contact cases that undergo psychological assessment. When a psychological assessment is ordered, other approaches to resolve conflict between the parents have failed previously, such as referrals to the Youth Welfare Services for counselling or mediation. A psycho-diagnostic assessment is ordered in Germany by the courts, not by the families. If not satisfied with the quality of the report of the court appointed expert witness, a party can get an additional expert opinion (Balloff, 2003).

The assessment includes typically an exploration and analysis of the family's background with respect to the question at hand, interviews with parents and the child, as well as observations of the child's behavior at home and of interactions between each parent and child. Depending on the case standardised tests and scales may also be used (Balloff, 2003). In families where contact has not taken place for a longer period, the psychological expert may also supervise contact visits (Buete, 2005).

The traditional approach to psychological assessment for the courts has been that the psychologist analysed and reported on the situation as observed without attempting to change anything in the family's dynamic (Salzgeber and Hoefling, 2004). With the arrival of the reform of the family law in 1998, the role of the court as changed. Before arriving at a judgment the court now has to try to actively resolve conflict between the parents as best as possible and let them arrive at an agreement (§§ 52, 52 a FGG). While the task of the expert witness used to be the assessment of the status quo, the role of the expert in the new law can also be to support the parents in their ability to reduce conflict, and to arrive at a more co-operative attitude (Kluck, 2003). This can be called a modification oriented assessment (Balloff, 2003). Implicitly this use of the psychologist as the 'peacemaker' existed before the change in the family law, but this function has become more explicit (Kluck, 2003; Rexilius, 2003).

There are movements towards are more interventionist conceptualisation of the role of the psychological expert away from a 'status diagnostic' approach (Kluck, 2003), in which they take the role of a distanced and neutral assessor, towards a 'case manager' approach, in which the psychologist works with the families to achieve change (Salzgeber and Hoefling, 2004).

Some speak already of a paradigm shift (Jopt and Zuetphen, 2004), but the admissibility of an interventionist approach is still debated: some courts say that judges are not allowed to instruct the psychologist to include therapeutic and modification oriented approaches (BGH, FamRZ 1994, 158, 160; OLG Hamburg, FamRZ 1996, 422, 424; OLG Brandenburg, FamRZ 2002, 976; OLG Karlsruhe, FamRZ 2004, 56) while other courts are of the other opinion (OLG Hamm, FamRZ 1996, 1557, 1558; OLG Stuttgart 2001, 932).

This modification based, interventionist approach works on the assumption that any assessment by the psychologist necessarily has an effect on the family under assessment. While the traditional approach tries to minimise this effect in order to get the most accurate measurement of the status quo, the modification oriented approach harnesses the effect in order to create more insight in the family members.

In such a modification oriented approach the psychologist, while assessing the parents and the child, uses this process in an interactive manner to guide the parents towards a changed perspective that puts the child's best interests in the foreground. The psychologist works together with each parent in assessing each parent's resources to deal with conflict and parenting challenges, conditions for certain behaviours as well as identifying possible alternative behaviours. In doing so, it attempts to improve the parental ability to cope and manage conflict as well as strengthening the child's interests through a better parental understanding of the child's perspective and needs (Balloff, 2003).

Guardian Ad Litem

After the separation of parents or the dissolution of a marriage, children have a right to be represented by a guardian *ad litem* (Anwalt des Kindes) in all court cases that concern the child as a person, and not merely their property rights (§ 50 section 1 FGG). However, the guardian *ad litem* is appointed not routinely but only where the conditions of the case warrant a child's independent representation (§ 50 section 2 (1) FGG). This is for instance the case where there is a conflict between the parents about contact such that the parents are not able to act in the child's best interest (OLG Duesseldorf, NJW 2000, 1274). Usually a guardian *ad litem* is only appointed after the Youth Services have reported back to court but it is possible to appoint the guardian *ad litem* earlier if there are specific indications for a severe conflict of interest between the parents (Buete, 2005). Very often it is the psychological expert who at an even later stage reports back to court that the parents are not able to act in the best interests of the child and as a consequence the guardian *ad litem* is appointed. Schulze (2005) estimated that guardians *ad litem* are appointed in only 5–10 per cent of divorce cases.

Contact Facilitation

The typical model of contact facilitation in Germany differs from that in England and Wales. In England and Wales most contact facilitation happens in the form of 'supported contact', in which families attend a contact centre in which there is typically a large room in which several contact parents interact with their children while a contact facilitator, frequently a volunteer, watches over them and monitors that the children are not endangered and not overly distressed (Furniss, 2000; Mueller-Johnson, 2005). Some centres also offer supervised contact, in which a professional provides one-to-one supervision of visits. Supported contact is the norm, often in church or Kindergarden facilities on alternating weekends rather than in specialised premises, mostly staffed by volunteers, and it tends to be kept deliberately low-key to minimise the artificiality of the situation (Mueller-Johnson, 2005). As most staff are volunteers this means that they may not be on duty during all the visits that the child attends. Thus it can happen that the child attends a contact centre but is not familiar with the volunteer on duty. Supervised contact is offered in cases where there are special concerns that make closer monitoring of the contact visit necessary, such as there is an ongoing risk of spousal violence or violence towards the child, or fear of abduction (Mueller-Johnson, 2005).

In Germany the standard model of contact provision (begleiteter Umgang) is similar to what would be supervised contact in the UK. Most contact is facilitated on a one-to-one basis by a professional, be it a psychologist, child psychiatrist, or social worker, possibly with additional training in contact facilitation. This one-to-one provision means that contact visits can be adapted specifically to the needs of the family, and where appropriate contact visits can also take place in locations other than the service's office (eg visits to the playground, etc). As contact sessions progress and the relationship with the parent improves, facilitators may also leave the parent and child alone in a room within the premises and stay in an adjacent room to be available should the child become upset (Buete, 2005). Most providers require that parents attend concurrent parent meetings.

There are also some services which provide contact similar to the English and Welsh model of supported contact, in that it is facilitated mainly by volunteers for several parents at one time and does not require concurrent parent counselling sessions, eg the charity Kinderschutzbund (Klotmann, 2005). The preliminary standards for contact facilitation, developed by the State Institute of Early Childhood Education and Family Research, Munich, state that due to the complexity of the cases and intensity of conflict a high degree of professional experience is needed and that therefore most contact should be facilitated by paid professionals rather than volunteers (Fthenakis, Goedde, Reichert-Garschhammer and Walbiner, 2001).

Reasons for referral to facilitated contact are similar to those in England and Wales: where there has not been any contact between parent and child for a longer period, where a child is fearful about contact, or where the residential parent has tried to influence the child against the contact parent. Other reasons include fear of abduction or concerns about the contact parent's ability to provide safe child-oriented contact, eg where is a background of substance misuse, psychopathology or mental disorder, or where there has been a history of domestic violence (Friedrich, Reinhold and Kindler, 2004; Guetthoff, 2004).

There is also 'controlled contact' (kontrollierter Umgang), in which the contact between parent and child is monitored closely and the contact facilitator is always present throughout the session. These can be ordered where there are specific indications of harm to the child, such as proof or suspicion of child sexual abuse (Buete, 2005).

For facilitated contact court referrals constitute only one third of referrals (30 per cent). Families are also referred by the Youth Welfare Service (37 per cent) or are self-referrals (27 per cent) (Stephan and Wolf, 2002).

Before starting the actual visits most contact centres in England and Wales conduct short intake interviews with the parents who will sign an agreement to abide by the ground rules of the centre (Maclean and Mueller-Johnson, 2003). Often centres also offer an opportunity for the child to visit the centre before sessions start in order to become familiar with the place and the staff, which families find very helpful for the child (Furniss, 2000). The standard procedure for facilitated contact in Germany begins with preparatory visits with the parents, either jointly or where this is not possible, separately. These sessions are held to ascertain if there is indeed a basis for contact and to try to work on the conflict. The number of meetings varies (Vergho, 2004) but there can be up to five preparatory sessions before the contact with the child is started. If there is no basis for contact it is regarded as better that contact should not be reinitiated for fear that it would come to nothing and burden the child unnecessarily (Vergho, 2004). Prior to meeting the contact parent at the contact service, the child typically attends one or two sessions at the contact service in order to get comfortable with the contact facilitator (Maclean and Mueller-Johnson, 2003). Throughout the series of sessions the family stays with the same facilitator.

Most services also mandate that parents attend separate counselling sessions concurrent with the contact visits. The purpose of these sessions is to work through concerns the parent might have about the contact visits, work on the underlying parental conflict and change the attitude towards the other parent (Haid-Loh, Normann-Kossak and Walter, 2000; Vergho, 2004).

Similar to England and Wales, contact facilitation is regarded as a temporary intervention. While in England and Wales the average is about ten sessions, in Germany contact facilitation used be ordered for six months in the first instance, with the possibility of an extension (Maclean and Mueller-Johnson, 2003). Most families move on within one year (Stephan and Wolf, 2002).

The Child's Experience of Facilitated Contact

As part of a large, as yet unpublished, evaluation project of contact facilitation in Germany led by Fthenakis at the State Institute of Early Childhood Education and Family Research in Munich, Friedrich analysed videotapes of children in their first and last contact session, and coded visible signs of stress and joy in their interactions with their parent (Friedrich et al, 2004). She found that children showed on average moderate levels of stress during parts of the session and an overall slightly positive attitude towards joint play. The joy expressed in this first session was related to parental sensitivity: where a parent was able to respond sensitively to the child even in the first session, the child showed greater joy and fewer signs of stress. Older children (older than 7 years) showed more symptoms of stress than younger children, and children, who attended the contact session together with siblings, showed greater stress symptoms that those who were an only child (although for families with several children at contact sessions it was always the oldest child that was included in the study and thus, as Friedrich suggests, age and attendance of siblings can have been confounded in this study).

After several contact sessions, 46 per cent of children showed a reduction in visible stress and 58 per cent an increase in the joyfulness of their play with the parent. Over the course of the contact sessions the more attentive the parent was and the more responsively and sensitively a parent interacted with the child, the more positive was the development of the child's experience (Friedrich et al, 2004).

Parent Satisfaction with Contact Facilitation

A small parent satisfaction survey (N = 25) of parents who had received contact facilitation directly at the Youth Welfare Service, augmented with a survey of the professionals that worked with these families (N = 61 cases) showed that most parents had positive attitudes towards the contact facilitation (Buchholz-Graf & Vergho, 2005). Ninety-two per cent of the mothers and 73 per cent of fathers found it a positive experience. Most families were court referrals (74 per cent) and 12 per cent were there by self-referral. All parents had to undergo a series of preparatory meetings. Eighty-four per cent of the parents said that they were satisfied with the number of preparatory meetings, 16 per cent said that they wanted more meetings. Sixty-four per cent found the session helpful and 92 per cent at least partially helpful. Concurrent counselling sessions with the contact facilitation were regarded as useful by 80 per cent of the parents, and 30 per cent would have liked more. About one-third of mothers (30 per cent) and about two-thirds of fathers (64 per cent) would have liked to see more joint meetings.

In this study about half the counselling sessions were conducted by the same person who was also the contact facilitator, in the other half of cases it was a separate person. Two-thirds of parents reported that they would prefer if the same person did the facilitation and the counselling. Some authors suggest that there are theoretical reasons of impartiality that would make it preferable if the counsellor was separate from the contact facilitator (Fthenakis et al, 2001). As could be expected, the role that parents wanted the contact facilitator to play differed across the sexes: Women wanted the facilitator to be mainly a person who monitored and controlled the contact visits, while fathers preferred the facilitator to concentrate on the supporting and facilitating function.

The parents' perception of the effect of supported contact on the child differed: 54 per cent of mothers, but only 9 per cent of fathers thought that contact visits were stressful for the child. On the other hand, 46 per cent of mothers and 73 per cent of fathers thought that the contact visits were an important experience for the child and 31 per cent of mothers and 73 per cent of fathers said that it was beneficial to the child's development.

While more than two-thirds of the parents had an overall positive impression of the contact centre facilities, the contact facilitator, and the counsellors, and said that they would recommend it to others, mothers and fathers disagreed strongly on the evaluation of outcome of the contact facilitation. No mother said that the contact facilitation had brought about a satisfactory outcome, while 82 per cent of fathers said that the outcome was satisfactory. The assessment of the professionals of the cases' success was similar to that of the fathers: 72 per cent of the cases were judged by the professionals as having made 'sufficient progress'. Although the preparatory and concurrent counselling sessions are specifically aimed at changing attitudes towards the partner and reducing conflict between the partners, no woman regarded the relationship to the other parent as having improved. Twenty-seven per cent of fathers reported a better relationship. More than three-quarters of the parents said that they could not rely on agreements with the other parents, or engage in meaningful conversations on logistic questions such as child rearing or educational issues. Despite this, 70 per cent of fathers had contact at least once or twice a month 2–18 months after leaving the facilitated contact arrangement (Buchholz-Graf and Vergho, 2005).

While this survey has several methodological limitations, notably different time intervals since completion of the contact facilitation and its small sample size, it provided some interesting and potentially sobering insights, such as to the change in parental attitudes that can be achieved in this intensive type of contact facilitation. More systematic and large-scale studies are needed to assess parent and child satisfaction with contact facilitation and to provide independent outcome evaluations.

Some Limitations of Contact Facilitation

A couple of studies have provided indications that a high percentage of families are not able to move on to safe independent contact as a result of the contact facilitation. Fifty-four per cent of the families in Stephan and Wolf (2002) were not able to arrive at an independent contact solution after facilitated contact, and in 75 per cent of families at a different contact service, contact stopped altogether before it could be moved onto a safe independent level (Familiennotruf, 2002). It was terminated by the staff, courts or by the parents (Familiennotruf, 2002). Stephan and Walter reported that in their sample showed it was more likely to stop particularly for families with a history of domestic violence (Stephan and Wolf, 2002). A small interview Swiss study followed up children who had been in contact facilitation in the 1980s and 1990s (N = 15) (Gassmann, 2000, cited in Staub and Felder, 2004). Five of these respondents reported that they could not remember the facilitated contact sessions, two remembered them as negative, and the half of the sample had positive memories. Similar to the studies above only in half of these families was contact with the parent maintained in the long term.

These data, albeit preliminary and based on small samples, do suggest that facilitated contact is not the panacea that some judges would like it to be. As in many cases, contact is either stopped while it is still facilitated by professionals or stopped once it was moved on to independent contact, calls have been made for better diagnostics of in what situations supported contact is likely to be successful (Buchholz-Graf and Vergho, 2005). These could help avoid a retraumatisation of the child through the stressful reinitiation of contact and the subsequent stop.

A study by Reinhold (2004, cited in Friedrich et al, 2004), part of the large evaluation project by Fthenakis and colleagues, aimed at predicting successful outcomes of contact facilitation. Using videotapes of contact sessions she employed standardised behaviour observation scales to code parental sensitivity at play and when supporting the child and coded the child's behaviour for signs of stress and joy. Parental sensitivity and children's level of stress in the first session both predicted the quality of the child–parent relationship at the end of the series of supported contact sessions: Children with parents who showed greater sensitivity in meeting the child's needs at the first session showed less stress at the end. And secondly, children who showed great signs of distress at the beginning were three times as likely to maintain similar levels of distress, or even experience an increase in distress and/or a reduction in expressed joyfulness over the course of the contact facilitation as children who showed fewer signs of distress at the beginning. Given this data, there is the risk for families with high levels of child distress coupled with low parental sensitivity that contact can become a negative, and cumbersome experience for the child. In order to avoid this, the authors recommend additional interventions for these families aimed at specifically improving the quality of the child–parent interactions (Buchholz-Graf and Vergho, 2005; Friedrich, Reinhold and Kindler, 2004).

These smaller studies are promising and a first step to the methodologically rigorous larger-scale research that is needed to evaluate the German provisions for contact facilitation. Future comparative studies might also be able to shed light on potential differences in parent/child satisfaction and outcome for the one-to-one high interventionist approach common to Germany with the lower-key group-oriented approach prevailing in England and Wales.

Contact Guardian

If a residential parent still does not comply despite a court order for contact or for facilitated contact, a 'contact guardian' (Umgangspfleger) can be appointed. Its current legal foundation is that of the 'additional guardian' (Ergaenzungspfleger) (§ 1909 BGB), whom the court can appoint to fulfil particular guardianship aspects, while the main guardianship or parental responsibility lies with someone else. As here the guardian has been given the duty to manage contact and is therefore also called contact guardian. If a contact guardian is appointed, the arrangement and management of contact visits are transferred from the parent(s) to the contact guardian. The contact guardian differs from all other non-legal professionals dealing with the family in that he has been invested with some of the parental powers by the court. The contact guardian also differs from the other psycho-social professionals whom the family may have previously met in that it is neither the facilitation of the visit itself, nor the psychological intervention in parental conflict that is addressed with this institute but rather the practical arrangement of visits and handover.

The court will usually specify the amount of contact that is to be arranged, eg fortnightly on weekends, but the practical realisation is with the contact guardian (Salzgeber and Menzel, 2004). Apart from arranging particular times for contact, arranging the handover or bringing the child to the contact facilitator, the contact guardian can also assist in the changing of agreements, such as for holidays and birthdays, without a need to go back to court for a new court order. Where the contact parent does not comply with the agreement and is unapproachable, the contact guardian can put a temporary stop to the contact visits until the parent is willing to comply with the arrangement. In cases where a court order had been obtained the contact guardian can go back to court to have it amended if it is considered that this is in the best interests of the child. In some cases additional contact facilitation may be indicated, such as where the contact parent has issues of substance abuse, mental disorder or a history of violence.

Prior to an appointment of a contact guardian would have been in many cases the involvement of other psycho-social professions, such as a counsellor, a psychological expert witness, or a contact facilitator. The court may have also tried to enforce contact through admonishment in court hearings or through the threat of fines or change of custody (Salzgeber and Menzel, 2004). The nature of the contact guardian is part enforcing, part enabling with the purpose of bringing the family eventually in a position in which they can have self-managed safe contact.

As the families for which contact guardians are appointed show very intense conflict a contact guardian needs a great deal of experience, communicative and mediative ability in order to deal with the families successfully (Salzgeber and Menzel, 2004). The most suitable candidates for this appointment are therefore also social workers or psychologists with experience in working with conflicted families. To date, no specific further training for contact guardians exists (Salzgeber & Menzel, 2004). In practice, it has been reported that due to lack of specialised staff in some Youth Welfare Services civil servants with degrees in public administration act as contact guardians (Deutsches Institute fuer Jugendhilfe und Familienrecht, 2004). Not surprisingly some of these have voiced that they feel overwhelmed by this task.

As it is a very recent development in German family law, there is hardly any empirical data on contact guardians. A phone survey of 107 randomly selected regional Youth Welfare Service agencies (Jugendämter), conducted by the German Institute for Youth Welfare and Family Law (DIJuF), an advisory institute for Youth Welfare Services of all German states (Bundesländer) and professional groups who work in the realm of youth welfare and family law, investigated the prevalence of this legal institute to facilitate contact (Deutsches Institut fuer Jugendhilfe und Familienrecht, 2004).

The majority of youth services surveyed (64.5 per cent) did not have any contact guardianships in place. Some of these mentioned that they had some general guardianship cases which also included contact issues, but did not have specific contact guardianship cases. Thirty-five per cent had at least one case of a contact guardianship on their books. Most states had at least one Youth Welfare Service with contact guardianships, only Bremen and Thuringia did not have any cases. As about one-third of this random sample had contact guardian cases with a total of 133 cases, the authors estimated that nationally there are currently about 200 youth services who manage about 750 contact guardianships. Some of these cases refer to families in which the child still resides with one parent, some of these cases refer to families where the other components of parental responsibility have been transferred to grandparents or other relatives as guardians, while the responsibility to arrange contact was transferred to the Youth Welfare Service because these guardians had difficulty coming to contact agreements with the parents.

The survey found that most contact guardianships that were known to the Youth Welfare Services were conducted by staff of the Youth Welfare Service. This was however kept completely separate from possible contact facilitation which might occur through the Youth Welfare Service (ie done by different members of staff). Many Youth Welfare Services that fulfil contact guardianship roles evaluated this type of guardianship quite negatively. It is regarded as very time intensive and necessitating intensive work with the parents. Those Youth Welfare Services who reported positive attitudes towards contact guardianship also reported good collaboration with the family court and regular exchange of information. Youth Welfare Services with positive attitudes also reported of preparatory meetings with the court prior to the appointment of contact guardians in a given case to discuss the aim for the contact guardianship and the expectations on both the court's and the Youth Welfare Service's side.

The contact guardianship is usually regarded as a temporary solution. Typically contact guardians are appointed for 6–12 months in the first instance, although there is an awareness that this short duration is usually not be long enough to resolve the situation (Salzgeber and Menzel, 2004). Contact guardianships are terminated once parents are finally able to move on to independent management of contact or once it becomes apparent that the conflict between the parents is so entrenched that independent management of contact by the parents will not become possible. In the survey it was suggested that a quite a number of contact guardianships fail and are terminated without success.

Youth Welfare Services also reported that family courts frequently overestimate the Youth Welfare Service's ability to make contact happen through contact guardianships when parents have not ceased to be actively opposed to contact. Although the contact guardian can mandate the time and place of contact, there are cases in which this is ignored by the parents, where doors are not opened, a contact guardian is not let into the home, the family is not present at the agreed time. Even when met, some parents will not hand over the child to the contact guardian as mandated. Some Youth Welfare Services described having been reproached by judges for having failed such families. They experience the appointment of the contact guardian as a passing on of responsibility from the judge's side to the contact guardian, without any clear plan of how these situations can be resolved. Some Youth Welfare Services mentioned that such families should better be referred to services that are specialised in contact facilitation rather than to the Youth Welfare Service. Such referral to third parties was said to be rare because courts would have to cover the costs when referring to specialised third party providers while they can refer families to the Youth Welfare Services without cost to the court.

Overall there was wide variability across the country in the reality of contact guardianships and uncertainties in how to implement them. This may be because of the lack of specific legislation governing contact guardianships that would make them specific and circumscribed. The DIJuF concluded that contact guardianships were not a valid measure to enforce contact against a parent's will. It is seen as a possible solution for some families in removing the responsibility for contact from the parents and thus eliminating the point at which conflict can crystallize. The transfer of the responsibility for contact to a third neutral party has also been suggested to help alleviate a child's potential loyalty conflicts (Salzgeber and Menzel, 2004).

CONCLUSION

This chapter discussed the legal provisions for contact in Germany. It reviewed the statutory enforcement provisions for contact and showed that enforcement is not very successful. Even those provisions that could theoretically be effective in creating compliance with contact orders, such as coercive fines, do not provide a long-term solution or are not in the best interest of the child, such as threat of detention or of change of custody. More promising seem enabling provisions, although there is little data on how promising they are exactly. In addition to mediation, families can get exposed to a long list of professionals trying to assist in contact: social workers and counsellors from the Youth Welfare Service, psychologists appointed by the courts to assess them and potentially help them change their perspective towards contact, guardians *ad litem*, contact facilitators and finally, if nothing else worked, contact guardians. Each of these professional groups tries to chip away at the contact problem from a slightly different perspective. It would be interesting to inquire what effect this cumulative exposure to the different helping professions has on these families.

As yet there is little empirical data available on how effective these different interventions are in supporting contact. This may be partially the case because many of these provisions are quite recent in their current form, and also because it is difficult to motivate these highly conflicted families to take part in research, especially if this involves long follow-up intervals. Another explanation may possibly be that empirical rigorous large-scale research in the family law area has traditionally not been given as much priority as in the criminal law area. There are, however, a number of promising smaller studies that provide a first insight into the practice and the challenges of these legal provisions. Further research will show how these provisions will fare in the long term.

REFERENCES

Balloff, R (2003) 'Begutachtung in der Familiengerichtsbarkeit–quo vadis Sachverstaendigentaetigkeit?' (*Familie, Partnerschaft und Recht* (10) 530–35.

Buchholz-Graf, W and Sgolik, V (2004) 'Familien in Trennung und Scheidung nach der Kindschaftsrechtsreform–Eine Elternbefragung im Jugendamt' *Zentralblatt fuer Jugendrecht* (3) 81–88.

Buchholz-Graf, W and Vergho, C (2005) 'Wie Eltern den begleiteten Umgang bewerten–eine katamnestische Befragung an Erziehungsberatungsstellen' *Kindschaftsrechtliche Praxis* (2) 43–52.

Buete, D (2005) *Das Umgangsrecht bei Kindern geschiedener oder getrennt lebender Eltern* 2nd edn (Berlin, Erich Schmidt Verlag).

Deutsches Institut fuer Jugendhilfe und Familienrecht (2004) Hinweise zu den gesetzgeberischene Ueberlegungen zur Regelung von sog 'Umgangspflegschafte' vom 11 Novermber 2004. Jugendamt (12) 571–74.

Familiennotruf (2002) Kurzbericht zum Modellprojekt: Evaluation integrierter, familienorientierter Beratungshilfen beim Begleiteten 'Umgang gemaess paragraph 18 (3) SBG VIII Munich: Familiennotruf.

Friedrich, V, Reinhold, C and Kindler, H (2004) '(Begleiter) Umgang und Kindeswohl: Eine Forschungsuebersicht' in M Klinkhammer, U Klotmann and S Prinz (eds), *Handbuch Begleiteter Umgang–Paedagogische, psychologische und rechtliche Aspekte* (Cologne, Bundesanzeiger Verlag) 13–39.

Fthenakis, W, Goedde, M, Reichert-Garschhammer, E and Walbiner, W (2001) Vorlaeufige deutsche Standards zum begleiteten Umgang Muenchen: Staatsinstitut fuer Fruehpaedagogik.

Furniss, C (2000) Research Findings in NAOCC Centres (ed), Conference Report 2000. 'Child Contact Centres in the new millenium: What are the issues arising from research done in the 1990s?' (Nottingham,: National Association of Child Contact Centres) 7–12.

Guetthoff, F (2004) 'Begleiteter Umgang als ein Instrument zur Umsetzung rechtlicher Regelungen des Kindschaftsrechts' in M Klinkhammer, U Klotmann and S Prinz (eds), *Handbuch Begleiteter Umgang–Paedagogische, psychologische und rechtliche Aspekte* (Cologne, Bundesanzeiger Verlag) 57–71.

Haid-Loh, A, Normann-Kossak, K and Walter, E (2000) Begleiteter Umgang-Konzpete, Probleme und Chancen der Umsetzung des reformierten Par. 18 SGB VIII.Berlin: EZI-Eigenverlag.

Jaeger, W (2005) 'Verlagerung von Sorgerechtskonflikten in Umgangsstreitigkeiten' *Familie, Partnerschaft und Recht* (3) 70–74.

Jopt, U and Zuetphen (2004) 'Psychologische Begutachtung aus familiengerichtlicher Sicht: A. Entscheidungsorientierter Ansatz' *Zentralblatt fuer Jugendrecht* 91(9), 310–21.

Klotmann, U (2005) 'Begleiteter Umgang am Beispiel des Konzepts des Deutschen Kinderschutzbundes in Rheinland-Pfalz' in M Klinkhammer, U Klotmann and S Prinz (eds), *Handbuch Begleiteter Umgang-Paedagogische, psychologische und rechtliche Aspekte* (Cologne, Bundesanzeiger Verlag) 97–122.

Kluck, M-L (2003) 'Entscheidungsorientierte Begutachtung im Familienrecht' *Familie, Partnerschaft und Recht* (10), 535–40.

Maclean, M and Mueller-Johnson, K (2003) 'Supporting Cross-Household Parenting: Ideas about the "the Family", Policy Formation and Service Development across Jurisdictions' in A Bainham, B Lindley, M Richards and L Trinder (eds), *Children and their Families* (Oxford/Portland, Oregon, Hart Publishing) 117–31.

Mueller-Johnson, K (2005) 'Supporting conflicted post-divorce parenting' in M Maclean (ed), *Family Law and Family Values* (Oxford/Portland, Oregon, Hart Publishing) 107–22.

Palandt, O (2005) *Buergerliches Gesetzbuch–Kommentar* 64th edn (Munich, C.H. Beck).

Proksch, R (2002) Rechtstatsaechliche Untersuchung zur Reform des Kindschaftsrechts.Koeln, Limburg: Bundesanzeiger Verlag.

Rexilius, G (2003) 'Intervention in der familienrechtlichen Begutachtung' *Familie, Partnerschaft und Recht* (10) 540–50.

Rheinhold, C (2004) 'Beobachung von begleiteten Umgangskontakten: Zusammenhaenge zu Indikationem und Beratung', unpublished Masters thesis, Regensburg University.

Salzgeber, J and Hoefling, S (2004) 'Familienpsychologische Begutachtung' *Kindschaftsrechtliche Praxis* (5) 163–70.

Salzgeber, J and Menzel, P (2004) 'Verfahrenspflegschaft und Ergaenzungspflegschaft' *Kindschaftsrechtliche Praxis* (1) 15–21.

Schulze, H (2005) 'Trennung, Lebenskrise und das Recht: Professionelle Handlungsparadoxien und die Rolle von Verfahrenspflegschaft im familiengerichtlichen Umgangsverfahren' *Kindschaftsrechtliche Praxis* (3) 98–103.

Staub, L and Felder, W (2004) *Scheidung und Kindeswohl* (Bern, Huber).

Stephan, HR and Wolf, C (2002) 'Betreuter Umgang–Wem hilft er? Ergebnisse einer landesweiten Evaluation beim Kinderschutzbund in Rheinland-Pfalz' *Kindschaftsrechtliche Praxis* 5(2) 44–46.

Vergho, C (2004) 'Die Vorbereitung auf einen begleiteten Umgang-Wie koennen gute Arbeitsbeziehungen zwischen den Beteiligten hergestellt werden?' in M Klinkhammer, U Klotmann and S Prinz (eds), *Handbuch Begleiteter Umgang-Paedagogische, psychologische und rechtliche Aspekte* (Cologne, Bundesanzeiger Verlag) 139–58.

8

The Changing Face of Contact in Australia

HELEN RHOADES

INTRODUCTION

IN COMMON WITH a number of other countries, Australia's approach to post-separation contact has recently been the subject of competing law reform demands by different stakeholders. As in England, fathers' groups have claimed the legal system is depriving men of time with their children and demanded a guarantee of contact and a presumption of equal residence with mothers.[1] Women's organisations are concerned about the system's treatment of intimate partner violence and want a specially targeted response to cases where this is an issue, in which protection from harm and not maintenance of contact is used to guide outcomes.[2] Advocates for children have argued for a more child-inclusive approach to shaping contact arrangements that would allow children to participate in the decision-making process.[3] And alternative dispute resolution practitioners have entered the fray, suggesting that more meaningful post-separation parenting relationships could be achieved if the government replaced legal advisers with social science trained professionals who have an in-depth understanding of child development.[4]

This chapter traces the shifts in Australia's policy approach to post-separation contact since the passage of its Family Law Act 31 years ago.[5] In doing so it seeks to explore the assumptions that have informed the

---

[1] See for this argument in the UK context, B Geldof, 'The Real Love that Dare Not Speak its Name: A Sometimes Coherent Rant', in A Bainham, B Lindley, M Richards and L Trinder (eds), *Children and Their Families: Contact, Rights and Welfare* Oxford, Hart Publishing, 2003), 171.
[2] See for this view, R Kaspiew, 'Violence in contested children's cases: An empirical exploration' (2005) 19 *Australian Journal of Family Law* 112.
[3] L Moloney and J McIntosh, 'Child-Responsive Practices in Australian Family Law: Past Problems and Future Directions' (2004) 10 *Journal of Family Studies* 71.
[4] T Fisher, 'Family Mediators and Lawyers Communicating about Children: PDR-Land and Lawyer-Land' (2003) *Journal of Family Studies* 201.
[5] The Family Law Act 1975 (Cth) came into operation on 5 January 1976.

different approaches and what these have meant for parents and children in post-separation families. The exploration focuses on the relevant case law, legislative developments and empirical research since the 1970s, with an emphasis on four themes of contact regulation: (1) concern to ensure children maintain a relationship with the parent they no longer live with; (2) concern to ensure children are not exposed to potentially harmful contact; (3) the use of presumptions about children's contact interests; and (4) recognition of children's citizenship. The analysis of this material suggests that while Australia's contact policies have attempted in varying degrees and at different times to meet the first and second of these goals, and have recently embraced a radical departure from the traditional (rhetorical) reluctance to presume what is best for children, a genuine commitment to enhancing children's agency has never been part of the law of contact in this country.

A CHILD WELFARE DISCOURSE

The 'family law system' as we know it in Australia has a relatively recent existence, commencing with the introduction of the Family Law Act 1975 and the creation of the Family Court of Australia in January 1976. At the heart of that new legislation was a concept of 'no fault' divorce, underpinned by a 'clean break' philosophy that aimed to help couples whose marriage had 'irretrievably' broken down move on with their separate post-divorce lives.[6] This idea obviously had implications for children, but concern for children's contact with their non-custodial parent was not a prominent part of the legal discourse or political debates at the time.[7] Nevertheless, the legislation's liberal attitude to divorce signalled the beginning of a new approach to custody arrangements, and instead of assigning children to the 'innocent' parent, judges were directed to regard the welfare of the child as their 'paramount' concern,[8] and to be conscious of the need to protect their 'rights'.[9] The Family Court's earliest jurisprudence praised this dual approach for its lack of paternalism and its recognition of:

> ... the fact that children have their own lives to lead and that they, as well as their divorced parents, have to make a wide manner of emotional readjustment, and in many cases determine for themselves attitudes of morality and responsibility.[10]

---

[6] HA Finlay, 'Divorce Without Fault' (1973) 47 *Australian Law Journal* 431; House of Representatives, Family Law Bill 1974, Second Reading Speech, *Hansard*, 28 November 1974, at 4323 (Mr Whitlam); House of Representatives, Family Law Bill 1974, *Hansard*, 28 February 1975, at 916 (Mr Erwin).

[7] The debates were overwhelmingly concerned with the proposed introduction of no-fault divorce.

[8] Family Law Act 1975 (Cth) s 64(1)(a).

[9] Family Law Act 1975 (Cth) s 43.

[10] *Mazur and Mazur* (1976) 2 Fam LR 11, 311 at 11, 316–17 per Wood J.

But references to children's 'own lives' and their capacity for self-determination are not manifest in the court's early case law, and discussion of their rights was limited to the question of whether children had a legal right to have contact with their non-custodial parent. This issue was addressed in the 1983 decision of *Cotton and Cotton*, in which Nygh J confirmed that the welfare principle was 'the one and only principle to be applied' and that any 'right of access' that might inhere in the child was subservient to its demands.[11] In what has become a classic statement of the court's discretionary approach to determining access orders, his Honour interpreted the Family Law Act provisions as dictating that 'in each case the court must make an independent investigation of what the welfare of the child requires, and the court is not very much assisted by recourse to general principles other than that principle'.[12] Nygh J went on to disavow any suggestion that judges should assume contact with the non-custodial parent will necessarily benefit a child and emphasised the importance of access being a 'meaningful' experience:

> It is true that we can fall back on generally accepted experiences and perceptions in so doing as a guide, but care should be taken not to elevate any of these generally accepted perceptions into presumptions which can only be displaced by evidence to the contrary. One of these generally accepted principles, as I see it, is that it is desirable for a child to maintain a meaningful relation with each of his or her parents. That is obviously desirable when the parents are living together in a united household, but it becomes even more desirable when the parents are separated. It is a trite observation that the parties to a marriage may divorce one another, but they can never divorce themselves from their children. In that sense, the parties remain tied to one another, at least, until those children can stand on their own two feet which may or may not necessarily occur at 18 years or 21 years of age. However, that desirability only operates where there is a chance of a meaningful relationship which is beneficial to the child. It is not, in other words, a question of contact for contact's sake.[13]

The reality of the court's early decision-making patterns, however, was less straightforward than this suggests, and its early case law reveals some contradictory impulses. In practice the discursive appeal of the welfare approach appears to have existed alongside a functional assumption that orders for contact should generally be made, with other cases from the time describing denial of access to a father as 'a serious step' which ought to occur 'only in exceptional circumstances'.[14] As Smart has pointed out, this was an era

---

[11] *Cotton and Cotton* [1983] FLC 91-330 at 78, 252.
[12] *Ibid*.
[13] *Ibid*, at 78, 252–53. See also *Re K* [1982] FLC 91-283, per Treyvaud J.
[14] *Cooper v Cooper* [1977] FLC 90-234 at 76, 250.

in which assessments of the *quality* of parent—child relationships had not yet formed part of the legal landscape.[15] Rather, the approach to determining children's living arrangements reflected the accepted child development theories of the period, which saw the child's welfare as best promoted by ensuring a stable emotional attachment to its mother.[16] Complementing this was a somewhat hardy 'common sense' approach to access, in which contact with the non-custodial parent was viewed as something that would be 'good for' children in the longer term, even if they expressed reservations about it at the time.[17] The Family Law Act's 'welfare checklist' at the time required the court to take the child's wishes seriously,[18] yet children it seems played little genuine role in shaping outcomes and the case law of the day provided judges with an array of legitimate means for disregarding their views.[19]

Whether or not fathers actually continued to see their children after orders for access were made is another (continuingly controversial) matter. Then,[20] as now,[21] there was some indication that a significant number of non-custodial fathers lost contact with their children following separation. Yet policy makers of the day showed little interest in post-separation parenting patterns until men's non-payment of child maintenance became a major issue for the public purse in the late 1980s.[22] On the other hand, the now familiar complaints about mothers who obstruct the father's contact with his children are not new, and the early cases reveal that judges have long been called on to deal with this issue. An example is *Sampson and Sampson*, decided in 1977, where Fogarty J addressed the situation of a custodial parent who had 'irrationally and wrongly' created difficulties with access. In a decision that warned judges not to become distracted

---

[15] C Smart, 'Towards an understanding of family change: Gender conflict and children's citizenship' (2003) 17 *Australian Journal of Family Law* 20 at 24.

[16] See J Bowlby, *Attachment and Loss vol 1: Attachment* (Harmondsworth, Penguin, 1969) and J Bowlby, *Attachment and Loss vol 2: Separation: Anxiety and Anger* (New York, Basic Books, 1973).

[17] Although see for an early example of access denial, *Parsons and Punchon* (1978) FLC 90-490, where the child became distressed when forced to have access with his father.

[18] Note that until 1983, the Family Law Act provided that the wishes of a 14- year-old child were to be given effect unless special circumstances made it necessary not to follow them. The current Family Law Act s 60CC(3)(a) refers to the relevance of the child's maturity and level of understanding in determining what weight should be given to that child's views.

[19] See, eg *In the Marriage of Witherspoon and Cooper* [1981] FLC 91-029, in which Wood SJ held that to give effect to a child's wishes, the judge must be satisfied that those wishes are 'soundly based': at 76, 281.

[20] S Hearst, and G Smiley, 'The access dilemma: a study of access patterns following marriage breakdown' (1984) 22 *Conciliation Court Review* 49.

[21] B Smyth (ed), *Parent-Child Contact and Post-Separation Parenting Arrangements* (Australian Institute of Family Studies, Research Report No 9, 2004).

[22] Australia's child support reforms, which created a legal obligation on parents to financially maintain their children after separation, came into effect in late 1989 with the passage of the Child Support (Assessment) Act 1889 (Cth).

by the inter-parental conflict, his Honour held that the matter 'must be determined only upon a test of the welfare of the child' and not 'by unconscious feelings of punishing the custodial party who appears to have brought the situation about or rewarding the innocent non-custodial parent'.[23] This approach, however, was not welcomed by fathers, with press reports from the court's early years suggesting it was 'hated by thousands' for failing to enforce access orders.[24]

At times, this reluctance to examine the relationship between the parents had negative consequences for the child's well-being, most notably in cases where there was evidence of spousal abuse. In this situation, the court's welfare discourse involved a refusal to see intimate partner violence as a question of parenting capacity, and a determination to separate the perpetrator's role as parent from their conduct as a spouse.[25] No doubt, as others have suggested, this approach reflected the early court's desire to avoid the (what were then seen to be uncivilised) investigations of 'fault' that had characterised pre-Family Law Act decision making.[26] Thus, in cases such as *Heidt*[27] and *Chandler*,[28] judges carefully distinguished evidence of assaults on the wife (which were considered to be irrelevant to the question of access) from abuse of the children (which was relevant), and stressed that their assessments of whether the father should have access to his child had 'largely disregarded his behaviour as a husband'.[29]

A CHILD PROTECTION APPROACH

Things started to shift in the early 1990s, around the time Australia ratified the United Nations Convention on the Rights of the Child,[30] when judges began to take a greater interest in ensuring children enjoyed *safe* access arrangements. Just prior to this, cases involving allegations of child abuse started to appear with more frequency in the reports, challenging the court to revise its approach to parental contact. In a judgment that proved sensitive to the emotional and psychological effects of abuse, the Full Court responded

[23] *Sampson and Sampson* (1977) FLC 90-253 at 76, 358 per Fogarty J.
[24] J Hocking, '100,000 hate family judges, court told' *The Australian* (16 August 1985).
[25] See for an early critique of judicial decision making in access cases, L Moloney, A Marshall, and P Waters, 'Suspension of Access Attitudes which have Influenced the Courts' (1986–87) 1 *Australian Journal of Family Law* 50.
[26] J Behrens, 'Domestic Violence and Property Adjustment: A Critique of "No Fault" Discourse' (1993) 7 *Australian Journal of Family Law* 9; The Hon KA. Murray, 'Domestic Violence and the Judicial Process: A review of the past 18 years. Should it change direction?' (1995) 9 *Australian Journal of Family Law* 26.
[27] *Heidt v Heidt* (1976) 1 Fam LR 11, 576.
[28] *Chandler* (1981) 6 Fam LR 736.
[29] *Heidt v Heidt* (1976) 1 Fam LR 11,576 at 11, 579.
[30] Australia ratified the Convention on the Rights of the Child in December 1990 and it entered into force on 16 January 1991.

to this challenge by cautioning judges to be aware of the limits of supervised access arrangements as a means of protecting children, noting the scope for an abused child to be re-traumatised by contact with a parent who has harmed them in the past. [31] The court in *Beiganski* in 1993 also proposed that greater attention be paid to the impact of the abuse on the custodial parent, suggesting an order suspending access might be appropriate if the obligation to facilitate contact with an abusive parent were 'likely to impact adversely' on her capacity to care for the child.[32] More generally judgments from this period revealed increasing judicial scrutiny of the quality of the non-custodial parent's parenting skills, and a willingness to refuse access where a parent was unable or unwilling to meet the child's emotional and psychological needs.[33]

In addition to these shifts, the 1990s witnessed the development of a new jurisprudence around the issue of domestic violence, including a new awareness of its consequences for children. In a series of cases decided in the mid-1990s,[34] judges took note of emerging research findings on this issue,[35] which showed that child adjustment was significantly impaired in families characterised by inter-personal violence and that men who abused their wives typically had a poor ability to discriminate their own needs from those of their children.[36] In *JG and BG* in 1994, Chisholm J criticised the court's earlier practice of disregarding violence that did not directly involve the children, and recognised its 'potential to cause them distress and harm' even when it occurred 'away from the children'.[37] In this new policy climate judgments began to focus more on the inter-parental relationship, suggesting that access arrangements should not expose children to 'a climate of a potentially violent and dominating relationship between their parents',[38] and the Full Court held that it was an error of law to exclude evidence of family violence from an access hearing on the basis that it is not relevant to the child's welfare.[39]

Around this time Family Court judges also began to pay increasing attention to children's wishes when making orders for access, and statements

[31] *In the Marriage of Bieganski* (1993) 16 Fam LR 353 at 368.
[32] *Ibid.*
[33] See, eg *Brown and Pederson* (1992) FLC 92-271, where the Full Court of the Family Court upheld a decision of the trial judge to deny access to the father because of the wishes of the (10-year-old) child, the poor father—child relationship, the risk to the stable mother—child relationship, and the father's failure to meet his son's emotional and psychological needs.
[34] *In the Marriage of JG and BG* (1994) 18 Fam LR 255; *In the Marriage of Jaeger* (1994) 18 Fam LR 126; *In the Marriage of Patsalou* (1995) 18 Fam LR 426.
[35] See, eg *In the Marriage of Patsalou* (1995) 18 Fam LR 426.
[36] J Johnston, 'Domestic Violence and Parent-Child Relationship in Families Disputing Custody' (1995) 9 *Australian Journal of Family Law* 12.
[37] *In the Marriage of JG and BG* (1994) 18 Fam LR 255 at 260.
[38] *Ibid*, at 261.
[39] *In the Marriage of Patsalou* (1995) 18 Fam LR 426. See for discussion of this case, P Parkinson, 'Custody, Access and Domestic Violence' (1995) 9 *Australian Journal of Family Law* 41.

about the child's 'rights' in this regard began to emerge.[40] The new weight given to children's views is underlined in the case of *Harrison and Woollard* in 1995,[41] in which Baker J in the Full Court made reference to research on children's decision-making capacities and their 'right to be heard' from the UN Convention, and held that a trial judge who departs from a child's wishes must give clear and cogent reasons for doing so.[42] In a judgment that reflects arguments that have since become familiar in law reform debates, his Honour made a case for including children in the decisional process, suggesting the quality of contact outcomes and potential for durable arrangements were likely to be enhanced if children were given an active role.[43]

A RIGHT TO CONTACT

Yet even as the child protection approach was unfolding, the groundwork for a very different contact policy was being laid. The emergence of Australia's 'right to contact' principle was foreshadowed in the Family Law Council's 1992 report on *Patterns of Parenting After Separation*, which recommended a move away from the proprietorial concept of custody as a way to encourage non-custodial parents to keep in touch with their children. The Australian Government warmed to this idea, which appeared to offer a salve to those divorced fathers who were tired of 'languishing' as access parents,[44] and who were demanding a joint custody presumption be enshrined in the law.[45] The replacement of 'custody' and 'access' with 'residence' and 'contact' had already been effected in the UK,[46] and encouraged by this,[47] the Australian Government moved quickly to enact similar reforms in a bid to enfranchise non-custodial parents.[48] However, the Family Law Reform

[40] See, eg *In the Marriage of Bieganski* (1993) 16 Fam LR 353.
[41] *Harrison and Woollard* (1995) 18 Fam LR 788.
[42] *Ibid*, at 819–25.
[43] *Ibid*.
[44] This description comes from P Nygh, 'The New Part VII–an overview' (1996) 10 *Australian Journal of Family Law* 4, at 16.
[45] M Kaye and J Tolmie, 'Fathers' Rights Groups in Australia' (1998) 12 *Australian Journal of Family Law* 19, at 33; R Graycar, 'Equal Rights Versus Fathers' Rights: The Child Custody Debate in Australia' in C Smart and S Sevenhuijsen (eds), *Child Custody and the Politics of Gender* (London and New York, Routledge, 1989).
[46] See for a comparison of Australia's Family Law Reform Act 1995 (Cth) and the private law provisions of the Children Act 1990 (UK), J Dewar, 'The Family Law Reform Act 1995 (Cth) and the Children Act 1989 (UK) Compared—Twins or Distant Cousins?' (1996) 10 *Australian Journal of Family Law* 18; and R Bailey-Harris and J Dewar, 'Variations on a theme—Child law reform in Australia' [1997] CFLQ 149.
[47] Family Law Council, *Letter of Advice to the Attorney-General on the Operation of the (UK) Children Act 1989*, 10 March 1994.
[48] Australia, House of Representatives, Family Law Reform Bill 1994, *Hansard*, 8 November 1994, 2841. See on this, J Dewar, 'Reducing Discretion in Family Law' (1997) 11 *Australian Journal of Family Law* 309 at 323–24; and L Young, 'Parenting Disputes Under the Family Law Act 1975: The New Regime' (1996) 1 *Sister in Law* 93.

Act 1995, which came into effect in June 1996, went further than this change of terminology, and provided children with what proved to be an important right to have contact with both parents on a regular basis.[49]

One of the interesting things that occurred following this reform, which distinguishes it from earlier times, was the conduct of empirical investigations into its effects on the advice and decision-making practices of the various professionals in the family law system—counsellors, mediators, lawyers, and judges.[50] These revealed something of a gulf between the pronouncements of principle handed down by the Full Court in the wake of the changes and the practices of trial judges and lawyers 'on the ground'.[51] According to the Full Court's interpretation, the right to contact provision had not created any legal presumption or starting point in favour of access, and the welfare principle (by this time called the 'best interests' principle) continued to be the determinative consideration.[52] Yet the empirical studies painted a very different picture that indicated a number of contact-related consequences were taking place. These suggested the reforms had increased non-resident fathers' expectations of contact with their children,[53] including in circumstances where their conduct might previously have ruled this out,[54] and revealed the emergence of a new 'pro-contact' culture in the making of court orders,[55] in which it was increasingly difficult to obtain an order suspending contact with a parent against whom allegations of harm were made.[56]

The research thus suggested there had been a retreat from the sensitive approach to family violence developed in the early 1990s and that previous concerns to promote children's safety had been replaced by a desire to maintain children's contact with their non-resident parent, even if the

---

[49] The child's right to contact (now 'right to spend time') with both parents is subject to the 'best interests' principle: Family Law Act 1975 (Cth), s 60B(2)(b).

[50] J Dewar and S Parker, *Parenting, Planning and Partnership: The Impact of the New Part VII of the Family Law Act 1975 (Cth)* (Family Law Research Unit Working Paper No 3, Griffith University, 1999); H Rhoades, R Graycar and M. Harrison, *The Family Law Reform Act 1995: The First Three Years* (Final Report, University of Sydney and Family Court of Australia, 2000); K Rendell, Z Rathus and A Lynch, *An Unacceptable Risk: A report on child contact arrangements where there is violence in the family* (Queensland Women's Legal Service Inc, 2000); Kaspiew, above n 2.

[51] See especially: J Dewar and S. Parker, 'The Impact of the New Part VII Family Law Act 1975' (1999) 13 *Australian Journal of Family Law* 96, at 116, where the authors refer to what they call 'the reverse effect' of appellate decisions.

[52] *B and B (Family Law Reform Act 1995)* (1997) 21 Fam LR 676 at 727–28 and 733–34.

[53] See on this, B Muehlenberg, 'Fatherhood under siege' *The Age* (11 July 1997).

[54] Rhoades, Graycar and Harrison, above n 50, at paras 4.10 and 5.8.

[55] This language comes from Rendell et al, above n 50.

[56] Dewar and Parker, above n 50, at 103; H Rhoades, 'The Rise and Rise of Shared Parenting Laws—A Critical Reflection' (2002) 19 *Canadian Journal of Family Law* 75, at 93.

quality of that person's parenting was suspect.[57] Instead of suspending contact with a violent father, judges were making orders for supervised contact or contact with a 'neutral changeover' arrangement to reduce the risk of physical harm to the mother,[58] and the former appreciation of a link between spousal abuse and child harm was forgotten.[59] As several commentators suggested, part of the problem was that judges and other players in the system had lost sight of, or had never come to understand, the complex 'special needs' of children exposed to domestic violence, and were treating all children as equally in need of an ongoing relationship with their father.[60] The result was that judges began to ignore what Kaspiew calls 'contextual' violence, and limited their protective responses to cases where the conduct was 'extremely severe'.[61]

Coinciding with these shifts, the idea of the selfish mother who was implacably opposed to the father's contact with his children gained political purchase.[62] Two years after the Reform Act was introduced, a Family Law Council inquiry found widespread dissatisfaction with contact orders among non-resident parents, and a widely held view that resident parents exercised an unreasonable degree control over contact arrangements.[63] As it had with the Reform Act, the Government responded to these concerns by amending the Family Law Act, this time broadening the courts' powers to enforce compliance with contact orders by allowing judges to send parents who failed to provide contact to parenting education programmes.[64] Yet the empirical investigations again revealed insidious repercussions of this policy acceptance of the 'no-contact mother' discourse, suggesting it was inhibiting women's ability to protect their children from harm by reframing their safety concerns as hostility towards their former partner,[65] or constructing them as overly anxious mothers.[66]

---

[57] *Ibid.* See also Rendell, Rathus and Lynch, above n 50.

[58] *Ibid*, at para 5.67.

[59] See CE Cox, JB Kotch and MD Everson, 'A longitudinal study of modifying influences in the relationship between domestic violence and child maltreatment' (2003) 18 *Journal of Family Violence* 5; A Tominson, 'Exploring Family Violence: Links Between Child Maltreatment and Domestic violence' (2003) 13 *National Child Protection Clearinghouse Issues Paper*, Australian Institute of Family Studies.

[60] A Shea Hart, 'Children exposed to domestic violence: Undifferentiated needs in Australian family law' (2004) 18 *Australian Journal of Family Law* 170.

[61] Kaspiew, above n 2.

[62] H Rhoades, 'The "No-Contact Mother": Reconstructions of Motherhood in the Era of the "New Father"' (2002) 16 *International Journal of Law, Policy and the Family* 71; C Smart and B Neale 'Arguments Against Virtue—Must Contact be Enforced?' [1997] *Family Law* 332.

[63] Family Law Council, *Child Contact Orders: Enforcement and Penalties*, A Report to the Attorney-General by the Family Law Council, 1998, at xi.

[64] This power is now located in the Family Law Act 1975 (Cth), s 70NEB.

[65] Rhoades, above n 62.

[66] Smart, above n 15, at 29.

One of the ironies of these shifts was the fact that the Reform Act had inserted into the legislation for the first time specific references to domestic violence, codifying the earlier case law on the issue. This included a provision that required judges to ensure the parenting orders they made would not expose a person to an 'unacceptable risk' of family violence.[67] Yet paradoxically this seemed to create a tension of principle, in which the child's 'right to contact' was clearly in the ascendancy. The right to contact was a key underpinning principle of the Reform Act, while the need for safe arrangements was an afterthought which was poorly integrated into the legislative scheme.[68] The right to contact appeared to reflect the weight of modern sociological and psychological thinking on child development[69] and resonated with the practices of counsellors and mediators working in the family law system,[70] whereas family violence was seen to affect relatively few families.[71] And the right to contact gave expression to a political desire to redress the apparent imbalance of power between mothers and fathers in family law system, in which the policy pendulum during the 'child protection' years was seen to have swung too far in favour of custodial parents.[72]

THE END OF CONTACT

There has been yet another reform instalment since the right to contact and enforcement amendments were passed in the late 1990s, and Australia is now in the throes of what the Government has called 'a generational change in family law'.[73] Once again non-resident parents played a prominent role in bringing about these changes, embodied in the Family Law Amendment (Shared Parental Responsibility) Act ('the Shared Parental Responsibility Bill'), which came into effect in July 2006. Despite the pro-contact practices that followed the introduction of the Reform Act, fathers remained

---

[67] This provision is now located in Family Law Act 1975 (Cth), s 60CG(1)(b). Note that the family violence provisions of the Reform Act comprised late additions to the legislation that resulted from lobbying by the National Women's Justice Coalition during the parliamentary consultation process: J Behrens, 'Ending the Silence, But ... Family Violence under the Family Law Reform Act 1995' (1996) 10 *Australian Journal of Family Law* 35, at 47.

[68] See SM Armstrong, '"We told you so ..." Women's legal groups and the Family Law Reform Act 1995' (2001) 15 *Australian Journal of Family Law* 129.

[69] See C Smart, B Neale, and A Wade, *The Changing Experience of Childhood—Families and Divorce* (Cambridge, Polity, 2001) ch 2.

[70] Rhoades, Graycar and Harrison, above n 50, at para 4.32; Kaspiew, above n 2 at 132; M Kaye, J Stubbs and J Tolmie, 'Domestic violence and child contact arrangements' (2003) 17 *Australian Journal of Family Law* 93, at 107–11.

[71] Rhoades, above n 62, at 83.

[72] See House of Representatives, Family Law Reform Bill 1994, *Hansard*, 9 November 1994, at 29–63.

[73] Attorney-General's Department, 'Bill Marks "Cultural Shift" in Dealing with Family Breakdown' *News Release* (8 December 2005).

dissatisfied with the state of the law and campaigned to secure enactment of a legislative presumption that would see children spend equal time with each parent following relationship breakdown.[74] After a two-year reform process, including a parliamentary inquiry which recommended against adopting the presumption sought by fathers' groups,[75] amendments were eventually passed that make substantial inroads into the traditional discretionary approach to determining children's arrangements, although the 'best interests' principle remains (ostensibly) the paramount consideration.[76]

Like the Reform Act before it, the Shared Parental Responsibility Act introduced new terminology to the field. In recognition of the previous regime's failure to 'eliminate any sense of ownership of children', all references to 'residence' and 'contact' have been removed from the Family Law Act.[77] Instead, the legislation now simply provides for orders that describe where a child 'is to live' and 'the time a child is to spend with' others.[78] Reinforcing this absence of distinction between different parenting roles is a new presumption of 'equal shared parental responsibility' for children, which presumes it is best for children if parents make joint decisions for them.[79] Judges are also now required to consider making orders for children to spend 'equal time' with each parent, and where this arrangement is not practical, an order for the child to spend 'substantial and significant time' with both, including on weekdays and not just weekends.[80] The Full Court has recently interpreted these provisions to mean that rather than preserving a well- settled parenting arrangement, as was the pre-reform practice in interim hearings,[81] judges must now consider making orders for a child to spend 'equal or significant' time with each parent.[82] Taken together, these changes effectively erase the idea of contact as distinct from parenting, and replace them with a single undifferentiated concept that assumes equal and

---

[74] See for discussion of this reform campaign, H Rhoades and SB Boyd, 'Reforming Custody Laws: A Comparative Study' (2004) 18 *International Journal of Law, Policy and the Family* 119; and H Rhoades, 'Yearning for Law: Fathers' Groups and Family Law Reform in Australia' in S Sheldon and R Collier (eds), *Fathers' Rights Activism and Law Reform in Comparative Perspective* (Oxford, Hart Publishing, 2006) 125.

[75] House of Representatives, Standing Committee on Family and Community Affairs, *Every Picture Tells a Story: Report on the Inquiry Into Child Custody Arrangements in the Event of Family Separation* (Australian Government Publishing Service, 2003) paras 2.41 and 2.44. (Hereafter '*Every Picture* report'.)

[76] Now contained in the Family Law Act 1975 (Cth) s 60CA.

[77] House of Representatives, Family Law Amendment (Shared Parental Responsibility) Bill 2005, *Explanatory Memorandum*, para 921.

[78] Family Law Act 1975 (Cth) s 64B(2).

[79] Family Law Act 1975 (Cth) s 61DA. This presumption does not apply if there are 'reasonable grounds' to believe that a parent has engaged in family violence or abuse of the child.

[80] Family Law Act 1975 (Cth) s 65DAA.

[81] See *Cowling* [1998] FLC 92-801.

[82] *Goode v Goode* [2006] Fam CA 1346, at paras 71 and 72.

active care by both parents, regardless of actual arrangements or pre-separation patterns.

The distinction between care work and contact is not the only erasure achieved by the latest reforms. Rather oddly, considering the parliamentary committee's suggestion that children be afforded increased opportunities to participate in decision-making processes,[83] the Shared Parental Responsibility Act also represents the demotion of children's views in determining how and when they will see their parents. During the inquiry that preceded the reforms, researchers offered the committee a wealth of empirical evidence of children's perspectives, which suggested children feel disempowered if they are excluded from negotiations about their living arrangements.[84] Yet the proposed amendments have disarticulated the 'best interests' checklist of factors into two tiers of importance,[85] elevating the need to maintain a relationship with both parents to a 'primary consideration',[86] and relegating the child's views to the second tier of factors.[87] Perhaps like the equality aspects of the Shared Parental Responsibility Act, this decision reflects the influence of the fathers' lobby, which criticised policymakers during the reform process for placing 'too much emphasis on what children think'.[88]

Other amendments may well make a difference to the way that potentially dangerous contact arrangements are considered. At the heart of the government's reform design is an expectation of peaceful parenting,[89] and the scheme reinforces this message in several ways. One of these is the insertion of a 'friendly parent' criterion[90] into the 'best interests' checklist, which directs judges to have regard to the extent that each person has been willing in the past to facilitate the child's relationship with the other parent.[91] As a number of critics have noted, this provision carries with it the potential for a woman's protective resistance to contact to be misread

---

[83] *Every Picture* report, above n 75, at paras 2.66 and 4.158.

[84] See, eg Smart et al, above n 69, at 122 and 167; AB Smith, NJ Taylor and P Tapp, 'Rethinking children's involvement in decision-making after parental separation' (2003) 10 *Childhood* 201, at 207.

[85] House of Representatives, Family Law Amendment (Shared Parental Responsibility) Bill 2005, *Explanatory Memorandum*, para 48.

[86] Family Law Act 1975 (Cth) s 60CC(2)(a).

[87] Family Law Act 1975 (Cth) s 60CC(3)(a)

[88] House of Representatives, Standing Committee on Family and Community Affairs, *Official Committee Hansard* (27 October 2003) at 53 (Mr Lenton, Dads in Distress).

[89] House of Representatives, Family Law Amendment (Shared Parental Responsibility) Bill 2005, *Explanatory Memorandum*, para 15.

[90] Note that recent research suggests that 'an implicit friendly parent criterion' already exists in litigation over children's arrangements in the Family Court, and that it is operating to discourage residence parents from raising concerns about their children's safety: see Kaspiew, above n 2, at 136. See for discussion of this criterion in Canada, SB Boyd, *Child Custody, Law and Women's Work* (Oxford, Oxford University Press, 2003) 121.

[91] Family Law Act 1975 (Cth) s 60CC(4)(b).

as belligerence.[92] The scope for marginalisation of a parent's fears about contact may also be widened by the Act's re-definition of family violence (in response to complaints by fathers' groups about unsubstantiated allegations),[93] which now requires that an apprehension of violence be 'reasonable', and not just genuine.[94]

Finally, the reforms have also introduced a new system of compulsory mediation for disputes over children, which aims to 'encourage a culture of agreement making' among separating parents.[95] The Government is giving effect to this direction by establishing a network of 65 'Family Relationship Centres' throughout the country over the next two years, that will offer families a range of 'non-adversarial' dispute resolution services,[96] and parents in conflict will be required to attempt one of these processes before applying for court orders.[97] Family dispute resolution practitioners have been assigned the task of policing this policy by certifying whether parents have made a 'genuine effort' to resolve their conflict,[98] and parents without a certification of this kind may be liable for costs if they proceed to litigate their dispute.[99] In recognition of its inappropriateness for family members who have been exposed to violence,[100] the latest amendments exempt parents who have a 'reasonable' apprehension of family violence from the mediation requirement,[101] and children's safety needs have been located

---

[92] Shea Hart, above n 60, at 176 and 182–85.

[93] See for examples of fathers' groups' submissions to this effect, House of Representatives, Standing Committee on Family and Community Affairs, *Official Committee Hansard* (4 September 2003) at 18 (Mrs Price, Men's Rights Association); and *Official Committee Hansard* (24 September 2003) at 79 (Mrs Bawden, Shared Parenting Council of Australia).

[94] House of Representatives, Family Law Amendment (Shared Parental Responsibility) Bill 2005, *Explanatory Memorandum*, para 20.

[95] House of Representatives, Family Law Amendment (Shared Parental Responsibility) Bill 2005, *Explanatory Memorandum*, para 81.

[96] See P Parkinson, 'Keeping in Contact: Family Relationship Centres in Australia' (2006) 18 *Child and Family Law Quarterly* 157; and T Altobelli, 'A Generational Change in Family Dispute Resolution in Australia' (2006) 17 *Australian Dispute Resolution Journal* 140.

[97] Family Law Act 1975 (Cth) s 60I(7).

[98] Family Law Act 1975 (Cth) s 60I(8).

[99] Family Law Act 1975 (Cth) s 117AB.

[100] CL Tishler, S Bartholomae, BL Katz and L Landry-Meyer, 'Is domestic violence relevant? An exploratory analysis of couples referred for mediation in the family court' (2004) 19 *Journal of Interpersonal Violence* 1042; H Astor, 'The Weight of Silence: Talking about Violence in Family Mediation' in M. Thornton (ed), Public and Private: Feminist Legal Debates (Oxford, Oxford University Press, 1995); G Clarke and I Davies, 'Mediation—When is it not an appropriate dispute resolution process?' (1992) *Australian Dispute Resolution Journal* 70; T Grillo, 'The mediation alternative: process dangers for women' (1991) 100 *Yale Law Journal* 1545. Note that compulsion also violates one of the core principles of mediation: S Gribben, 'Mediation of family disputes' (1990) 5 *Australian Journal of Family Law* 126; H Astor, *Guidelines for Mediating in Cases Involving Violence Against Women*, National Committee on Violence Against Women (Australian Government Printing Service, 1992).

[101] Family Law Act 1975 (Cth) s 60I(9).

as a 'first tier' consideration in the new 'best interests' checklist.[102] But a number of commentators have raised questions about how these protective qualifications will compete in practice with a dominant shared parenting message,[103] and there is some anxiety that both legal and dispute resolution practitioners may fail to recognise clients with safety needs,[104] and reframe their concerns as parental conflict.[105] Nevertheless, dispute resolution practitioners are predicting that families affected by violence are likely to appear in their services in greater numbers than ever before, challenging them to adapt their practices for these clients.[106] All of which suggests that while contact as a concept no longer exists, parents with protective concerns may be left to negotiate it as an actuality in a policy environment that is geared towards cooperation and equality, rather than safety.

CONCLUSION

The shifting contact policies described in this chapter reflect broad patterns that have dominated decision making and negotiation practices—or look likely to. There have been, of course, resistances to these—there are judges and lawyers who eschewed the pro-contact approach that developed after the Reform Act, just as there were those who challenged the Full Court's protective stance in the early 1990s.[107] The officially sanctioned approach has, until recently, centred on the notion of the welfare (or best interests) of the child, and an aversion to the use of legal presumptions about what this might mean. As numerous commentators over the years have pointed out,[108] the paramountcy principle is a 'radically indeterminate' one,[109] and Australia's case law and empirical evidence suggest there have long been implicit assumptions about children's contact interests operating in practice that have prompted judges and others to respond to the issue of contact in different ways at different times.

---

[102] Family Law Act 1975 (Cth) s 60CC(2)(b).

[103] Shea Hart, above n 60, at 191.

[104] See on this, D Greatbatch and R Dingwall, 'The Marginalization of Domestic Violence in Divorce Mediation' (1999) 13 *International Journal of Law Policy and the Family* 174; Kaye et al, above n 70, at 109.

[105] See on the use of 'reframing' by mediators, T Fisher, 'Advice by Any Other Name ...' (2001) 19 *Conflict Resolution Quarterly* 197.

[106] D Flynn, 'The social worker as family mediator: Balancing power in cases involving family violence' (2005) 58 *Australian Social Work* 407.

[107] See, eg: *Koutalis and Bartlett* (1993) 17 Fam LR 722 at 744 per Kay J; and PA Doolan, 'The "Unacceptable Risk" of What? Access Orders in the Wake of M v M' (1994) 8 *Australian Journal of Family Law* 178.

[108] See, eg J Eekelaar, 'Beyond the Welfare Principle' (2002) 14 *Child and Family Law Quarterly* 237.

[109] J Behrens, 'The form and substance of Australian legislation on parenting orders: a case for the principles of care and diversity and presumptions based upon them' (2002) 24 *Journal of Social Welfare and Family Law* 401, at 403.

Underpinning the Family Court's earliest reported cases was an assumption that contact was good for children, even if children themselves failed to appreciate this at the time, and little if any inquiry was made into the quality of the parent—child relationship or the capacity of the contact parent to meet the child's needs. In part this was a function of judges' determination to avoid 'undignified' investigations of 'fault' that had characterised the previous system.[110] But with Australia's accession to the Convention on the Rights of the Child in the early 1990s, the court began to rework its case law guidance to emphasise the child's right to be heard on the question of access, and to have safe contact with their non-custodial parent. The assumptions informing these decisions seemed to be that contact should be beneficial for children and that both questions about the quality of the parent—child relationship and the quality of the inter-parental relationship were central to this.

The introduction of the right to contact reforms in 1996 heralded yet a new direction, and the belief that 'it is almost impossible to overstate the importance to the child of the maintenance of an on-going relationship with their non-custodial parent' became normative.[111] Decision making in this period started to focus on maintaining contact regardless of parental capacity, and became less interested in the history of care than the promise of it.[112] The operating assumption seemed to be that disruption of the relationship with a father was more damaging for children than exposure to distressing contact, unless there was a risk of serious abuse, such that mothers who expressed concerns about a man's parenting abilities came to be viewed as overprotective or vindictive. With the passage of the most recent reforms, Australia's contact law has seen a number of (politically driven) presumptions about children's interests become explicit legal guidelines for the first time, which will direct judges to assume that children should spend as much time as possible in each parent's household. Ironically, given what we now know about children's self-determination desires, this latest move embraces a return to the paternalism of old, when decision makers presumed to know what was best for children.

What are the implications of the different approaches to contact for family members? According to researchers who investigated decision-making patterns after the Reform Act was introduced, the right to contact principle produced a shift in the balance of power between resident and non-resident parents.[113] Mothers effectively lost their ability to assert a protective stance

---

[110] This was the language used by politicians to describe fault-based divorce during the debates of the Family Law Act: see House of Representatives, Family Law Bill 1974, Second Reading Speech, *Hansard*, 28 November 1974, at 4323 (Mr Whitlam).

[111] This phrase comes from *Koutalis and Bartlett* (1993) 17 Fam LR 722 at 744, per Kay J.

[112] See on this distinction, C Smart, 'The Legal and Moral Ordering of Child Custody' (1991) 18 *Journal of Law and Society* 485.

[113] Dewar and Parker, above n 50, at 104.

without coming under suspicion, while fathers came to see themselves as being entitled to have contact with their children. Where mothers had once been encouraged to be protective, they were now demonised for suggesting a father's quality of care was problematic or that he might be a danger to the child. As occurred in England following the Children Act reforms, the idea of the dangerous father 'practically disappeared'.[114] The various 'innovations' of the Shared Parental Responsibility Act—its emphasis on equal time and mandatory mediation, its re-definition of violence and 'friendly parent' provision—may entrench this pattern further, and see women with genuine fears about contact having to negotiate arrangements for their children in a setting that excludes advocacy and expects co-operation.

Another consequence of Australia's newest contact policy is that contact as a legal phenomenon has been removed from the scene. The shift in legal terminology will not of itself make a difference to family practices, particularly given the significant material obstacles to making shared parenting arrangements work.[115] The removal of 'fault' from the legislative scheme in the 1970s did not put an end to recriminations between separating spouses,[116] and the shift away from custody and access in the 1990s did not lessen proprietorial contests over children. It is just as unlikely that removing 'residence' and 'contact' will create genuine joint care arrangements. But the merger of contact and care into a single undifferentiated concept will mean that parents who find themselves doing most (rather than half) of the day to day work of looking after children will no longer have any authorised language with which to distinguish their experience from that of the less involved parent.

The impact of these shifts, of course, is not confined to parents, but has real meaning for children, both for their security interests and their ability to affect the shape of their post-divorce lives. Family violence rarely occurs in isolation from children's lives,[117] and children are acutely sensitive to conflict between their parents, whether the parents live together or not.[118] Smart's research suggests that parental separation provides children with an opportunity to evaluate and withdraw from an oppressive parent.[119] This and other studies have revealed the importance of giving them a voice in decisions that affect them, including for those who have been exposed

[114] A Barnett, 'Contact and Domestic Violence: The Ideological Divide', in J Bridgeman and D Monk (eds), *Feminist Perspectives on Child Law* (London, Cavendish, 2000) 129.

[115] See Smyth, above n 21.

[116] V May and C Smart, 'Silence in court?—Hearing children in residence and contact disputes' (2004) 16 *Child and Family Law Quarterly* 305.

[117] P Parkinson, 'Custody, Access and Domestic Violence' (1995) 9 *Australian Journal of Family Law* 41, at 44.

[118] Smart et al, above n 69.

[119] Smart, above n 15, at 31.

to domestic violence,[120] and advocates for children have already expressed concerns about the current powerlessness of children in this regard.[121] Yet Australia's latest reforms, which assume an equal relationship with both parents is best for children, are a missed opportunity in this regard. Sadly it appears that the warning Smart issued several years ago—that the political attention being paid to adults' rights claims was threatening to silence children's nascent voices[122]—has not been heeded in Australia.

---

[120] J Irwin, F Waugh and M Wilkinson, *Domestic violence and child protection: A research report* (The Department of Social Work and Sociology, University of Sydney, 2002).
[121] Shea Hart, above n 60.
[122] *Ibid.*

9

Moving On: The Challenge for Children's Contact Services in Australia

GRANIA SHEEHAN, JOHN DEWAR AND RACHEL CARSON

ABSTRACT

C HILDREN'S CONTACT SERVICES in Australia are designed to assist separated parents manage the contact arrangements with their children. The services provide a safe environment for children to maintain contact with a non-resident parent. This and the following chapter draw on the findings of the Children's Contact Services Project to explore how parents and children move through contact centre services and on to self-managed contact independently of the centre (this chapter),[1] and how families come to use children's contact services (next chapter). In this chapter, an exploration of what is meant by the term 'self-management' is presented and the role of the contact services in assisting parents to self-manage contact is discussed. Factors that appeared to facilitate parents and children's movement from supervised contact to supervised changeovers and on to self-managed contact away from the centre are identified. The chapter concludes by proposing an expanded role for contact services in Australia from one of maintaining the contact parent–child relationship to a model of therapeutic intervention and referral that (where possible) focuses on both transforming the contact parent–child relationship and the parents' relationship with one another.

Acknowledgements: The empirical research that informs this chapter was conducted with the assistance of a grant from the Australian Research Council via its Strategic Partnerships with Industry for Research and Training (SPIRT) scheme (C00106942: *Children's Contact Services: Expectation and Experience*, John Dewar, Rosemary Hunter, Belinda Fehlberg and

---

[1] G Sheehan, R Carson, B Fehlberg, R Hunter, A Tomison, R Ip and J Dewar, *Children's Contact Services: Expectation and Experience* (Brisbane, Socio-Legal Research Centre, Griffith University Australian Attorney-General's Department, The University of Melbourne and the Australian Institute of Family Studies, 2005) www.ag.gov.au/familylawpubs/.

Grania Sheehan in collaboration with the Australian Attorney-General's Department). The Australian Institute of Family Studies (AIFS) supported the conduct of the research and Adam Tomison was the AIFS' partner investigator on the project. The presentation of this chapter as a paper at the International Institute for the Sociology of Law workshop: '*Contact between children and separated parents*' (chaired by Mavis Maclean) was supported by a grant from the Ian Potter Foundation. Our appreciation is extended to the many participants in the research who willingly gave up their time to participate in the study.

INTRODUCTION

Children's Contact Services (CCSs) are designed to assist separated parents manage the contact arrangements with their children in circumstances where private arrangements could pose a risk to the welfare of the children. The two main forms of assistance provided are supervised changeovers (enabling parents to 'exchange' children at a contact centre without meeting each other), and supervised contact (enabling children to be with their contact parent in a safe and supervised environment at the centre).

People's pathways into CCSs are varied, although services have a significant relationship with the Family Court of Australia and the Federal Magistrates' Court of Australia, with most CCSs receiving a majority of their referrals from the courts and legal practitioners.[2] The services are primarily used by parents characterised by a range of significant problems, including actual or alleged instances of domestic violence and child abuse. For many parents, parental drug and alcohol problems, mental health issues, child abduction concerns and financial disadvantage further compound these problems.[3]

Over the last decade, CCSs in Australia have burgeoned in number. This is largely a consequence of the pro-parent/child contact shift that has characterised developments in family law in recent years.[4] In 1996

---

[2] *Ibid* at 77; Strategic Partners Pty Ltd, *Contact Services in Australia: Research and Evaluation Report—Year One Report* (Canberra, Legal Aid and Family Services, Commonwealth Attorney-General's Department, January 1998), Appendix 5; G Sheehan, R Carson, B Fehlberg, R Hunter, A Tomison, R Ip and J Dewar, *Children's Contact Services: Expectation and Experience* (Brisbane, Socio-Legal Research Centre, Griffith University Australian Attorney-General's Department, The University of Melbourne and the Australian Institute of Family Studies, 2005) www.ag.gov.au/familylawpubs/.

[3] Above n 1, at 39–50; see also Strategic Partners Pty Ltd, *Contact Services in Australia: Research and Evaluation Report—Final Report* (Canberra, Legal Aid and Family Services, Commonwealth Attorney-General's Department, December 1998) 31.

[4] J Dewar and S Parker with B Tynan and D Cooper, *Parenting, Planning and Partnership: The Impact of the New Part VII of the Family Law Act 1975* (Brisbane, Family Law Research Unit, Griffith University, 1998) 68; S Boyd, H Rhoades and K Burns, 'The Politics of the Primary Caregiver Presumption' (1999) 13 *Australian Journal of Family Law* 236;

the Family Law Act 1975 was amended to expressly set out a number of guiding principles, including the right of a child to have regular contact with both parents, subject to the child's best interests.[5] Since these amendments, the Family Court has demonstrated a greater willingness to order interim contact in high-risk situations (particularly those involving a risk of domestic violence and allegations of child abuse) than prior to the reforms.[6] In this new legal environment, even in perceived high-risk situations, there has been a shift from a choice between ordering contact and no contact, to a choice between unregulated and supervised cont act, particularly at the interim stage of the proceedings.[7] CCSs in Australia provide the courts with a way of balancing the rights of children to have regular contact with both parents and to be protected from harm in cases where private contact arrangements would expose children to an 'unacceptable risk' of harm.[8]

At the time of the 1996 amendments, the Australian Government introduced a national programme of CCSs. The programme was piloted in 1996–97 and evaluated by Strategic Partners Pty Ltd in 1998.[9] By 2001 the Australian Government's CCSs programme had grown to 35 centres nation wide. The Australian Government's June 2005–06 Budget announced a further expansion of this programme to 65 CCSs. This programme expansion is part of a range of proposed government reforms to the family law and associated relationship services. The amendments also included amending the Act to introduce a presumption of joint parental responsibility, except in cases involving child abuse and domestic violence.[10] The principles that guide the court in making orders for contact will be amended to attach dual primacy to parental involvement post-separation and to the protection of children from violence and abuse.[11] The expansion of the CCSs programme,

---

H Rhoades, R Graycar and M Harrison, *The Family Law Reform Act 1995: The First Three Years* (Canberra, Family Court of Australia, 2000); K Rendell, Z Rathus and A Lynch, *An Unacceptable Risk A Report on Child Contact Arrangements where there is Violence* (Brisbane, Women's Legal Service, 2000); M Kaye, J Stubbs and J Tolmie, *Negotiating Child Residence and Contact Arrangements Against a Background of Domestic Violence'* (Brisbane, Families, Law and Social Policy Research Unit, Griffith University, 2003).

[5] Family Law Act 1975 (Cth) s 60B(2).

[6] Rhoades, Graycar and Harrison, above n 4, at 78–86.

[7] Rendell, Rathus and Lynch, above n 4; Kaye, Stubbs and Tolmie, above n 4.

[8] See, eg: *M v M* [1988] 166 CLR 69; *In the Marriage of A v A* (1998) FLC 92-800 J for a legal definition of 'unacceptable risk'; J Peirce and J Gorman, 'New Developments in Children's Contact Services' (1996) *Law Institute Journal, Special Issue* 38; G Sheehan and R Carson, 'Protecting Children's Rights in Contact Disputes: The Role of Children's Contact Services in Australia' *Family Court Review* (in press for October 2006).

[9] Strategic Partners (January 1998), above n 2; Strategic Partners (December 1998), above n 3.

[10] Australian Government, 'A New Family Law System: Government Response to *Every Picture Tells a Story'* (Canberra, Australian Government, June 2005).

[11] *Family Law Amendment (Shared Parental Responsibility) Bill* 2005 s 60B(2). Exposure Draft 23/06/2005.

coupled with these new family law reforms, may herald a surge upwards in the relatively small number of cases currently being referred by the courts to the CCSs as the existing tension for the courts between protecting the child's right to contact and keeping children safe from harm becomes more legislatively salient.

The research report, *Children's Contact Services: Expectation and Experience* concluded that in spite of the relatively small number of cases referred to CCSs in Australia, the CCSs are struggling to cope with a demand for service that outweighs the current intake capacity.[12] A factor that may be contributing to this problem is the difficulty faced by the CCSs in moving clients on from using the contact centre to safely self-manage their contact arrangements independent of a centre's services and staff. 'Self-management' of contact is thus an important issue for CCSs and clients alike.

Past research has demonstrated that the role of CCSs in facilitating 'self-management' raises important strategic and operational questions for contact centres and their government funding bodies. The issue of self-management generates strongly conflicting expectations about the purpose of CCSs as Aris, Harrison and Humphreys observed in their study of service provision in the United Kingdom:

> ... views about moving on from a contact centre were characterised by an inten-sification of ... tensions and differences. In general terms, referrers ... considered contact centres as short-term provision, rather than a long-term arrangement. Contact centre staff experienced the pressure of demand exceeding supply and sometimes inappropriate referrals. Fathers often saw the contact centre as unnec-essary in any event, and wanted more contact and less surveillance. Mothers were often very fearful indeed about the prospect of moving away from the perceived safety offered by the centre.[13]

Similarly, Strategic Partners found that there existed different expectations of the Australian Government's pilot CCSs between residential and non-residential parents—the former saw them as providing increased safety for them and their children, while the latter saw them as unnecessary mile-stones on a road to unsupervised contact.[14] To our knowledge, no research to date has examined the possible tensions that self-management generates for the children who use these services.

Self-management can be considered a practical necessity for CCSs that operate in an environment of short-term, competitive funding arrangements and high service demand. Past research, however, suggests that it presents a significant and at times insurmountable challenge to parents using the

---

[12] Above n 1, at xiv.
[13] R Aris, C Harrison and C Humphreys, *Safety and Child Contact: An Analysis of the Role of Child Contact Centres in the Context of Family Violence and Child Welfare Concerns* (Lord Chancellors Department, Research Series No 10/02, 2002) 110.
[14] Strategic Partners, above n 3, at 109.

CCSs. The Strategic Partners research found that only one third of parents were able to make their own arrangements after ceasing to use the CCS, and that the longer a former couple used a CCS the less able they were to consider self-management.[15] Research conducted in the United States by Thoennes and Pearson provided little evidence that the hostility between parents decreased through the use of CCSs, or that parents were able to move away from the centre and on to safely self-manage their contact arrangements.[16]

These findings suggest that separated parents require significant support to be able to move away from the CCS and safely self-manage contact, particularly support aimed at improving the quality of the parents' relationship with one another. The Strategic Partners research found that lack of communication between the parents was a significant factor impeding movement towards self-management, but that most services were either unable to provide parties with support in improving the quality of the parents' relationship with one another because of resource constraints, or viewed the provision of such support to be outside the role of the CCSs which were designed to keep parents apart and provide a safe and conflict free environment for contact to take place.[17]

The aim of this chapter is to examine the movement of parents and children towards self-management in the current Australian context of government funded CCS provision, and to highlight some of the conceptual and operational issues to which self-management give rise.

THE CHILDREN'S CONTACT SERVICES PROJECT

The findings presented in this chapter are drawn from the Australian Children's Contact Services Project. The project comprised two studies that were conducted concurrently on the same study population. The first study was qualitative and based on 142 interviews. The second study was an analysis of client data from 396 families who attended six different Australian government funded CCSs in August 2003. The methodology for both studies is presented in full detail in the research report *Children's Contact Services: Expectation and Experience.*[18]

Qualitative Study

The qualitative study involved conducting in-depth interviews with 142 participants from a variety of groups. Purposive sampling was used to

---

[15] *Ibid*, at 102–04.

[16] N Thoennes and J Pearson, 'Supervised Visitation: A Profile of Providers' (1999) 37 *Family and Conciliation Courts Review* 469.

[17] Strategic Partners, above n 3, at 103–04.

[18] Above n 1, at 17–36.

provide a wide range of respondents who had a diversity of experiences. The groups included: (1) senior representatives from the Australian government departments charged with developing, funding and administering the CCSs programme, along with senior industry representatives from the three national relationships service providers that operate CCSs in Australia (n = 9 interviews); (2) CCS providers including the staff (ie service co-ordinators and contact supervisors) and representatives from service management committees and the auspicing organisation (n = 22). Twelve different services were selected that operated in the Australian states of Victoria and Queensland. Both government funded and volunteer based services were included in the sample along with metropolitan, regional and rural based services; (3) referral agents including private solicitors, judicial officers from the Family Court and the State and Federal Magistrates' Courts, child representatives, mediators, psychologists and social workers (n = 40); (4) residence and contact parents who had orders to use one of the 12 selected CCSs for supervised contact or changeovers (n = 46) and their children (n = 25). The children interviewed for the study were aged between 6 and 15 years and the parents interviewed had on average been using a CCS for 2.2 years. The interviews included questions on the role of the CCSs, the factors that facilitated or impeded service delivery, children's best interests in the context of service provision, the referral process and self-management. The interviews with the children were focused on their experiences of contact before, during and after (where applicable) using the CCSs.

Client Data

An analysis was conducted of client data collected by the CCS staff from 396 cases comprising parents and children who used six different Australian government funded CCSs in August 2003.[19] Information was collected about each adult and child who used the CCSs during this time period. This included information on the socio-demographic characteristics of clients, the personal and relationship issues that clients presented with on referral to the CCS, the types of contact services accessed, and the client's history of service use. For those clients who had stopped attending the CCS in August 2003, additional information was gathered on the reasons for leaving the service. This de-identified data was sampled from a larger pool of client data collected by Australian government funded CCSs as part of the centre's funding contract and intake procedures.

---

[19] There were a small number of cases included in the analysis where it was a grandparent, foster-parent or guardian who brought the child or children to a CCS for visits with the contact parent.

Findings

Self-management Defined

Self-management is an important operational objective for the CCSs,[20] yet the exact point at which parents and children are considered to be 'self-managing' their contact was not clearly defined by the Government or the industry bodies in documented policy related to CCS provision. Government policy and funding requirements provided the CCSs with little guidance on the extent to which self-management was a required outcome of service provision, or on how best to facilitate parents and children safely moving on from using a contact centre. The comments made during interviews with government and industry representatives and the service staff reflected this lack of clarity in relation to self management of contact. For example one government representative commented:

> The government isn't really clear on what it expects and the services don't have a clear model of what that really means and I think we need to make some decisions around that, but do we keep families there? Admittedly some will never resolve or get to a point of self-management, but do we keep them forever?

In theory there exists a number of different models of self-management. First, parties can be considered to be self-managing contact when they have safely moved on from using the centre. This model of self-management does not include parents and children who are forced by circumstances outside their control to conduct contact on their own or with the assistance of family and friends, who would otherwise need the protection provided by a CCS. Secondly, families are considered to be self-managing contact when they have moved on from using the centre for supervised visits to using the centre for supervised changeovers, and require little or no assistance from the service staff. In this paper, the term 'self-management' is used to indicate the first model—that of safely self-managed contact conducted independently of the centre.

There are alternative options for parents and children who are unable to safely move on to self-managed contact. They can remain using the centre's services for as long as the services are needed. At the point at which it is no longer viable for a CCS to allow the parents and children to continue using the service, or when attending the service become too

---

[20] See, eg: Australian Children's Contact Services Association, *Standards for Supervised Contact Services,* para 1.5: 'where appropriate, [CCSs are] to work towards the independent management of contact by the parties' www.accsa.org.au/contact.html. The contract between the Australian Government and the funded CCSs specifies that an objective of the service is to enhance children's relationships with the non-residential parent, and improve parents' management of relationship difficulties through making progress on, managing and resolving issues which created the need to the contact service (Service Type Specifications, 17).

onerous for the children, service can be withdrawn or contact stopped by the court.

The Role of CCSs in Assisting Parents and Children to Self-manage Contact

In practice, the role played by the CCSs in moving parents and children though the centre's services and on to self-managed contact reflects the range of possibilities described above. Government and industry representatives, referral agents, CCS staff and parents were asked to identify the central role of the CCSs and to comment on any other functions of the CCSs. With the exception of the parents, respondents from each of these three groups identified that the CCSs have some role to play in moving parents and children on from using CCSs. There were, however, differences of opinion between interviewees as to how appropriate it was for the CCSs to make such a role a central concern for service provision, and which model of 'self-management' the CCSs should apply.

The parents who were interviewed were asked to discuss their intentions with regard to moving on from using the centre. As a group parents did not generally view the CCSs as having a role in moving them on from using the centre.

Many of the CCS staff interviewed considered self-management to be an outcome of service provision, not a role of the CCS. For example, one CCS supervisor commented:

> I really don't see the goal of our service as being self-management. If it happens, fabulous! We can help along the way in some small ways by modelling appropriate behaviour, by being there and helping facilitate those small steps. Great! But that's not why we're here.

There was disagreement among the CCS staff as to what constituted self-managed contact. Many CCS staff commented that self-management was achieved when parents and their children used the CCS for supervised changeovers—the cheapest and least labour intensive of the services provided by the contact centres. For example:

> They [the children] just come and they say, 'Hi' and they go through and you don't have to sort of follow them along and make sure they feel comfortable and when you get that, that's what I call self-management. ... we're just there, the building is here.
>
> The length of time that you can use a changeover service is eternal. So if you never ever want to see that parent, we never say to people you need to self-manage your changeovers.

Government and industry representatives as well as referral agents considered that moving parents and children on to self-managed contact was not a role of the CCSs, rather it was viewed as a possible outcome of service provision for some, but not all, of the parents and children referred to CCSs. For example, one government representative commented that:

> I don't think that we see that [self-management] as the primary reason for people using the contact service. I think it's more a bonus if that happens and certainly we don't want people stuck in the contact services if they could be actually assisted, but we need the contact. The most important thing is to have that supervised or have a handover opportunity. If they don't do any more than that well they're still fulfilling the major objective. Our view really is that it [self-management] is terrific and it can be done but it's not the core thing that they're funded for.

The notion that achieving self-management (as we have defined it) is a product of service provision rather than an active role of the CCSs is consistent with what Bastard has labelled the 'low threshold' nature of the services provided by contact centres—that is, the services do not seek to actively change people, but rather to affect their relationships and to assist them to maintain social links between parents and children.[21]

Self-management Achieved

Parents and children's experience with a CCS can begin with the first visit to a centre for one-on-one supervised contact. They can move on from this service to supervised changeovers for overnight contact visits, and then on to conduct their contact visits safely and independently of the centre. This transition usually takes place within the one centre and involves decreasing over time the level of staff vigilance and staff involvement during contact visits, while simultaneously increasing the contact parent's responsibility for, and time spent with, the children. The findings suggest that for many parents and children this transition can take a number of years, if it happens at all.

Of the 46 parents interviewed, only six residence parents and three contact parents spoke of being able to one day move on to self-manage contact. The analysis of the client data suggested that a relatively small number of clients were able to move on to self-managed contact. Only 11 of the 396 cases sampled had moved on to self-managed contact in the month of August 2003. More families (n = 24) had stopped attending the centre because service had been withdrawn out of concerns for the welfare of the child or the safety of the staff, or because of a decision made by a court or state welfare department to stop contact visits taking place at the CCS.

---

[21] B Bastard, 'Different Approaches to Post-divorce Family Relationships: The Example of Contact Centres in France', in J Dewar and S Parker (eds), *Family Law: Processes, Practices and Pressures* (Oxford, Hart Publishing, 2003) 275.

While few clients had moved on to self-managed contact, there was considerable movement of clients through the centres' services from supervised contact to supervised changeovers. In half of the cases sampled (52 per cent) the family had begun using a centre for supervised contact visits. Only 4 per cent of cases were families who had been using the centre for supervised contact visits for more than two years. A closer examination of long-term clients who had been using a centre for more than two years revealed that 85 per cent of them were using the centre for supervised changeovers. These findings suggest that most parents and children make the transition from supervised contact visits to supervised changeovers within a two-year period. The average length of time that clients remained using the CCS for a particular service such as supervised contact was unable to be determined using the client data.

Compared with the earlier findings from the Strategic Partners research, parents and children using the Australian government funded CCSs in 2003 spent on average a much longer period of time attending the contact centres (5 months vs 1.5 years).[22] This difference in the findings between the two studies may reflect the CCSs current approach to 'self-management' (ie moving parents and children on from using the CCSs for supervised contact to supervised changeovers by not actively intervening to move clients away from the centre altogether). It is also possible that the characteristics of the clients referred to CCSs by the courts and legal practitioners since 1996 may have changed in ways that promote long-term service use. The relative proportion of high-risk clients referred to the CCSs by the Family Court and the Federal Magistrates' Court on interim orders may have increased since the 1996 family law reforms of the Act, making it more difficult for the CCSs to move parents and children on to safely self-managed contact. Rachel Carson has argued that since the 1996 reforms emphasising the child's right to regular contact with both parents, the courts have been less conservative in their approach to the assessment of an 'unacceptable risk' and of the child's 'best interests' in contact cases involving domestic violence and allegations of child abuse. This has led to high-risk clients entering the CCS sector who perhaps would have received orders for 'no contact' in the pre-reform legal environment.[23]

Factors that Facilitate Moving Through Centre Services

Interviews were conducted with parents and children who had moved on from having supervised contact visits to supervised changeovers, and (in

---

[22] Strategic Partners, above n 3, at 57. The average 'length of stay' in a contact service had risen from three to five months during the two-year period of the Strategic Partner's evaluation.

[23] R Carson, 'Complex Contact Disputes' presentation made to the Current Issues in Family Law class (Melbourne, Faculty of Law, The University of Melbourne, 24 August 2004).

some cases) on to self-managed contact. These interviews, along with the interviews with the CCS staff, referral agents, government and industry representatives provided insight into the factors that assisted parents and children in making these transitions. These factors are discussed in detail below and relate to aspects of the referral process and the nature of orders made, staff behaviour and the extent to which centres are networked to other support services and programmes, as well as parent and child characteristics.

One obvious catalyst for the movement of parents and children through a centre's services and on to self-managed contact is a court order that specifies that the parties will move on to using a different service type, or stop using the service altogether, in a set period of time or after a set number of visits. Supervised contact has not generally been regarded as an appropriate long-term measure.[24] In Australia, the Family Court together with representatives from the contact service sector have developed guidelines for the referral of matters to contact services.[25] These guidelines released in 2004, recognise that the use of CCSs 'is only of benefit to a child for a defined period of time, and that long term use of a Children's Contact Service may not be in a child's best interests'.[26] Below, a CCS co-ordinator commented on the types of orders that her CCS has been involved with in the past:

> A lot of people will come with orders that will say: six visits at [the centre], then unsupervised. Some might say supervised but for three hours every Saturday, for three months, then for six hours, and then after another six months, overnight. So they've got that progression laid out before them. They know what's happening.

Industry representatives, referral agents and service staff noted that orders made that have a fixed progression away from supervised contact without provision for return to court or review by service staff or other professionals involved in the case were problematic. One industry representative commented:

> If you say in the wrong case, 'You've got three more weeks' then the effects could just be disastrous. I can imagine the effect of that being a mother or a father killing their children.

---

[24] The Full Court of the Family Court *In the Marriage of Bieganski* (1993) held that: 'Supervised access is not appropriate as a long term measure': *In the Marriage of Bieganski v Bieganski* [1993] FLC 92-357, Fogarty, Baker and Purvis JJ at para 54. The Full Court of the Family Court in *C and J* [1996] FLC 92-697 at para 83342 has since clarified that the *Bieganski* decision did not mean that supervised access may never be ordered in a final as opposed to an interim order, rather that 'The court has the widest discretion to make whatever orders are appropriate in the best interests of the child by way of access or contact'.
[25] Family Court of Australia, *Guidelines for Referrals to Children's Contact Services*. http://www.familycourt.gov.au (date retrieved 7 June 2005).
[26] *Ibid*, at 3–4.

Service staff in particular were acutely aware of the dangers involved in moving parents and children on before it is safe to do so.

There have been calls locally and internationally for standards for supervised contact to be developed that contain provisions requiring courts to set review dates in orders for supervised contact.[27] As noted above, in 2004, the Family Court released its new guidelines for referral to CCSs. The guidelines provide that orders to attend a CCS be made to allow variation by permitting CCS providers to assess whether the period in supervised environments is too long for children, or conversely to allow service staff to extend contact or move the parents and children on to self-management.[28] There is, however, no mandated process of review by the courts of long-term CCS arrangements.

Centre staff facilitated parents and children moving through the centre's services by arranging for the family to trial supervised changeovers or periods of self-managed contact. One CCS staff member described this process in the following way:

> They'll probably come to me and they'll say, oh they want to go and try outside and I'll say, 'Well how do you feel about it?' I usually ask them how they feel about it. Do they feel confident enough to do it? And okay, if they want to, I'll say, 'Yes well give it a go and see how you go and then you've always got the centre to fall back on if you want to come back' and some of them have gone away and sort of done it one or two times and then they've come back a couple of times, and then they've gone away and we've never seen them again.

The process by which CCS staff negotiated with parents to change their visiting arrangements was described by some staff and industry representatives as a form of 'mini-mediation':

> They [parents] go to the service, particularly when it's time for moving-on-type arrangements and want us to mediate meetings between them, which is outside of what we're set up to do but it's a very valuable thing to do nonetheless because it may mean the difference between moving people on and having them in the system a lot longer. (CCS staff)
>
> [It] is really a sort of little pocket of mediation about: 'If we weren't to have our contact here, where would we have it, when would we have it, how would it work, who would come where?' You know, and really get something pinned down, absolutely pinned down. Then allow them trial periods, allow them to come back to their support base. (Industry representative)

The referral of parents and children to other support services and programmes networked to the centre was nominated by CCS staff, government and industry representatives as a way of moving clients on from using the

---

[27] See especially: M Bailey, 'Supervised Access: A Long-Term Solution?' (1999) 37 *Family and Conciliation Courts Review* 485; Sheehan et al, above n 1, at xii.

[28] Family Court of Australia, above n 25, at 5.

CCSs. This is not surprising given the range of serious personal and relationship issues that clients present with on their arrival at a CCS. The analysis of the client data suggested that the majority of clients using CCSs had a range of therapeutic service and support needs in addition to the supervision of contact visits and changeovers. In order of frequency, parents and children using the government funded CCSs were considered to require the following additional support services and programs, as nominated by the CCS staff:

- services and programmes that address parents' individual problems (ie individual counselling (73 per cent of the cases sampled), anger management programmes (38 per cent) and substance abuse programmes (18 per cent));
- services and programmes that focus on parenting (ie parenting skills training (16 per cent) and parenting after separation education (57 per cent));
- services focused on resolving disputes between parents (ie mediation (46 per cent) and conciliation (10 per cent)); and
- services tailored to assisting children (ie counselling for children (47 per cent)).

Despite the serious nature and complexity of the personal and relationship problems of the CCS clients, some CCS staff were adamant that it was not their role to refer parents or children on to other support services and that doing so would compromise the neutrality of the services the centre provided. Below a residence parent commented on the reluctance of the CCS staff to refer her on to a counselling service:

> Where do I go when you're on a pension to get some counselling? I've asked several times and usually the response is well it's not their [the CCS staff] place to recommend anybody and they don't want to be seen as favouring anybody. Well I guess when I'm stressed out and think well who else am I going to ask? Because these are the people I'm seeing twice a week, and I felt like 'If you guys don't know then where else will I go?'

Past evaluations of the operation of CCSs have recommended that the services provided by the contact centres be expanded to include other therapeutic services,[29] and/or that the CCS staff refer parents and children on to outside support services and programmes.[30] While there is little consensus regarding the best model of therapeutic intervention for CCS clients, the research is unanimous that the role of contact centres needs to be broadened to be able to move parents and children on to safely self-managed contact.

---

[29] Thoennes and Pearson, above n 16, at 476.
[30] Strategic Partners (December 1998), above n 3, at xvi; M Peterson-Badali, J Maresca, N Park and J Jenkins, 'An Evaluation of Supervised Access III: Perspectives from the Legal System' (1997) 35 *Family and Conciliation Courts Review* 75.

For some residence parents, an important catalyst for moving on from supervised visits to supervised changeovers was confidence in the contact parent's ability to look after the children. The interviews with both parents and children confirmed that this was an important characteristic of parents who had successfully made this transition. Jane (12 years) commented that:

So how did it get changed [from supervised visits to supervised changeovers]?
Um, well Mum decided it because she thought everything was going fine because I think we've been doing it for about two years now, and she saw it was going fine and she decided to let it be changed. She decided to let us stay overnight in his house and all that, because she thought she could trust us kids, and she trusted him that nothing would really happen. So she trusted him so it all got changed. *And has that been okay for you?*
[Yes] it's been fun going to his house and all that.

Jane gave a different reason for having moved on from supervised change-overs to self-managed contact a few months later:

And then Mum had a big decision over it and decided to let us stay and we went [to father's place of residence]. So it was Dad's Saturday night and then she, because we had to come here [the contact centre] she started to get really annoyed having to drive into [country town] two times every month. Like having to drive all the way in here and because he lives at [father's place of residence] he had to drive all the way here as well. ... and like there was no point driving all the way to [country town] just to drop [the children] off because Mum had to drive in and he had to drive in too. So she decided to let him pick us up after school.
Okay
So it was just easier instead of Mum driving to [country town]. And she wanted us to see more of him so we went every two weeks. So like it's all changed because it was once a month and it went to every two weeks.
And how has that been?
Good.

Below, a Family Court judge described this important function of the CCSs in building the children's and the parents' confidence in the contact process and one another:

[by referring parties to a CCS] we are trying to engender a sense of security in the child about the contact, security in the residence parent that the child is going to be okay, and the security of the contact parent that they're not going to be exposed to allegations of bad behaviour, so it's a breathing space in a sense when they can perhaps have a relationship rather than that not being the case, and that they will be able to move on.

Parents being able to communicate effectively and safely about their children without an intermediary, and having the ability to be flexible around making arrangements for contact were further important factors that appeared to facilitate moving through a centre's services and on to self-managed contact. One CCS coordinator commented:

> Where they've become more relaxed around their time, their timing of coming in, where they've become more flexible around arrangements. For example the little one's got a birthday party, the residential parent feels confident about saying: 'Can we make it the other weekend?' the other parent says 'Yes that's fine' or they might, say, come to some middle ground that satisfies the need for contact but is based on looking after what the child wants.

Below, a residence parent and a contact parent who had moved through a centre's services described the way they now communicate with the other parent in discussions over the phone about the children:

> But I can talk to him now. I rang him up yesterday and said, 'Look, I've got this interview. Do you want to have her early?' and he goes, 'Oh I've got to finish work' and I said, 'Well what time can you be there?' and if he can't make a decision about time, I'm like, 'Some time today would be good'. But I don't say anything and I don't stir the pot. I just leave it and eventually I've got an answer. (Residence mother)
>
> So we do quite well for about 20 minutes and then after that it gets a bit [difficult]. I think it's because we run out of things to say and it only has to be one of us bring up something from the past and it all goes whoosh. We try to avoid that. We just talk about [child's name] and we find that works. (Contact father)

These findings suggest that over time some parents are able to change the way they related to one another while using the CCSs. For some parents this change was mediated by the residence parent's observations of their children's consistently positive reactions to contact visits with the other parent over an extended period of time.

For other parents, using the CCSs over an extended period of time appeared to have done little to reduce the distrust and anger they felt towards one another. Some parents commented that the time will inevitably come when they will have to stop using the centre, and their children will initiate this change to the current visiting arrangements when they are old enough to stop contact altogether, or manage the contact arrangements on their own. These parents appeared to advocate delegating the responsibility for self-management to their young adolescent children. In some cases this position may have been generated by a sense of powerlessness on the part of the parent that they are themselves able to initiate such a change. For example:

> In six to ten years I would hope that they're old enough and I've given them enough skills that perhaps even the service won't be needed, or yes a case of okay, they can get on a train and meet Dad down at [town name] or vice versa or whatever, but do it without me being a third person but knowing that they've got skills to ensure their own safety, to say, 'No Dad, I'm not going in the car'. Get on the mobile: 'Mum, we're at a party and I don't want to be here. Come and get me'. (Residence mother)

I think the older the girls get, probably when, I don't know, yes, three or four years' time when they're both, say, in their teens, early teens, eleven, twelve or whatever, I don't think there'll be any reason for us to go to the contact service then. … It'll not be up to me to decide, I think it will be up to the children to decide. It'll be a day when I'll phone, say on a Sunday, to talk to the kids and then one day they'll say 'Oh well Dad instead of going there, can we just meet you at McDonald's and then go to the pictures from there?' (Contact father)

On one view, the approach of these parents demonstrates an abrogation of parental responsibility for moving through the centre's services and on to self-managed contact and are consistent with what Kaganas and Diduck described as the 'good' child of separation or divorce—a child who is an agent of their own welfare and takes responsibility for shaping their post-separation parenting arrangements.[31] In the context of CCS provision this agency would take place within a framework where the choices children are permitted to make are confined to those, which the legal and CCS sectors have determined are in their best interests.[32]

For other parents moving on to self-managed contact or even communicating directly with the other parent would never be advisable. Below, the comments made by one residence mother highlight the potential danger involved in pressuring parents and children to self-manage contact where there has been domestic violence and child abuse:

We'll we've been separated now for almost five years and I'm scared stiff of the man. He's done nothing to gain any of my trust in that matter, in that way. He's continually taking me to court and accusing me of things. … the only thing I can ever see in the future is that he will take [child's name] one day and [child's name] will end up dead one day and I'll probably end up dead as well.

In general, the above findings relating to parent characteristics are consistent with earlier research by Trinder, Beek and Conolly that examined the experiences of highly conflicted parents negotiating their contact arrangements after divorce. They concluded that a wide range of factors interact over time to influence the quality and quantity of contact arrangements for high conflict parents. These factors included mediating factors such as the parents' beliefs about contact and their relationship skills, and direct determinants such as the quality of the relationship between the contact parent and child.[33]

Of crucial importance to children being able to move through a centre's services, and on to self-managed contact, was the quality of their relationship

---

[31] F Kaganas and A Diduck, 'Incomplete Citizens: Images of Post-separation Children' (2004) 67 *Modern Law Review* 959.

[32] *Ibid*, at 981.

[33] L Trinder, M Beek and J Conolly, *Making Contact: How Parents and Children Negotiate and Experience Contact After Divorce* (Joseph Rowntree Foundation, 2002) v–vi.

with the contact parent. Data from the interviews with CCS staff, parents and children suggested that there were three main ways in which the CCSs facilitated the development of the contact parent–child relationship over time. First, staff were able to control a parent's inappropriate or harmful behaviour while at the centre. This appeared to help those children who had supervised contact visits to regain their confidence in the contact parent that her or she would behave appropriately and attentively during contact visits. Secondly, the staff worked with the contact parent during supervised visits to develop their basic skills in 'child focused' parenting. Staff did this primarily by modelling parenting skills during contact visits at the centre. Thirdly, staff encouraged children to express their wishes in relation to going on contact visits and then liaised with parents to help them modify the visiting arrangements to better suit the children's expressed needs.[34] These findings are consistent with the research evidence to date that highlights the importance of the *quality* of the relationship with both parents to children's well-being post-separation and divorce.[35] Sustaining an emotionally close and warm relationship requires time.[36]

A child's age was related to their desire to move on from supervised visits to supervised changeovers, or to move on from using the CCS altogether. Some of the young adolescents interviewed reported that they were very restricted by having to attend a CCS for supervised contact or changeovers, and they wanted to move on from using the CCS. Sarah (12 years) didn't like the lack of control she felt she had over what she could do with her contact parent during her supervised visits:

> Here [at the centre] you felt like you were a little bit trapped as well. You could, like you'd think, 'Oh I want to go down to the shops and do something. Oh no I can't'. But then again, if you wanted to spend time with Dad.

These feelings were not specific to supervised contact arrangements. Susan (12 years) had been attending the CCS for weekend changeovers for four years. At the time of her interview she resented the way her regimented arrangements for visits to the CCS were restricting the time she could spend with her friends on the weekends:

> *Do you like to see your dad?*
> Yes. Sometimes.
> *Sometimes?*
> No I get sick of it.

[34] See especially: Sheehan and Carson, above n 8 for a detailed presentation of the ways in which CCS staff facilitated the development of the contact parent–child relationship.

[35] P Amato and J Gilbreth, 'Non-resident Fathers and Children's Wellbeing: A Meta-analysis' (1999) 61 *Journal of Marriage and the Family*, 557–73; J Pryor and B Rodgers, *Children in Changing Families: Life After Parental Separation* (Oxford, Blackwell Publishers, 2001).

[36] B Smyth, *Parent–Child Contact and Post-Separation Parenting Arrangements* (Melbourne, Research Report No 9, Australian Institute of Family Studies, 2004) 7.

What do you get sick of?
Oh well because I have to come over here every second weekend and I have to
be home for Tuesday night phone calls and so I can't really go anywhere, like on
the weekends.
So that is a problem?
Yeah well because I normally go to Youth [Club] and like my friends always ask
me and I miss out on a lot of birthday parties and things like that.

Of all the children who were interviewed, Simon (11 years) appeared to
struggle the most with the restrictions that the centre environment, and
court ordered arrangements for supervised contact, had imposed upon him.
Below, Simon commented on the things he didn't like about using a contact
centre for supervised contact:

> Well the fact that like half the toys are for two year olds. Like it just gets me
> angry because, yes, the fact that, like part of the big kids' toys have to be played
> with outside.
> *So are there things that are good about [the staff]?*
> Mm, not really.
> *So what would you like them to do that might be different that would make you
> feel a little bit better about [the centre]?*
> Mm, like just if they got some more toys for older kids and like, yes. I think that
> would make the older kids more happy and all.
> *So have you ever talked to [the staff] about that or have [the staff] ever asked
> you about that?*
> No, because once I also said, like I think asking, like because ah, I think it's when
> you reach a certain age you can choose whether you want to come to the visits
> or not. Um, yes, and anyways, I asked [a staff member] that about three times in
> one visit and she said, 'No, you can't'. And I went, 'Yes [I can]'.
> *You kept asking [the supervisor] whether you could choose to come?*
> Yes. I asked her three times before Saturday because, like, because I said 'These
> tournaments are on sometimes'.
> *And so what does that mean for you?*
> Well like if a [sporting] tournament is on, like it is today, and I have to miss out
> on the[sporting] tournament, it's kind of bad.
> *Right, so if you could choose, what would you choose?*
> If like you could reschedule the visit for, like next week … or the week before.
> *You would like a bit more flexibility?*
> Yes.

Simon and his younger sister Kate had been having supervised contact with
their father once a month for a period of two hours for more than three
years at the time that they were interviewed. The parents were ordered
by the Family Court to attend a CCS. The family had a history of domestic violence by the contact parents and the relevant state child welfare
authority had investigated the residence parent's allegations of child abuse.
No criminal charge was laid against the father, nor was a protective order

put in place. At the time the parents were interviewed, they were planning the return to the Family Court to change the court order to supervised contact. The residence mother wanted the new order to be for 'no contact', while the contact father wanted to self-manage the contact visits. Simon and Kate reported wanting to continue having contact with their father but not in a supervised environment at the centre. Simon's case demonstrates the tension that can exist between an adolescent child's desire to move on from supervised visits at a contact centre, and the absence of any resolution on the part of a parent (or parents) of the issues that brought them to the CCS in the first place.

The analysis of the client data suggested that the courts, lawyers and parents were rarely called on to address the issues that could arise for young adolescents attending CCSs during the referral process for the simple reason that older children were infrequently referred to CCSs. The average age of children at the time of their first visit to the service was 5.6 years.[37] At the time of the children's first visit to the service, 10 per cent of the sample was comprised of adolescents (ie children aged 10 years or older). A quarter (26 per cent) of the cases sampled involved adolescents currently using the government funded CCSs.[38] These findings are consistent with the proposition that many children are entering the CCSs during early to middle childhood, a significant proportion of whom remain in the service sector at least until they reach their early adolescence.

CONCLUSONS AND RECOMMENDATIONS

The exact point at which a family is considered to be self-managing their contact was not clearly defined by the funded CCSs, the Government or the industry representatives. There existed in practice two different models of self-management: parents and children moving on from supervised contact visits to supervised changeovers; and parents and children moving away from the centre to safely self-manage contact. The first and second models appeared to require the residence parent and children to have confidence in the contact parent's ability to care for the children during contact visits. The second model of self-management appeared to require some degree of resolution of the issues that characterised the relationship between the parents on referral to the extent that the parents could be flexible about arrangements and communicate with one another safely without an intermediary. The first model dominated parents and children's experiences of the CCSs and self-management. Despite the sustained focus over time on maintaining

---

[37] Sheehan and Carson, above n 8.
[38] *Ibid.*

and developing the parent–child relationship, some parents remained emotionally engaged in conflict with one another, even though this conflict was rarely acted out in front of the children during supervised contact visits or at supervised changeovers.

The widespread adoption of the second model in Australia would require a new approach to contact service provision that incorporates the active referral of CCS clients to other support services and programmes networked to the contact centre, with the intention of addressing individual problems such as anger management and substance abuse as well as the relational or dyadic problems that characterised the parents' relationship with one another. This was identified by government, industry representatives, the CCSs and parents alike as an important step forward in assisting parents and children to move on from using the CCSs.

These issues were earlier brought into focus by Bastard's observations of the operation of contact centres in France.[39] He suggested that contact centres in France fell into one of two categories. The first are what he called 'pro-mediation' centres, which 'consider that visiting rights can be implemented only if the conflict between parents is reduced'.[40] As a result, these centres place heavy emphasis on improving parental communication through mediation. On the other hand, there are 'anti-mediation' centres, which assume that 'it is neither useful nor feasible to try to restore the relationship between parents who are in high conflict'.[41] Instead, these centres focus on restoring separate links between the child and each of their parents after divorce.[42] These differences in approach reflect, he suggested, different assumptions about how best to maintain contact between parents and children post separation and divorce. In the first, pro-mediation model, the assumption is that the child–parent relationship is mediated by the parental relationship. On the second, the two relationships are considered separate from each other.

While the findings do not suggest that there is a similar polarisation of service provision philosophies in Australia, the data do indicate that there is a mixture of views and practices that could be described as leaning towards one or other of these models. In particular, there was often recognition of the desirability of staff working to improve parents' relationships, and staff mediated small changes in the visiting arrangements in order to move parents and children on from supervised contact to supervised changeovers, and on to self-managed contact. It was also commonly thought that to actively facilitate the parents' relationship with one another would entail a paradigm shift in the core work of CCSs—in effect, that in shifting to

---

[39] Bastard, above n 21.
[40] *Ibid*, at 275
[41] *Ibid*, at 276.
[42] *Ibid*.

what Bastard calls the 'pro-mediation' model, they would be providing different services from the ones they are currently funded to provide. It is perhaps not surprising that moving parents and children on to supervised changeovers and then on to self-managed contact appeared to be a difficult task for many clients and took a number of years to accomplish. Simon's experience of long-term supervised contact encapsulates the risks to children when the courts, the CCSs and parents abandon them at the *centre of the post-separation family structure.*

Some families will never be able to safely conduct supervised changeovers, or move on safely from using the centre. Currently, parents and children who are unable to ever move on to supervised changeovers can have the CCSs respond by withdrawing service. This can stop contact and force the parents to return to court to review their order for supervised contact at the CCS, or alternatively it can lead to them continuing to conduct the contact visits privately, once again exposing parents and children to harm.

Considered together, the research findings presented suggest that clear policy and practice guidelines in relation to self-management are needed in Australia so that the number of parents and children who move successfully and safely on to self-managed contact can be maximised, and those who are unable to move to supervised changeovers over time are protected by redirecting these cases back to the courts to have the orders for supervised contact reviewed and changed.

Despite the obvious challenges that self-management poses for the courts, service staff and clients, the government funded services involved in the project were successful in minimising children's exposure to parental conflict and violence. This conflict minimisation, Lamb argued in chapter 1, is one of the most important interventions that reduce the likelihood that children will be adversely affected by parental separation and divorce.

10

Children's Contact Services in Australia: The Referral Process

BELINDA FEHLBERG AND ROSEMARY HUNTER

ABSTRACT

IN AUSTRALIA, THE possibility of using a Children's Contact Service arises in a relatively small number of cases, but on a regular basis. This chapter, as chapter nine, draws on the findings of a recently completed project on Children's Contact Services. While the previous chapter looked at families' movement through Contact Services and on to self-managed contact, this chapter looks at entry into Contact Services, in particular, referral agents' accounts of the process of referral to Children's Contact Services, the types of court orders made for supervised contact or change-over, and the contents of those orders. It also looks at the factors identified by referral agents as prompting an increase in recent years in the number of orders for the use of Children's Contact Services, and the impact of the advent of Children's Contact Services on their legal practices. The chapter concludes by identifying best practices for referral to Children's Contact Services to emerge from the project.

1. INTRODUCTION

This chapter, like the previous chapter, draws on data from a project recently conducted in Australia on Children's Contact Services (CCSs).[1] The focus of the previous chapter was on *families' movement through CCSs and on to self-managed contact*, along with background information on the project design and methodology. The focus of this chapter is *entry into*

---

[1] G Sheehan, R Carson, B Fehlberg, R Hunter, A Tomison, R Ip, and J Dewar, *Children's Contact Services: Expectation and Experience* Final Report, 2005, Griffith University, Melbourne University, AIFS. The project was funded by an Australian Research Council SPIRT Grant, which had the Federal Attorney-General's Department as the Industry Partner. The major role in the project's design and conduct of Dr Sheehan, assisted by Rachel Carson, is gratefully acknowledged.

CCSs. Given the current Australian family law context, in which there is an increasing emphasis on identifying and streamlining the various 'pathways' of families through the family law system,[2] it was important that our investigation should extend to explore expectations and experiences of the process of referral to contact services.

The chapter draws mainly on the 40 interviews conducted with referral agents, a group comprising: representatives from the Family Court of Australia (n = 6), the Federal Magistrates' Court (n = 5) and the Magistrates' Court of Victoria (n = 1); legal practitioners (both barristers and solicitors) (n = 21); and other referral agents including psychologists, domestic violence workers and community service counsellors (n = 7). These data are contextualised by drawing on results from the client survey.

2. THE PROCESS OF REFERRAL

Although the processes of referral to CCSs described by referral agents in our sample were varied, referral was usually by court order. Use of a CCS was usually suggested by lawyers, at court, and just before orders were made. This meant that it was not always possible to contact the CCS before orders were made, which could result in problems, the most common being a delay in contact commencing.

2.1 Referral is usually by Court Order

Referral to a CCS was usually by court order (80.6 per cent of cases surveyed), although it was also clear that '[s]ome people go to the contact centre without any orders. They just do it by agreement' (solicitor). This was often after receiving some information (for example, a pamphlet or a telephone number) about a CCS from a solicitor or counsellor (often based at a Legal Service or a Family Violence Service).

There appeared to be two main reasons why referral to a CCS was usually by court order. First, CCSs were viewed as scarce resources and there was a general perception among solicitors that the chance of access was greater via court orders:

... it's very limited in the accessing of it. So it's limited mainly to court-ordered clients. (family/domestic violence worker)

---

[2] The first step in this process was the Federal Government's appointment of the Family Law Pathways Advisory Group in 2000, which explored the ways in which individuals discover and utilise particular options for resolving family law disputes: *Out of the Maze: Pathways to the Future for Families Experiencing Separation*, Report of the Family Law Pathways Advisory Group, Commonwealth of Australia, July 2001 Recent reforms are discussed at the end of this chapter.

Secondly, client co-operation was viewed as more likely if court orders were obtained:

> ... if you're acting for a dad and there is possibly a no-contact mum on the other side and she's going to put up all sort of barriers and delays and all the tactics that they usually engage in, if there's a court order that says along the lines that the mother and father must participate in the process, [CCS] process, must fill out an application form, must attend an interview, must be assessed, whereas if that's a court order and mum doesn't do any of that, then we can take it back to court and say, 'Well hey! She hasn't done it'. (Solicitor)

This issue of client co-operation is explored at 3.1 in relation to the typical contents of orders.

2.2 Use of a CCS was usually suggested by Lawyers, at Court

Regardless of the court involved, or the stage in proceedings, the idea of involving a CCS was usually suggested during negotiations at court by lawyers for one of the parties, or the child representative if one was appointed:

> ... you probably assume from the outside that being the judge, I'm the one who decides everything that happens. In fact I probably shape the least of it, in a sense. So I'd be driven a lot by what the practitioners have arrived at. ... there'd be very few cases where I've been called upon to decide whether it's the contact centre or not, and there are very few instances where I've been, you know, the brilliant one that said, 'I know. What about a contact centre?' because the practitioners know. And generally if one person is unrepresented, the other one will be represented so their lawyer would have raised it. So it's not often left up to me to have to think about it. (Family Court judge)

In cases that went to trial and resulted in a judicial determination, it was also likely that the lawyers would be responsible for working out the final details regarding attendance at a CCS, unless problems arose:

> ... in fact my preference is always to indicate in general terms what sorts of orders I consider appropriate and leave it to the parties to work out the finer details. If they can't, they come back. ... [If] for example, there's an argument about whether contact begins at 11.00 am or 1.00 pm, then of course I will resolve that on the basis of whatever evidence is before me. But I don't usually want to buy into those things. That isn't to say that I haven't done such things. I mean I had a case where the actual arrangements at [CCS] in that particular case became very relevant because the centre had made arrangements for the mother and father to be assessed and attend interviews and there were problems with both of the parents. And I managed that pretty firmly and in fact arranged for evidence to be given to me by the administrator at the centre, just to work out exactly what happened and I brought it back before me to make sure that the parties had attended and that they were suitable. (Federal Magistrate)

Given that accessing a CCS was often raised at court, a degree of pressure on litigants to consent to orders to attend a CCS was sometimes evident:

> Well some people object and you say to them, 'Well look', you know, 'do you want contact or don't you?' especially in situations where we'd like to think it's a short-term measure and I always put it to them in terms of: 'This is a protection for you. Allegations have been made. Now if you don't want allegations to continue, what we're doing here is making sure that you're safe and the child's safe'. So I always try to put it in rosy terms. (State Magistrate)

There was also some acknowledgement that lawyers and courts have seen CCSs as an easy way of getting rid (at least temporarily) of difficult cases (see 5.1).

2.3 CSSs were not always Contacted before Orders are Made, which had Consequences for the Content and Workability of Orders

Lawyers often said they usually did, or preferred to, contact the relevant CCS before orders were made, or requested their clients to contact the CCS before the court hearing date. Some judges also preferred to telephone the relevant CCS before making orders so that they could tailor their orders to reflect the operation of the service.

However, because the prospect of using a CCS usually arose at court just before orders were to be made, it was not always possible to contact the CCS in the short time available:

> Well, I always used to insist that phone calls be made ... I wouldn't make an order without the outside community agency having agreed. But I think the way the lawyers quite reasonably have gotten around that, probably out of frustration at times when they're trying to get through to a busy contact centre and they can't, and they're trying to give the Court the answer on the orders, is that they often just make orders that are subject to the approval of the contact centre ... on the basis that usually, between the lawyers and the judge, you've got a pretty good feel for what a contact centre would take. It's only going to be because they hadn't got time or whatever. You know, it's going to be something like that, but the majority of cases will be taken, so it's better than hanging around on the phone or not being able to get an answer. (Family Court judge)

In most cases in the survey the CCS concerned was able to provide the contact as specified in the order (76.5 per cent), but the approach of contacting the CCS post-orders could result in problems, the most common problem being a delay in contact commencing due to the CCS operating hours and/ or long waiting list:

> ... once the orders had been made, we found out when [CCS] could facilitate the contact, the mother couldn't provide the child at those times because she was

at university. So then we had to go through the process of renegotiating. Now whether, I suppose in their defence, [CCS] could argue, 'Well you should have rung us and found out what times', but in the heat of trying to negotiate contact, where you've got a party that says, 'Okay, I'm going to finally let you have some contact' at court, that's the last thing that you're thinking about doing, is asking whether that can be done. ... Also with [CCS] there was a fairly substantial waiting list. (Solicitor)

In the survey, the CCS was unable to provide the contact as specified in the order in only 11.7 per cent of cases. The major reasons for being unable to provide the contact specified were that the CCS did not provide the specified type of service (32.6 per cent), the CCS was not open at the specified time (30.2 per cent) and the CCS was unable to provide the service for the specified length of time (16.3 per cent).

3. THE TYPES OF ORDERS MADE

Court orders for contact or changeover to be supervised at a CCS may be made at the interim stage or as final orders, and may be made by consent (reflecting the agreement of the parties) or by judicial determination. It appears that that interim consent orders are the most common types of orders made. Final orders raise the issue of long-term or indefinite supervision, options which were rarely considered appropriate by the referral agents interviewed.

3.1 Consent Orders vs Judicial Determination

Referral agents consistently said that many or most orders for supervised contact or supervised changeover are made by consent. One judge claimed never to have imposed an order for supervised contact on a party.

As noted at 2.2, lawyers had various ways of persuading their clients to consent to an order. In the case of a contact parent, a lawyer explained:

Well you can sit them down in the Magistrates Court and say, ... 'We've got concerns about your behaviour. You can disprove our concerns by agreeing to this controlled contact'. And you can sell it. You can sell it to a party against whom accusations have been made and he's indignant about it, by saying, 'Listen, if it's not happening it won't be seen to be happening and it will take the weapon out of the other party's hands. You'll be right'. (Solicitor)

And in relation to a residence parent:

You see it when you've got one party not, you know, not wanting the other party to have contact to force a no-contact situation, and then, it is incumbent on the court system and the lawyers, I think, to make extremely clear to the recalcitrant parent that this isn't acceptable, and that they'd better get used to the idea. And then if they don't consent to contact being ordered then it will be ordered over their heads and they will then not be able to control the amount of time and contact which is involved ... . So it behoves the lawyers to make that abundantly clear before the parties turn up to ... allow contact under supervision. (Solicitor)

Other referral agents were more neutral, or actively critical of the fact that residence parents had little option but to consent to supervised contact:

And the reality of it is, I think, more and more lately, is that you cannot advise residence parents that the other party, you know, this person is so bad they probably won't get contact. In fact you almost have to advise them, I think, that especially in the interim stages, that they're better off, even where there are allegations of abuse and so on, that in order not to lay themselves open to suggestions that they're being difficult, or that they're trying to prevent contact, you almost have to suggest to people where there is abuse that they should allow contact. (Solicitor)

Judicial officers varied regarding their level of scrutinisation of proposed consent orders. Some judicial officers indicated that they would not question minutes of consent orders involving supervised contact or changeover that were handed up to them. Others were prepared to be more interventionist if they considered the orders might be unworkable, either for reasons related to the operation of the contact centre or related to the family situation:

I have a checklist, which is in my mind which every time you get a consent order on children's matters, as soon as you see them making these referrals out, the first question you ask is:
  1. Have you contacted the appropriate centre?
  2. Are they aware of the order that you're making?
  3. Do the times that you're asking for this supervision to occur actually fit in with their operating hours?
  4. Is there a waiting period? ...
If it's a lawyer who says, 'Well this is the contact centre the clients will accept because we're recommending it, but no one's approached them yet', I'd be saying, 'Well look, I'm hesitant about making the orders. Would you like to make a phone call and check with them as to what you're asking is appropriate and they are the appropriate place to go?' (Deputy Registrar, Family Court)
I refused to sanction a consent order on an interim basis because I was so concerned about the matter, and it was one where the parties, no doubt with much misgiving, had agreed to contact at the contact centre, and I didn't have a problem with the contact centre, I had a problem with the contact. And it's a case where there's going to be psychiatric assessment done on everybody in the family and I just did not think it was appropriate in those circumstances to be ordering contact before that assessment was done. (State Magistrate)

The view of referral agents that consent orders for supervised contact or changeover are more common than judicial orders following a contested hearing is probably not surprising, given that generally consent orders outnumber judicial determinations in family law proceedings.[3] The survey data, by contrast, showed that similar proportions of orders were made by consent (47.1 per cent) and by judicial determination (45.1 per cent). This data may be unreliable, however, as the distinction between a consent order and a judicial determination may not always have been obvious and understood by CCSs, from whose records the survey data were drawn.

3.2 Interim Orders

Several referral agents contended that most contact orders are made on an interim basis. The predominance of interim rather than final orders was variously attributed to the court's reluctance to make supervision orders on a final basis (see 3.3), and the incapacity of CCSs to supervise for long periods of time.

The potentially lengthy duration of interim supervised contact orders attracted some comment from referral agents. One noted that in the Federal Magistrates' Court, interim orders tend to be in place for only a short time, with matters coming back for final hearing relatively quickly. In the Family Court, on the other hand, a backlog of cases awaiting final hearing means that interim orders can be in place for 12–18 months, giving rise to the complaint that:

> Sometimes children are going there for too long and it's not necessary. ... It's a very easy fallback position for a resident parent and what should be a very temporary situation becomes a long-term thing, and that's a problem. I mean I've had contact parents who have been going to the contact centre for two years. (Solicitor)

Another solicitor observed that when the Magellan project (in essence, an expedited list for cases involving serious allegations of physical or psychological violence towards children) was running in the Family Court, cases were getting to final hearing in 4–6 months. In that kind of time frame, the Court could make the decision not to allow contact during the interim stage without causing irreparable damage to the parent-child relationship. But if the interim period took between 12 and 18 months, suspending contact was not an option.

---

[3] Regarding the Family Court, see Family Court of Australia, *Annual Report 2005-2006*, Family Court of Australia, 2006, 33–35. Available via the Family Court's website: http://www.familycourt.gov.au/.

A third solicitor, however, presented a different perspective. She noted that the first 18 months after separation is the most dangerous time for women and children, and this coincides with the approximate length of interim orders. So the result of interim contact orders, even for supervised contact, is that children are being forced to have contact with a perpetrator of family violence at the time when he is at his most aggressive.

3.3 Final Orders

While some referral agents considered that interim supervision orders are far more common than final orders, others gave various instances in which final orders had been made, either by judicial determination or by consent, or claimed that there was no predominance one way or the other as between interim and final orders. In contrast, the client survey indicated almost twice as many interim orders (52.3 per cent) as final orders (27.9 per cent), which is probably a fair reflection of the general picture.

Even where final orders were made, there was general agreement that supervised contact should be ordered for a finite rather than an indefinite period. Some respondents referred to Full Court authority to support the view that if indefinite supervision is contemplated, then it is doubtful whether contact should occur at all.[4] More often, any period of supervision included in final orders will be limited in practice (cf the terms of final orders themselves, which are more likely to be open-ended on this issue—see 4.5). A range of reasons was given for this, including the fact that contact centres offer a time limited service and lack the resources to supervise for long periods, the impracticality of a child having supervised contact for the whole of their childhood, and the potentially damaging effects on the child and the parent–child relationship for contact only to take place in a contact centre:

> We have actually requested ongoing supervision of the contact as the final orders in that one. But I can see there is going to be a major issue because the contact centre cannot just give endless supervised contact so there's the whole issue of who could even do it basically. ... It's really hard to get it as final and when you do get it as final orders it's got a cap on it and you've still got to come up with another solution. (Solicitor)
> ... so you might get some court orders that are laid down when children are quite young, you know, three or four, but those court orders have to be carried

---

[4] In *B and B* [1993] FLC 92-357, Fogarty, Baker and Purvis JJ held that 'Supervised access is not appropriate as a long term measure'. This view has not commanded universal assent, however. See, eg *M and H* [1996] FLC 92-695; and *C and J* [1996] FLC 92-697. In the latter case, Fogarty and May JJ in their joint judgment stated that 'Ultimately the determinant is the best interests of the child. That discretion should not be circumscribed by absolute rules which appear to exclude one of the otherwise available possibilities'.

through till that child gets to an age where they're no longer practicable and it can encroach on their social lives to the extent where the child then starts to really resent having to go. (Family violence worker)

... if we use them for too long, after the need for them has objectively evaporated, then we can do damage I think, because we can teach the child that there's something in the relationship with that parent which is unsafe and which needs intervention. ... Sometimes the child has to learn that, but I think we have to be careful about long-term orders. (Family Court judge)

What happens after supervised contact is another matter. Other arrangements may be phased in, for example moving from supervised contact to unsupervised contact, perhaps with changeover in a neutral location, but at least one referral agent (a solicitor) argued that after the period of supervision, 'there are a lot of children going into unsafe contact'.

Circumstances for making Long-term Orders for Supervised Contact

Various circumstances were suggested in which it might be appropriate to order supervised contact for an extended period of time. A number of judicial officers mentioned cases in which the contact parent has serious and permanent problems, such as brain injury, intellectual disability or psychiatric disorder, which mean that they will never be able to cope with the child or guarantee the child's safety unsupervised. This does not mean that contact can always occur at a CCS, however, and graduated orders could be made. According to one referral agent, clients would be able to make a maximum of 10 or 12 visits to the CCS, after which:

may be they've got a very good mother or partner, she would be the one who would do the backup just to make sure that the nappies are changed, just to make sure kids get to bed on time and those sorts of things. (Primary Dispute Resolution co-ordinator)

A judge considered that a lengthy order for supervision could be made in sexual abuse cases, but appeared equivocal about this approach:

... once you determine that the abuse has occurred, I mean you can sometimes make a supervised order, but once you've determined—I won't say you've determined that the abuse has occurred, but there's an unacceptable risk, yes, you could make a lengthy supervised order and report back to see what the relationship was. ... But they're very difficult. You tend at that point to say, 'Well sorry, but that's the end of it'. (Family Court judge)

By contrast, a solicitor reported a case in which contact had been supervised for 12 months, there was evidence of unacceptable risk to the child, and the father consented to a further 18 months' supervision, after which unsupervised contact would be phased in. By that time, the child would be seven or eight and 'it was felt that ... if there is an issue with Dad, [the child] could express her opinion'. This seems to place an extraordinary burden on the child to protect herself in the absence of protection from the family law system.

Circumstances for making Long-term Orders for Supervised Changeover

A few respondents noted that final orders may be made for supervised changeover as well as for supervised contact. One referral agent considered that for a minority of parents, changeover would always need to take place at a contact centre, and another expressed the view that long-term changeover at a contact centre would be preferable to long-term changeover at a police station. It was also considered that long-term supervised changeover presented less of a resource problem than did long-term supervised contact.

4. CONTENTS OF ORDERS

Referral agents were asked whether there were particular matters that they would specify in orders for supervised contact or supervised changeover. This question elicited a wide variety of responses. Some of the most common categories of responses are identified in this section.

4.1 Specifications Relating to the Contact Service's Intake Procedure

Most referral agents interviewed were aware of CCS intake procedures, which involve the completion of an application form by both parties, and an assessment by the CCS, sometimes including an interview, before the case will be accepted. A Family Court judge noted that this means that court orders should not require the CCS to accept the parties concerned, as they may not complete the screening process or meet the service's criteria. Another considered that the contact order must always be expressed to be subject to the CCS assessing the family as appropriate.

A solicitor recounted a case in which:

> We had to wait four months before the other side filled in her application. She was simply using it as a stalling mechanism and therefore my client was not getting any contact for that period of time. Now that's a huge period of time that we lost because she wouldn't fill it in. I ended up having to threaten bringing a Form 8 application and bringing her in contempt, for her to do that. But that's something that needs to be addressed. I don't know whether the practitioners need to look at having the assessment forms there and getting them filled in and attaching them to the orders, and then they are simply sent to [CCS].

This solicitor described such stalling tactics as 'a huge problem'. Other referral agents, however, reported a variety of well-developed strategies that they use to ensure that parties do in fact complete the intake procedures in a timely manner:

> I try to have that application form at court with me, on the date when I'm hoping to get the orders for [CCS], so I can have my client fill in the form. I'll try and organise that there be another form for the client on the other side, so that everybody fills the forms in. (Solicitor)
>
> [I get] a court order that says along the lines that the mother and father must participate in the process ... must fill out an application form, must attend an interview, must be assessed ... (Solicitor)

As noted above (at 1.1), if a party fails to comply with such specifications, they can be taken back to court for enforcement.

4.2 Frequency of Contact, Dates and Times

Referral agents were agreed that specific dates and times for supervised contact or changeover should not be included in orders unless the CCS had been contacted and agreed to those times. Otherwise, it was unlikely that the particular dates and times specified would be able to be met by the CCS. Because, as discussed at 1.3, it is sometimes not possible to contact the CCS before orders are made, the orders might instead provide that the particular times for contact or changeover are to be as determined by the CCS. This allows contact services to slot people in according to their own timetable and current bookings.

4.3 Empowering the CCS

One solicitor said that she always specified in orders that the parties must co-operate with the CCS. Apart from this, it was judges who tended to speak about including conditions in orders to empower the CCS:

> Well first of all the order has got to be made subject to the contact centre assessing the family as appropriate for the centre. I can't require them to take the matter. Secondly, I require the family to comply with all reasonable directions of the contact centre. Thirdly, I will normally give some degree of autonomy to the contact centre to terminate contact if the matter goes outside the orders or their rules. (Family Court judge)
>
> I think sometimes you need to make it absolutely clear that it's at the discretion of the staff that if they ask a person to leave that person is to leave forthwith and those sorts of matters. So I have on occasion had quite detailed orders or rung one of the centres to ask do they have a policy about alcohol. What did their protocols that they had people sign say about if they formed a view that someone was alcohol or drug affected and those sorts of matters? ... [I] try and tailor orders if I thought it needed more than a bare order, to really empower in a way the contact centre. (Family Court judge)

As well as empowering the CCS, two referral agents were concerned that orders should also empower the child representative, for example by allowing the CCS to contact the child representative if necessary, or allowing the child representative to exercise discretion to provide relevant material to the CCS, and discuss the case generally with the CCS.

4.4 Duration of Orders

A few referral agents mentioned that they would place limits on the duration of orders. For example a federal magistrate said they would generally make orders for supervised contact for six months, after which the order may be reviewed, while another federal magistrate explained that their orders would generally specify supervised contact for two hours a fortnight for a period of X months, or X weeks. Two referral agents saw a need for orders to be time-limited, either because orders made when a child is quite young should not be carried on inappropriately when the child is older, or because in their experience, the services of a CCS would only be available for a limited time, such as one year.

4.5 Provision in Court Orders for Phasing Out of Supervised Contact/Changeover

The issue of the duration of supervised contact orders is related to that of the phasing out of supervised contact or changeover, in accordance with the received wisdom identified at 3.3 that long-term supervision should not be ordered. To what extent, then, is the phasing out of supervision provided for in contact orders which are expected to be final orders?

Respondents suggested that the Federal Magistrates' Court has adopted a practice of judicial supervision of moves to self-management, which involves bringing parties back to court after a specified period of time at a CCS, in order to make further arrangements.

This practice does not appear to be common in the Family Court, however. The phasing out of supervision may occasionally be left directly under the control of the CCS but more often, supervision orders appear to be open ended, and phasing out is left implicitly to the CCS or to the parties themselves. For example:

> ... when you make an order for contact centre, generally it's an open-ended order, and times change, the circumstances change. So whilst you might start off with a contact centre when you've got a three-year-old, very quickly in two years time they're a five-year-old and off to school, and there's not the necessity for the people to have to go back to the contact centre. But generally that's agreed between the parties and we mightn't know that they're still at the service, because our files would be closed and until they come back to us to change it, we don't necessarily keep tabs on all of those people going through. It's just impossible. (Solicitor)

Another referral agent put a less positive spin on this process of making open-ended orders and leaving the duration to the discretion of the CCS:

in the case of the violence directed to the mother, I mean we see a lot of those cases and the reality I think is that in the long term they do move on to manage their own contact but it's usually not their choice. It's usually more because the service cannot keep going for them and it just has to happen. And they're the ones that will often, the contact changeover will be at McDonalds, or it will be at the police station, because that's the only place the woman feels safe ... . (Solicitor)

Another referral agent raised the question of how, in practical terms, orders could be reviewed. In cases of proven sexual abuse in particular, it would be inappropriate to simply move to unsupervised contact:

if the child representative's still in it, it might be able to be reviewed by the feedback from the contact centre. There might be sort of like an implicit agreement that if all goes well and the contact centre says it's okay, that it might go to non-supervision, but that it's not actually included in the order because people aren't prepared to commit to it. Another option is it might go back to court again. I mean the Court is very reluctant at the moment to do that, but that's an option. (Solicitor)

4.6 Judicial Guidelines and Pro Forma Orders

While one solicitor was concerned that there was still a haphazard approach and a lack of clear processes for ordering supervised contact or changeover, deputy registrars and judges of the Family Court referred to pro forma orders and guidelines on referrals to CCSs. The process of developing the guidelines began at a workshop funded by the Federal Attorney-General's Department in 2002, and was continued by a cross-sector drafting group headed by a judge of the Family Court, Justice Jennifer Boland.[5] The pro forma orders have been incorporated into the Family Court's electronic bench book, and since the completion of this project, both the guidelines and pro forma orders have been placed on the Family Court's website.[6]

The guidelines cover three areas: intake procedures, use of the CCS, and moving on from the CCS's intervention. Their purpose is to raise awareness and improve the knowledge of court personnel and CCS personnel about each other's processes and procedures, and ensure that up to date information about CCSs is available to the court. They draw the attention of judicial

---

[5] Family Court of Australia website, http://www.familycourt.gov.au/, 'Business Administration'.
[6] http://www.familycourt.gov.au/

officers to the following matters in considering orders for supervised contact or changeover at a CCS:

- is the proposed CCS available to offer the supervision required?;
- is there a sufficient time lag in the order to permit the CCS to properly undertake its intake procedures?;
- is the proposed CCS open at the time of the proposed orders?;
- does the CCS have age-appropriate facilities for the children? (eg some CCSs are conducted at weekends in church halls and do not have suitable facilities for infants);
- will the CCS accept the parent? (eg intake criteria issues);
- are the participants able to meet the costs of the CCS?;
- does the order permit variation? (eg CCS may consider that the family should be moved on to self-management);
- should the order include provision of other support services provided at the CCS? (eg counselling);
- does the order provide that the CCS may terminate its services?;
- are the orders sufficiently precise, given that clients of CCSs tend to be 'high conflict'?

The current pro forma orders, however, do not deal with all of these matters. In particular, the pro forma orders appear to be designed as interim orders, and do not contain any specifications concerning duration, phasing out of supervision, or movement to self-management. The pro forma orders contain:

- detailed specifications concerning compliance with the CCS intake procedure in a timely manner;
- if the parties are accepted by the CCS, specifications as to the frequency of contact and how it shall occur—assuming at least some knowledge about the days of operation and services provided by the CCS, although incorporating sufficient flexibility to enable alternative arrangements to be made if those specified in the order are unachievable;
- directions as to the payment of fees;
- provision for the matter to be returned to court if, following its intake procedure, the CCS is unable or unwilling to take the family; and
- provision for the matter to be returned to court if the CCS declines or is unable to continue to provide its services, or if the Director of the CCS recommends in writing to the parties that the orders be varied.

From the discussion above, it is also notable that the pro forma orders do insist on the specification of a particular CCS, rather than leaving the choice of CCS open. By contrast, however, they contain only implicit rather than explicit provisions empowering the CCS, and nothing about the interaction between the child representative and the CCS.

5. FACTORS AFFECTING THE ORDERING OF SUPERVISED CONTACT

Referral agents were asked to identify factors that they consider have affected the ordering of supervised contact and supervised changeover in the past ten years. In response, they expressed a range of views on the extent of the impact on contact orders of the Family Law Reform Act 1995 (Cth) (FLRA) which introduced a number of changes to the Family Law Act 1975(Cth) regarding parenting disputes. These changes reflected similar provisions in the Children Act 1989 (UK) and were largely aimed at helping to encourage on-going involvement of contact parents in their children's lives. Referral agents also referred to a wide range of broader social factors that they considered relevant to the increased use of orders for supervised contact and supervised changeover.

5.1 Impact of the FLRA

Some respondents were firmly of the view that the enactment of the FLRA had increased the likelihood of orders, especially interim orders, for supervised contact and supervised changeover being made. Of particular relevance was section 60B(2) of the Family Law Act 1975 (Cth), inserted by the FLRA, especially paragraphs (a) and (b) which refer respectively to the child's right to know and be cared for by both their parents, and to have contact with both parents and others significant to the child's care[7]:

> I've got to say that since the recent changes to the Family Law Act, the general view amongst solicitors is that you can rarely if ever advise people that the non-resident parent won't get contact, that he won't get contact if they push hard enough. (Solicitor)

The Chief Justice of the Family Court cited the research of Helen Rhoades, Reg Graycar and Margaret Harrison[8] to support this view:

> I think as the Graycar/Harrison study shows, it actually did probably lead to more interim orders being made and perhaps questionable interim orders in relation

[7] Following significant amendments to the FLA effective from 1 July 2006 and resulting from the Family Law Amendment (Shared Parental Responsibility) Act 2006 these principles still comprise s 60B(2)(a) and (b) respectively, but two additions have been made to the objects (which the principles are said to underlie) set out in s 60B(1). The new objects are: ensuring that children have the benefit of both parents having a meaningful involvement in their lives to the maximum extent consistent with the best interests of the child, and protecting children from physical or psychological harm resulting from being subjected to, or exposed to, abuse, neglect, or family violence (s 60B(1)(a) and (b)). These two objects are also now the primary considerations for courts to consider when deciding what is in the child's best interests: s 60CC(1) and (2). The prioritising in the legislation of potentially conflicting goals—being the maintaining the parent/child relationship and protection of children from harm—is now more evident than it was before, and logically the role of contact services in reconciling these conflicting goals will increase.

[8] H Rhoades, R Graycar and M Harrison, *The Family Law Reform Act 1995: The First Three Years. Final Report*, University of Sydney and Family Court of Australia, 2000.

to that. That's the only objective evidence of that. I doubt if judges would have subjectively thought that they were often doing that but it may be that the effect and emphasis of the Family Law Reform Act did have that effect.

In contrast, other referral agents (especially judges) were of the view that the FLRA had no impact at all on ordering of supervised contact and supervised changeover:

> I can't see any difference in the last 10 years. In my view the amendments from 1995 did not make the slightest bit of difference. They were just words without substance. (Federal Magistrate)
> I think the majority of people, particularly the majority of practitioners, see the 1996 amendments as being simply moving deck chairs but providing no real change to the way in which they practise.
> *A confirmation of the previous position?*
> It simply meant you've got to draw your orders differently to take account of the legislation but ...
> *Not a practical change?*
> I don't think there's been a practical change at all. (Family Court judge)

5.2 Changes in Judicial Thinking, and in the Approach of Courts and Lawyers more Broadly

Referral agents (particularly judges and magistrates) often noted that changes in judicial thinking in the High Court and the Full Court of the Family Court had *preceded* the FLRA, leading to more orders for supervised contact and supervised changeover:

> I'm inclined to think that ... I think a lot of the running was being done by the Full Court of the Family Court and the Reform Act tended to reflect what the Full Court was already doing. (Federal Magistrate)

Referral agents also noted other changes related to the court and the legal system that had encouraged use of supervised contact and changeover arrangements. These changes included:

- 'the increase in the number, in the last decade ... of cases involving allegations of child abuse, particularly child sexual abuse' (Chief Justice, Family Court of Australia);
- the enactment of domestic violence legislation;
- the 'pro-contact culture of the Family Court' (Manager, sexual assault/ family violence/domestic violence centre);
- the trend for more contact to be sought and given; and
- lawyers' and clients' increasing awareness of the need to preserve some form of contact between parent and child as a holding position pending final determination of the case.

5.3 The Relevance of Broader Social Changes

Some referral agents saw the FLRA as part of, or a contributor to, a broader societal change in attitudes to contact over the past ten years:

> I think it's more reflective than anything else. But, after it ... there were little bits of publicity that came out in the paper about a proposed change. The next day, people would be ringing up saying, 'Now I've got, you know, now I can have equal time with my children' or they would just tell their spouse that's what they're going to do because they read it in the newspaper or something.
> *Yes.*
> So I've no doubt that the Reform Act bolstered that movement, so there was a bit of the 'chicken and the egg' in it.
> *The perception that there was a change in rights as such.*
> Yes, and it amplified the pressure for change too. (Solicitor)

Broader social changes identified by referral agents as relevant to the increased use of supervised contact and changeover were as follows:

- increased community awareness of the need to protect children from domestic violence and sexual abuse, including violence witnessed by children;
- increased awareness of children's rights, (including the United Nations Convention on the Rights of the Child);
- increased awareness (including media) of the importance of children having contact with their non-resident parent (including allegations of 'parental alienation syndrome');
- increased lobbying by fathers' rights groups to local MPs who put pressure on governments to act on their concerns (including reducing their child support liability);
- increased drug and alcohol abuse;
- increased community acceptance that some parents need assistance with parenting skills, and
- an increasing level of family breakdown, along with increasing consideration of the risk factors for children associated with that and public debate regarding family life.

6. IMPACT OF CCSs ON LEGAL PRACTICE

Most referral agents thought that the existence of CCSs had impacted on legal practice in terms of more orders for supervised contact and changeover being made. CCSs were generally viewed as providing a viable, convenient solution for lawyers and the courts, especially in high-risk cases where contact would not have occurred previously:

> *So do you think the very existence of contact services then has enabled more contact orders to be made?*

In my view unquestionably. There are cases where you'd find it very difficult `to order contact because of the high level of dispute between parents unless you have the availability of a contact centre. But I mean certainly there were cases where contact wouldn't have been as frequent because of the difficulties in having an appropriate safe venue. You often had to find people willing to do it and that wasn't always easy and sometimes it was impossible. It didn't happen or it broke down because we couldn't find appropriate people. And if there was a level of hostility that was too great you just would never find anyone to do it. So contact I think in those cases wouldn't have happened. (Chief Federal Magistrate)

CCSs were also said to have encouraged lawyers to view the option of supervised contact more positively:

> *What sort of factors do you think have affected the ordering of supervised contact and changeovers over the past decade or so?*
> Whether or not there's a contact centre. I think that's a biggy. If there's no contact centre and you can't arrange private supervision, well contact [won't take place] I suppose.
> *Yes, so you think that existence of contact services has had a significant impact on practice?*
> I think it has, yes. It's certainly changed how we thought about supervised contact.
> *Yes? And what do you mean by that?*
> For the better, I think. (Primary Dispute Resolution co-ordinator)

Some referral agents emphasised that the high quality of the service provided by CCSs was also a relevant factor:

> I think that the contact centres have behaved so professionally. There has been broadly speaking within the Court, we believe, the professional acknowledgement of them and a desire to use the services now.
> *So the very existence of contact services has had an impact?*
> Absolutely. It's had an impact because it provides a good result so then it's seen as a very useful thing for the families.
> *So do you think the very existence of contact services has impacted in the way that perhaps orders are being made for contact that perhaps mightn't have been in the past because there was no other way to facilitate contact?*
> I get a lot of consent orders using contact services now, and that's because the solicitors are comfortable with them and tell their clients about them. (Family Court judge)

CCSs could also have a number of practical advantages for lawyers and the courts, by assisting them to resolve conflicts more quickly and easily:

> We don't argue as much. ... I think it gives you a degree of certainly about your client's position, because if they've been accessing the service for a while, it gives you an opportunity to check the records to find out. We can get a report from the service. ... I think that the contact service cuts down on court time, one way or the other. It cuts to the chase. (Solicitor)

What do you think the impact of contact services has been on your legal practice and family practice in general?
Oh it's sensational. It just makes my job so much easier. In the past I would have been perhaps tearing my hair out thinking of some appropriate independent person, where that person might not have even existed, and we might have had to try a number of stop-start regimes to try and get something happening, whereas these days we just simply pick up the phone and book them in and it's just so easy for us. It's just marvellous. (Solicitor)

Some lawyers also viewed contact services as providing peace of mind to judges, and judges thought the same about lawyers:

So I think the Court sees supervised contact as the perfect solution, really, because they are so loathe to give zero contact because of this whole pro-contact culture that's happening. But they do recognise that there may be a risk to the child, so, supervision. That's the solution. (Solicitor)
... referrals to contact centres, in my experience ... have been in an interlocutory phase of the case, where it's basically ordained by the parties ... and the rationale to that I think is safety, because it's the interlocutory phase and you just can't undertake any risk, even though it may be, in the result, unnecessary. (Family Court judge)

However, while there was a broad level of agreement among referral agents that the existence of CCSs had positive impacts on legal practice, there were some distinct points of disagreement. In particular, the convenience of CCSs led some referral agents to think that sometimes, CCSs were being over-utilised:

Lawyers, quite honestly, are trying to get a problem off their own plate. I think that's what they're all trying to do. Like, what the hell are we going to do here? Let's send them to a contact centre. It the easy way out but it's the only way out a lot of the time, and so you just see it as ... Look it's not the curer of all ills, but you hope it is. You sort of think, well if I send them to a contact centre the problem will go away. I don't think it does. (State Magistrate)
... sometimes it's too easy a solution and I believe there are cases where it's used when it's not necessarily required. (Solicitor)
This attitude, however, was not consistently held and may be changing:
... well I think there's kind of a consciousness-raising exercise going on for the practitioners in terms of what might be the appropriate sort of orders to make. There's always been that sort of slight presumption that the contact centres are just available to take anything and so you just whack them into the orders and it becomes their problem. (Solicitor)
The view was also expressed that CCSs were a last-resort option:
I would like to sort of leave our interview on the basis that from my point of view I see the service as being fundamental to the salvation of family relationships in the most extreme of circumstances.... It's almost the last port-of-call and if that fails, ask yourself: Where do you go from there? It's the last port, and therefore it should be given the greatest of respect from people. (Family Court judge)

Referral agents were also divided on whether CCSs served children's best interests, especially whether they protected children. Some referral agents were firmly of the view that the best interests of children were served and children were protected:

> With high risk I think the option is you have some supervision, so the contact centres have been important in creating an environment where there can be contact that is appropriate, but without risk to the children. (Family Court judge)
>   It might be overcautious and it might give us an easy way out, but at least, I think the bottom line is, it protects the kids. (Solicitor)

In contrast, other referral agents had concerns about whether children were being protected. This was often related to the concern that CCSs were being too readily resorted to by judges and lawyers, especially at the interim stage of cases involving allegations of child sexual abuse or other serious problems:

> Whether the contact centres exist or not, we're always faced with the dilemma of ... I mean in most cases of sexual abuse, we don't know whether it really occurred or not, and the Court gives the benefit of the doubt generally in a situation where the allegations have been made.

But if you've got a child who genuinely believes his [mother] or thinks that the Court hasn't looked after him, or a mum or a dad who believes that it's happened but is forced into a contact situation, I think that's a really hard issue, and I don't think a contact centre addresses that problem. ... But I don't think the Court addresses that problem either. (Solicitor)

> So they really need to be having a bit of a think about the alcohol and other drug stuff. And also unmanaged mental health where you've got major bipolar and major personality disorders stuff. Often that's not appropriate to be referring straight off to the contact service. Get that stabilised and then let's have a look at the issue with the contact with your children. ... That's why I think the Court just misses it a bit. (Manager, counselling service)

As these quotes suggest, some referral agents were concerned about the limits of CCSs to resolve the significant problems often faced by the families who accessed them:

> The problems that are problems now are going to remain problems. The problems that I think are intractable are going to remain problems, and they are: clients who lack insight or maturity or intelligence or stability. Not much you can do about that. Those who are intractable in that regard are going to remain intractable and they, I'm sorry, are going to be the people who are going to be found not suitable for contact services like this, because either their attitude is going to stand out like a sphinx right from the beginning, and they might get through the interview process but the moment they hit the contact, their agenda's going to show. It's going to be picked out and got rid of. (Solicitor)
>   It's a very useful bandaid, but we just need to know it is a bandaid. (Psychologist)

7. CONCLUSIONS AND RECOMMENDATIONS

The advent and growth in the numbers of CCSs has had an undoubted impact on legal practice. CCSs are perceived by lawyers, courts and other referral agents as presenting a viable option for facilitating contact that did not previously exist. The questions of whether CCSs are resorted to too readily, and how useful they are in all cases, remain in dispute among referral agents, however. These disagreements are related to broader differences of opinion and emphasis concerning the FLRA, related judicial developments, and broader social changes that have resulted in an increased focus on maintaining contact between parents and their children. Some see contact as always in the child's best interests, others are concerned to weigh up pros and cons. Some see the current 'pro contact culture' as appropriate and beneficial, others see it as unbalanced and potentially dangerous for some children.

Despite these philosophical differences of approach, some clear patterns emerged from the referral agent interviews regarding the process of referral to CCSs, and good practices in relation to referrals to CCSs via court order. The extension of these good practices would have implications for the resourcing of CCSs, the role of the courts, and their own resourcing.

The fact that the great majority of referrals to CCSs are currently made by court order puts the courts in a position to monitor the referral process and to enforce good practices. The fact that it appears that the majority of court orders are made by consent, however, means that such monitoring and enforcement has not occurred systematically. We would argue that courts ought to undertake a monitoring and enforcement role, involving, among other things, greater scrutiny of consent orders. This role may be facilitated by the further development of judicial checklists, guidelines and pro forma orders, and the dissemination of these to all relevant courts (the Family Court, Federal Magistrates' Court, State Magistrates' Courts and Children's Courts), and to solicitors, barristers, child representatives and community legal centres.

The Family Court's current pro forma orders appear to deal effectively with the need to ensure that parties comply expeditiously with the CCS's intake procedures, the possibility that a family may be rejected by the CCS, the fact that it is necessary for the CCS to determine what times are available for contact, and the need to provide flexibility in the event that the frequency or other timing of contact as specified in the order is unable to be met by the CCS. To this list may be added a requirement that lawyers establish whether the relevant CCS currently has a waiting list or is able to take families immediately after assessment. At the same time, it is arguable that federally funded services need to be sufficiently resourced so as to be able to meet demand as it arises rather than having to operate waiting lists. The recent injection of $A17 million in federal funding (see 1, earlier) is unlikely to resolve the problem of demand for CCSs exceeding supply.

Interim orders for supervised contact or changeover are usually expressed to apply until further order (though, according to the pro forma orders, with liberty to apply if the CCS terminates its services or recommends a variation in the orders). The duration of interim orders is dependent on the backlog of cases awaiting trial in the particular court. There appears to be quite a disparity between the duration of interim orders in the Federal Magistrates' Court and the Family Court, although time delay in the Family Court has also been reduced in some instances (such as under the Magellan Project) and the time delay in the Federal Magistrates' Court is increasing. The crucial difference between a relatively short interim stage (six months or less) and a longer one (12–18 months) is that a short interim stage increases the options available to the court in making interim orders in the best interests of the child. In appropriate cases (eg those involving serious allegations of sexual abuse) a short interim stage gives the court a real choice between no contact and supervised contact, whereas a long interim stage takes away that choice, because the consequences of suspending contact for 12–18 months are potentially much more damaging for the parent–child relationship. If the Family Court was sufficiently resourced to enable it to process cases more quickly, it could make more considered referrals to CCSs at the interim stage.

The duration, review and possible phasing out of final orders for supervised contact or changeover are not addressed by the current pro forma orders, but are the issues most contested among the referral agents we interviewed, and apparently most fudged in current practice. A good practice solution to this set of issues should incorporate the following:

- recognition that final orders for use of a CCS are appropriate in some cases and may be made;
- sufficient resourcing of federally funded CCSs to enable them to provide longer-term supervision services in appropriate cases;
- the principle that no family should be forced to move to 'self-management' simply because time or the number of visits have run out at the CCS;
- specification in final orders for supervised contact or changeover of a fixed duration for supervision, or a regime for phasing out supervision, as appropriate to the particular case;
- if a fixed duration is specified, return to court at the end of that period (or if the CCS terminates the service or recommends variation at an earlier date) for formal review and continuation or variation of orders;
- if the parties have agreed to an alternative arrangement by the end of the specified period, this can be embodied in consent orders, but there should be no expectation that parties must do this or pressure exerted on them to do so; and
- provision of legal aid for parties needing to return to court to review supervision orders.

Finally, provisions noted by some referral agents that positively empower the CCS to give reasonable directions to parties and to exercise discretion to stop contact, on a particular occasion or permanently, should form part of standard orders, as should provisions enabling the child representative to provide information to and receive information from the CCS.

Since the completion of this project, the Federal Government has begun to establish 65 Family Relationship Centres (FRCs) around Australia to help parents work out post-separation parenting arrangements without lawyers or courts being involved, and has amended the Family Law Act 1975 (Cth) to encourage shared parenting post-parental separation, discourage use of the legal system to resolve parenting disputes, and make the court system less adversarial. The changes require parents to attend a session with a 'family dispute resolution practitioner' at a FRC or other service before they can file an application in court for a parenting order with limited exceptions, including cases involving family violence or child abuse (the prime categories for CCS involvement) which, it is intended, will proceed straight to court.[9]

The new family dispute resolution requirements are still being implemented. However, it is interesting to contemplate how the introduction of FRCs/family dispute resolution practitioners will fit into the overall referral process. There appear to be three options: (1) that they screen appropriately for violence/child abuse and refer those cases to lawyers and the court, and the system will continue to operate much as it has done to date; (2) that they do not screen appropriately for violence and child abuse, but rather attempt to 'resolve' those matters out of court, which may mean that fewer cases than ought to reach CCSs (or reach CCSs later than they ought to), with resulting increased risk to children and their mothers; (3) that FRCs/family dispute resolution practitioners themselves become referral agents, perhaps sending families directly to contact services when family violence/child abuse is identified. If option (3) occurs, then they will need to be aware of protocols and best practices in the referral process, and CCSs will gain another constituency that they will have to liaise with and train in referral protocols.

---

[9] Family Law Amendment (Shared Parental Responsibility) Act 2006 (Cth).

11

Intervening in Litigated Contact: Ideas from Other Jurisdictions

JOAN HUNT

INTRODUCTION

The Current Position in England and Wales

IN ENGLAND AND Wales only a minority of parents, around 10 per cent, use the courts to make arrangements for their children after separation and divorce (Blackwell and Dawe, 2003). There is no requirement to seek a court order for either contact or residence; indeed this is positively discouraged by the minimum intervention principle in the governing legislation—the 1989 Children Act—which states that the court shall not make an order unless satisfied that it is necessary to do so. Thus the courts only deal with disputes. Levels of conflict even among families who use the courts only once are already strikingly high (Trinder, 2004). About half the applications before the court at any one time are repeat applications, of which around a third are brought because of alleged breach of court-ordered arrangements (DCA, 2004). Many of these families are likely to be trapped in entrenched conflict.

Services to assist litigating families and/or the courts are still fairly rudimentary. Publicly funded mediation is available on a voluntary basis. Further opportunities for dispute resolution are available in some courts, usually in the form of an interview with an officer of the Children and Family Court Advisory and Support Service (CAFCASS) prior to the first directions hearing. It is planned to extend this across the country. Currently CAFCASS's main role in private law is to provide welfare reports to the court and, increasingly, though still not frequently, representation for children (in conjunction with a solicitor). Further expert advice may be sought from other experts, usually jointly instructed.

There is also provision for post-order help through a Family Assistance Order, typically serviced through CAFCASS. This potentially useful mechanism is currently rarely used though this may change with the passage of legislation currently before Parliament (now the Children and Adoption

Act, 2006) which removes the requirement that it can only be ordered in 'exceptional circumstances' and extends the maximum duration from 6 to 12 months. Families may also be referred to contact centres for supported or supervised contact. And of course there are a range of community facilities (such as counselling and family therapy) available either through the NHS or voluntary/private agencies though these are not commonly used and cannot be ordered by the court.

Recent Developments

As in many other countries contact has become a highly controversial and politicised issue, with groups representing non-resident parents, typically fathers, demanding changes in legislation to enact, variously, a legal presumption of contact, a presumption of shared residence or minimum levels of contact. To date government has resisted these calls, defending the individualised 'best interests of the child' criteria laid down in the Children Act. It has also, however, come under pressure, particularly from the senior judiciary, to enhance the ability and powers of the courts to deal with difficult contact disputes, most especially those where contact is deemed to be being denied or obstructed without reasonable cause. While the extent and nature of this 'problem' is not known, there is a dominant perception that it exists and needs to be tackled.

Central to developments in this area has been the report *Making Contact Work* (Advisory Board on Family Law, 2002) the result of a national consultation exercise by the Children Act Sub-Committee of the Family Law Advisory Board, a body set up to advise government. It is worth noting the report's sub-title: *A Report to the Lord Chancellor on the Facilitation of Arrangements for Contact between Children and their Non-resident Parents and the Enforcement of Court Orders for Contact*. Although the original remit was non-compliance, the Committee decided to extend this to the broader question of facilitation, taking the view that enforcement should be very much a last resort and that the key was to find ways of preventing difficulties escalating to this point, including community-based services. The report recommended enhanced powers for the courts, including powers to order litigating families into a range of services as well a wider range of enforcement options.

Although the Government quickly accepted virtually all the recommendations of the report, those dealing with the services and powers available to the courts, most of which required legislation, are only now being actioned in the Children and Adoption Act 2006. This contains new penalties (financial compensation and community service) for resident parents who fail to comply with contact orders, though the most draconian new measures (curfews and electronic tagging) proposed in a draft bill (DfES, 2005) have been dropped following trenchant criticism by a parliamentary committee (House of Commons, 2005). Courts will also be able to order parents to take part in 'contact activities'. These are defined as attending an information session, or taking part in a programme, class, counselling or guidance session or other activity devised for the purpose of 'assisting a person to establish, maintain or improve contact'. CAFCASS is to be given duties to monitor compliance with both contact orders and contact activities and, as mentioned earlier, there are changes to Family Assistance Orders.

In order to implement the legislation a great deal will need to be done to develop new services, and the experience of other jurisdictions is obviously very relevant. Indeed a striking theme in many of the often heated debates about contact is that it is handled much better elsewhere, and that particular interventions have been proved to work. Such claims can rapidly acquire the status of proven fact, simply by repetition, when on close examination some turn out to be based on a misunderstanding of other legal systems or a limited appreciation of what constitutes 'evidence' of effectiveness.

The Research Study

The study on which this chapter is based was undertaken in an attempt to facilitate a more informed and evidence-based approach to the legitimate desire to learn from other jurisdictions. The aim was to identify forms of intervention which were not a routine part of the UK court system for dealing with disputed contact, and to examine what evidence there was for their effectiveness. It is important to emphasise the limitations of the study, determined by constraints of time, resources and language. In particular, since it could not be set up as a collaborative exercise with researchers in other countries, the number of jurisdictions covered was restricted to Australia, Canada, New Zealand, the United States and western European countries. It was largely dependent on English language published research or material available on the internet, which together produced a bias towards US research. Although considerable efforts were made to contact a range of people who were thought likely to be able to supply information and provide leads, the response was somewhat patchy. Finally, although in the course of the study a considerable amount of material was collected on what does and does not happen in other jurisdictions, the aim was not to document this and thus to provide a comprehensive descriptive comparison, but to extract from the material information relevant to the UK context.

EDUCATION IN POST-SEPARATION PARENTING

In the US and Canada, classes are a common and often mandatory stage in the legal process, either for all divorcing parents or for those litigating children's issues (Bacon and McKenzie 2001; Erickson and Ver Steegh, 2001). They are under active consideration in New Zealand and the Netherlands. The Australian Family Court requires attendance at basic information meetings and has a number of more elaborate community-based programmes, although currently only parents in breach of contact orders can be ordered to attend. In England and Wales a very basic form of parent education—information meetings—based on the Australian model, were trialled a few years ago as part of the process all parents would have had to go through before obtaining a divorce under what was expected to be a reformed divorce law. However, although the results appeared promising, the relevant sections of the legislation were not implemented (Walker, 2001). Currently a more sophisticated form is being piloted as part of the Family Resolutions Project for parents litigating contact issues.[1]

The myriad different programmes in the US vary in length, aims and teaching methods. However, broadly, they aim to increase knowledge of the impact of separation on children; improve parental communication; reduce children's exposure to conflict and as a result and facilitate their post-separation adjustment. Most programmes are short (1–2 sessions of up to three hours) with limited participant involvement, relying on lectures, videos and handouts to increase knowledge and understanding (Geasler and Blaisure, 1999). Some programmes, such as the Children in the Middle programme (Arbuthnot et al, 1996) use more interactive approaches to help parents develop practical skills in conflict management and communication and there is some evidence that these are more effective (Kramer et al, 1998; Krolczyk, 2001).

Are Programmes Effective?

The almost wholesale endorsement of these programs has occurred prior to the conducting of ongoing serious systematic research into their effectiveness. (Whitworth et al, 2002: 14).

Educational programmes clearly meet a need, typically reporting high levels of parental satisfaction (90 per cent and above), even among those ordered to attend. The importance of this should not be discounted. They are also highly regarded by professionals (Bacon and McKenzie, 2001; Fischer, 1997; Geasler and Blaisure, 1999; Hughes and Kirby, 2000). However, the

---

[1] Under this scheme parents are encouraged to attend two classes aimed at sensitising parents to the impact of conflict on children and developing their skills in dealing with each other. They are then offered one or more meetings with a CAFCASS officer to develop a parenting plan. The scheme, which is based on methods used in Florida, is being trialled in three areas.

effectiveness of most has not been proved (Grych, 2005; Goodman et al, 2004; Whitworth et al, 2002). Only a minority have been evaluated, typically, by means of exit surveys. There are some studies measuring impact by means of before and after measures but few using control groups. Where robust research has been carried out the findings are mixed, suggesting that programmes are not of equal efficacy. Indeed, a systematic review of research on the impact of parent education on inter-parental conflict found only four short, court-related programmes which had been researched to the necessary standards. Of these there was some evidence that one programme (Children in the Middle) had an effect but sparse evidence that the others did (Goodman et al, 2004).

Programmes have been found to achieve their objectives of enabling parents to acquire and retain useful knowledge, understanding and skills (Arbuthnot et al, 1996; Arbuthnot, Kramer and Gordon, 1996; Pedro-Carroll et al, 2001; Thoennes and Pearson, 1999a) and giving them more confidence in dealing with the children and even their ex-partner (McKenzie and Guberman, 1997; Thoennes and Pearson, 1999a). These may translate into improvements in *parental* well-being although findings using comparison groups are mixed (Arbuthnot, Kramer and Gordon, 1996; Buehler et al, 1992; Kramer and Washo, 1993). There is some evidence of attitudinal change and expressed intentions to make more effort to work with the other parent (Loveridge, 1995; Mayes et al, 2000; Pedro-Carroll et al, 2001). Not all parents act on these—in one study six months on only two-thirds had used suggestions relating to contact (Thoennes and Pearson, 1999a). But many do try (McKenzie and Guberman, 1997) and some report improved relationships, with better communication and reduced conflict (Bacon and McKenzie, 2001; Criddle et al, 2003; Gray et al, 1997; Stone et al, 1999), including conflict specifically about contact. These are probably not just the result of time passing: two of three studies using comparison groups show greater changes among attendees (Arbuthnot et al, 1997; Buehler et al, 1992; Thoennes and Pearson, 1999a).

Protecting children from conflict is one of the key messages educational programmes try to get across. They are not always successful–focus groups with children in one project reported parents engaging in behaviour specifically discouraged by the programme (Hans and Fine, 2001). However, positive findings are reported in several studies (Arbuthnot et al, 1996; Bacon and McKenzie, 2001; Gray et al, 1997; McKenzie and Guberman, 1997), including one of the more robust, while one study, although finding no overall differences, reported significant differences in the behaviour of higher conflict parents (Kramer and Washo, 1993). Moreover, this study reported parents' perceptions of the behaviour of their ex-partner, which provides somewhat stronger evidence of impact than self-reported behaviour which might be somewhat idealised.

The ongoing involvement of the non-resident parent may be facilitated. One study of a number of Canadian programmes (Bacon and McKenzie, 2001) reported a slight increase post-attendance in encouraging the child's relationship with the other parent, willingness to accommodate changes in arrangements, and discussion of parenting issues, and although the amount of contact did not change, satisfaction with the arrangements did. Another multiple site study in the US (Thoennes and Pearson, 1999a) found that only 19 per cent of attenders had irregular or no contact (compared with 30 per cent where there was no programme). Levels of contact may be higher (DeLuse, 1999). Participants in one programme (Children in the Middle) were reported to be more willing than a comparison group to share children's time almost equally (Arbuthnot and Kramer, 1998).

Despite a professional perception that parenting education promotes dispute resolution the research is insubstantial. While many parents report greater willingness to use mediation on completing the programme (87 per cent in one study: Pedro-Carroll et al, 2001) few appear to do so (Seippert et al, 1999; Bacon and McKenzie, 2001) though some are reported to have reached agreement informally or at least made more efforts to do so. There is some evidence that attendance is correlated with fewer court hearings and shorter proceedings (Ellis and Anderson, 2003) and higher settlement rates in mediation (Dyer, 1989). However, most evaluations do not measure settlement patterns.

The evidence on re-litigation is sparse and inconsistent. While a few studies (Arbuthnot et al, 1997; Leitz-Spitz, 2002; Criddle et al, 2003) report reduced rates (half that of a comparison group over a two year period being the most dramatic); others find no difference (Free, 1998; McKenry et al, 1999; De Luse, 1999; Thoennes and Pearson, 1999a) and one even reports higher rates (McClure, 2002). One programme produced positive results in one evaluation but not in two others. However, a more encouraging finding comes from a study which, while recording no overall reduction in litigation, did find a difference for the most conflicted parents (Kramer and Kowal, 1998). There is also a little evidence to suggest that participation early in the court process may affect litigation rates (Arbuthnot et al, 1997; Vanhoy and Pitts (1995, unpublished, cited in Bussey, 1996).

Probably the most disappointing finding is that court-related programmes have not been able to demonstrate a positive effect on child well-being. The children may become better adjusted, but so do those whose parents have not attended (Arbuthnot et al, 1996; Kramer and Washo, 1993). The passage of time, not attendance, would appear to be the crucial factor. This contrasts with the positive impact consistently demonstrated by a programme focusing on improving the parenting capacity of the resident parent, the New Beginnings programme in Arizona, an eight-week, university run programme. Work has now begun on trying to adapt this programme for use by the courts (Wolchik et al, 2005).

The Case for Compulsion

The effectiveness of parent education programmes as a genre has not been conclusively proven. Such positive impacts as have been demonstrated are not dramatic and researchers caution against unrealistic expectations: such a short-term, limited intervention does not, and cannot be expected to, revolutionalise post-separation parenting (Hans and Fine, 2001; Bacon and McKenzie, 2001; Thoennes and Pearson, 1999a). However, on the whole commentators seem to consider that programmes can make a useful contribution as part of a spectrum of services.

It is hard to argue on the basis of the available evidence of effectiveness that programmes should be compulsory. The fact is, however, that without compulsion most parents, and perhaps particularly those most in need, are unlikely to attend (O'Connor, 2002; Mayes et al, 2000), which will severely handicap any attempt to develop more effective programmes. Being required to attend does not appear to reduce the effect of the programmes (Gray et al, 1997); initial resentment tends to dissipate (McKenry et al, 1998); and most parents express satisfaction with the experience (Loveridge, 1995) and agree that attendance should be required (Bacon and McKenzie, 2001). Provided adequate attention is paid to the issue of domestic violence (through screening, exemptions or targeted content) programmes are unlikely to do any harm and may help—and as far as many parents are concerned they do help. On balance, therefore, a degree of compulsion may not be unreasonable.

SERVICES FOR HIGHER CONFLICT FAMILIES

While standard parent education and mediation may help many parents to resolve their disputes over contact, jurisdictions where these interventions are well established are increasingly recognising that some high conflict families cannot benefit (American Bar Association Family Law Section, 2001; Doolittle and Deutsch, 1999; Elrod, 2001) and need more specialised interventions. Some of the services which the international literature sees as necessary (Schepard, 2004) are already available in the UK, even if perhaps not in sufficient quantity or able to be ordered by the court (eg supervised contact and handover; neutral assessment; child representation; individual and family counselling and therapy; substance abuse and domestic violence programmes). Others, such as the ones examined here, are more innovative. Typically, however, these are still in the early stages of development and evaluations are rare and usually limited.

Multi-method Interventions

One of the most ambitious attempts to meet the needs of high conflict/ enforcement cases is Australia's Contact Orders Pilot. The three agencies involved in the project, which all had a track record in helping separated families on a voluntary basis, have had to adapt their services to meet the rather different needs of court-ordered families. While the detail of pro-grammes differ, all employ a range of interventions, tailored to individual needs, including group work; education; counselling; modified mediation; children's programmes; supervised contact; overall case management and telephone support. The Government has expressed itself satisfied with the results of the pilot:

> The very successful Contact Orders Programme has used a mixture of interven-tions to address the needs of families struggling with the emotional and practi-cal consequences of family breakdown. Through this programme, high conflict couples are able to move towards self-management of their child contact arrange-ments and, as a result, both parents become more involved in caring for and guiding their children. The Government will expand this very valuable service (Attorney-General's Department, 2003a).

It should be noted, however, that the evidence on which this assessment is based is extremely limited. It is understood that there were problems carrying out the original ambitious research design and the full report is not being published. All that is available is a summary, which indicates that clients are struck by the mix of services available, which is different from anything else they have been offered; and 88 per cent are positive, reporting that they learned communication techniques and dispute resolution skills; felt less isolated and had greater understanding of their children's experiences. However, this falls far short of the original specification of what would constitute proof. If the programme is to be successful, then separated or divorced families' management of relationship difficulties will be improved. Children's contact and relationships with both parents will be facilitated in a manner which encourages consideration of what is in the child's best interests, while ensuring the safety of all parties. The adversarial nature of family disputes will be reduced and there will be less use made of the Family Court or other legal processes in relation to issues about contact with children. Children's relationships with their non-residential parent will be established or maintained and a workable relationship will be negotiated between separated or divorced parents in relation to their ongoing parenting responsibilities (Department of Family and Community Services, undated).

Another example of multi-method intervention is the Court Care Center for Divorcing Families in Florida's Ninth Judicial Circuit, which offers assessment and assignment to a range of services either provided in-house or through referral to other agencies. Evaluation is in progress (Homrich et al, 2004).

Educational Programmes

Standard educational programmes are likely to include at least a proportion of higher conflict families and, as indicated earlier, research on one programme suggested that they were likely to experience more benefit (Kramer and Washo, 1993). There is also an interesting (voluntary) programme in Manitoba (For the Sake of the Children) which offers one common three-hour session to all parents, who then choose to attend either a class for low to moderate conflict families, or one for high conflict families. Parents are helped to make the choice by completing a questionnaire on their relationship. The high conflict option is more skills-based, and aims to help parents manage conflicted relationships. The programme evaluation (McKenzie and Guberman, 1997) reported that parents who registered higher levels of conflict prior to attendance demonstrated greater gains in personal adjustment, positive parenting, satisfaction with custody, access and child support and conflicts with the other parent that put children in the middle. They also reported more positive changes in their children's adjustment and in some respects those attending the second level programme reported greater changes in this than those who opted out after level one. However, while the results suggested that high conflict parents could benefit, the evaluation concluded that a six-hour programme was not sufficient to address the needs of very high conflict families and that while it provided an important initial resource, more was needed.

Educational programmes specifically for higher conflict families have recently become a growth area in the US. While universal programmes typically emphasise co-operative parenting, some of these aim to teach 'parallel parenting' approaches, recognising that co-operative parenting is impossible for many high conflict families and, by requiring parental interaction, may even exacerbate their problems (Elrod, 2001). For example, *Parents Apart*, in San Diego, California, is a five-hour programme which aims to reduce opportunities for conflict by advising parents to eliminate all direct contact for two years, communicate even indirectly as little as possible, operate on the basis of an unchanged parenting plan and create separate worlds within which to parent the children (Stacer and Stemen, 2000). Unfortunately no evaluation data is yet available. Oregon's ten-hour Parents Beyond Conflict programme aims to reframe parents' negative perceptions of each other. Initial data are positive but very limited: parents are appreciative and most are able to make use of the concepts; judges perceive that families are less likely to return to court and when they do their behaviour is improved (McIsaac and Finn, 1999).

Maricopa County, Arizona, has recently introduced a four-hour educational programme—the Parental Conflict Resolution programme—which focuses on the (controversial) topic of parental alienation, though not, it appears, in the sense of a syndrome with a single cause. Rather the programme explains the complex dynamics involved, emphasising it is more likely to be the unintended effect of inter-parental hostility than deliberate brainwashing, and that both parents may be contributing to the problem. It addresses the long-term consequences, not just for the children but for the parents, and what each can do to change things. The programme is unusual in that, rather than seeking to work through engaging parents' concern for their children, it 'appeals heavily to each parent's self-interest', on the basis that:

> a high proportion of parents in high conflict are personality disordered and that the most effective intervention is to point out, clearly, simply and repeatedly, the consequences of continuing their present course of action (Neff and Cooper, 2004).

Perhaps surprisingly, participants are reported to engage with and learn from the programme and express high levels of satisfaction both immediately and at follow-up, with 80 per cent reporting that their children were doing better and 61 per cent that there was less inter-parental hostility. Given the nature of the client group these findings are encouraging but in the absence of a comparison group they can only be regarded as promising (Neff and Cooper, 2004).

The only course which appears to have been substantially researched is an older programme in Los Angeles now called Parenting Without Conflict, but which when originally set up in 1989 went by the forbidding but unambiguous title of the Pre-Contempt/Contemnors Program. As this name suggests, the programme mainly targets parents in breach of court orders or involved in intense conflict/chronic litigation. Most are court-ordered although lawyers can also refer. Both parents attend (separately) six two-hour sessions, run weekly by Family Court Services. Between 25–75 people attend each class. A certificate of attendance is required by the judge, who may also order parents to produce a paper or return to court to demonstrate what they have learned. The programme includes lectures; small group discussion using vignettes; videos; role play and skill practice sessions with extensive written material provided in advance (Elrod, 2001; Kibler et al, 1994).

The programme has been the subject of at least three evaluations although one was part of an evaluation of several different types of programme and results were not reported separately. Findings are mixed. In the only published study (Pearson and Thoennes, 1998), 62 per cent of non-resident fathers reported improvement and 27 per cent an increase in contact. However, half reported continuing problems and 53 per cent of mothers had safety concerns. There was no comparison group and no evaluation of re-litigation or impact on the children. A more substantial study, only available from the author (Johnston, 1999) reported positive client evaluations, and found that nine months on parents were significantly more co-operative and communicative, had a greater understanding of children's needs and their own role in disputes and were better able to protect children from conflict. Domestic violence had diminished. However, results were not quite as good as the comparator programme (the Alameda therapeutic mediation model, see later). Moreover, one year on, compared with parents not included in the programme, there was no difference in the number of new applications, actions for contempt of court, rates of agreement in mediation or the number of hours of mediation required, results which were described as 'disappointing'.

Therapeutic Mediation

This form of intervention aims to meet the needs of highly conflicted couples who cannot mediate because they are blocked by the emotional baggage from their relationship. It combines mediation techniques with therapeutic counselling, the mediator taking a directive role, assisting the parties to identify and tackle the obstacles impeding negotiation and adopting an active educative and advocacy role in relation to the needs of the child (Pruett and Johnston, 2004; Smyth and Moloney, 2003). There are a number of emerging variants, including one using a mediator/therapist team (Smyth and Moloney, 2003) and one actively involving lawyers (Pruett and Johnston, 2004).

Central to the development of this form of intervention has been the work of Janet Johnston in Alameda County, California, where both individual and group models have been developed. Projects based on her ideas have been trialled in other parts of the US (Neff and Cooper, 2004), Australia (ALRC, 1995) and Canada (Elrod, 2001).

The individual model takes about around 27 hours' of work over 12 weeks. The first phase involves assessment and individual counselling with each parent and child. Crucially, knowledge from the children's sessions is used to sensitise and counsel parents. This is followed by the dispute resolution phase after which any agreement reached is reviewed by parents' lawyers. The practitioner remains available to the family for emergencies and continuing mediation. An evaluation of this model found that 83 per cent of court-referred parents, who had all failed to resolve their disputes in standard mediation, reached agreement and two years on 60 per cent had adhered to, or been able to renegotiate, the arrangements. Parents reported a marked decline in hostility and conflict and both physical and verbal aggression had declined to the level of the whole divorcing population. On the downside, 36 per cent had returned to court, 23 per cent twice or more, and 15 per cent of the whole sample were actually doing worse than before (Pruett and Johnston, 2004).

An even more intensive individual model involves counselling for 3–5 hours per week for two months, plus frequent phone calls, diminishing to 1–2 hours per week for the next 2–6 months plus a follow-up period of 1–2 hours per month and telephone counselling. A follow-up evaluation found significant shifts in levels of hostility, distrust of the other's parenting and dissatisfaction with custody/contact. Relitigation was reduced to a sixth of previous levels (though 34 per cent returned to court over contact). Children were coping better in some respects. Nonetheless, the researchers considered many remained at risk because of parental hostility, albeit muted by the intervention. (Pruett and Johnston, 2004).

In the group model, which takes 16 hours over eight weeks, parents meet separately in gender-mixed groups for four weeks during which time parallel group sessions are held for children, with the objective of providing them with peer group support. The parent groups then combine and receive feedback from the children's group leaders, including information about how each child is coping. The final sessions are used by some parents to mediate a parenting plan although the primary aim of the programme is said to be to help the family through the transition, rather than settlement per se. Other aims are: to help parents communicate better and understand their child's perspective and the impact of their conflict on their child; reduce excessive litigation and dependence on the court and increase compliance with parenting plans and court orders.

Two evaluations have been carried out on this model, though it should be noted that neither has involved an independent researcher. The first, which compared it to the individual model, found it as effective, with about two-thirds of parents able to keep or renegotiate agreements and stay out of court for a 2–3 year period. The second, which involved a comparison with the Los Angeles Parenting Without Conflict educational programme, found that though it was less popular with parents outcomes were similar and in some respects better. Parents reported more substantial gains: women reported less violence and more communication; men reported greater co-operation. Moreover, unlike the Los Angeles programme, there was a reduction in re-litigation compared with parents not offered the intervention (of the order of one third). The number of hearings reduced as did the number of hours of mediation required. Mediators rated families significantly better than before, while the comparison group remained the same or worse (Johnston, 1999).

Post-order Support

As mentioned above, the UK already has a formal mechanism—the Family Assistance Order—for helping litigating families manage post-order parenting. This appears to be unusual, few other jurisdictions seem to provide specific post-order support, although families can presumably make use of any services, such as counselling, available to the broader separated community. In Germany, for instance, all separating parents are entitled to help with contact from the equivalent of social services (Maclean and Mueller-Johnson, 2003).

Despite the existence of the Family Assistance Order, however, which is little used (James, 1999) in reality little is currently available in the UK in the way of post-order support (Buchanan et al, 2001). In the US, however, post-proceedings intervention for high conflict/repeatedly litigating families is a fast developing area, with the introduction by many states of what are generically called 'parenting coordinators', though names differ (Coates et al, 2003, 2004). These are mental health or legal professionals appointed by the court, usually with the consent of both parents, and almost always at their expense, for a period of up to two years. What is particularly novel is that not only do co-ordinators seek to help parents implement their parenting plan, educate them about the needs of their children and mediate disputes, they are also typically authorised to arbitrate certain post-order issues and may be able to order parents to obtain services. Parents can seek a court hearing if they are not satisfied, and the co-ordinator can also return the case to court. According to a recent overview:

> The parents ideally learn more functional dispute resolution strategies and conflict management that cannot occur through repeated exposure to the legal/adversarial process. At a minimum the parents have a stable, knowledgeable and readily accessible professional to resolve day to day disputes (Coates et al, 2004).

There is said to be positive clinical and anecdotal evidence of effectiveness (Coates et al, 2003) with parents, lawyers and judges reportedly satisfied, and conflict reduced, although it is also noted that parent co-ordinators see many families who do not respond. However, research appears to be confined to three localised studies, all unpublished. A survey of parents and co-ordinators in Colorado reported most clients were satisfied and conflict diminished (Vick and Backerman, 1996, cited Sullivan, 2004). In California court review of the co-ordinator's decisions is said to be rarely requested (Kelly, 2002, citing own unpublished work). Another Californian study reported that a group of parents who had had an average of six court appearances in the year preceding the appointment of the co-ordinator had reduced this to 22 the following year (Johnston, 1994, cited Sullivan, 2004).

Amplified Contact Supervision

Supervised contact facilities now exist in many countries, including the UK. One developing area internationally is the addition of complementary services within or closely linked to the centres (eg counselling, education and facilitative/therapeutic supervision aimed at improving parental relationships or parent/child interaction) which are still fairly unusual here. According to a survey in the US, for instance, 35 per cent of centres offer psychotherapeutic intervention (Thoennes and Pearson, 1999b). Of particular interest are developments in Germany where since 1998 public welfare services have been responsible for ensuring the provision of supervised contact as part of their general responsibilities for children (though typically accomplished through contracts with private agencies). Each family has their own facilitator, who works out individual plans, which have to be agreed with the welfare authority and supervision, including off-site, is provided by highly qualified professionals. Counselling is mandatory since facilitating contact without addressing the parental relationship is considered pointless (Maclean and Mueller-Johnson, 2003). However, as reported by Mueller-Johnson (this volume) early research is limited and shows mixed results, with quite high levels of parental satisfaction with the process, but little evidence of changed relationships.

TACKLING ALLEGED NON-COMPLIANCE WITH COURT ORDERS

It is a striking feature of the UK debates about contact that the 'problem' of non-compliance with court orders is almost always construed in terms of the resident parent denying contact. Non-resident fathers who do not comply with the terms of the order rarely feature. While there are a number of interventions outside the court system designed to increase parental involvement post separation, it is very unusual for resident parents to be able to take court action to require this, even where contact is construed as the right of the child rather than, or as well as, the right of the parent. The interventions covered in this section all reflect this bias.

Few jurisdictions have developed a response to non-compliance which goes beyond punitive/deterrent sanctions: typically fines and imprisonment, occasionally bonds, community service; compensatory or even supplementary contact, reimbursement of expenses or legal costs and fines payable to the other parent. In the Netherlands it is possible to temporarily suspend child support and to terminate adult maintenance, while some US states can additionally suspend occupational, driving or sports licences. Powers to invoke assistance with collecting the child where contact is denied are common, as is the facility to change custody/residence/parental rights. Indeed in Rhode Island there has been a presumption that residence will be changed on a third breach.

There appears to be no research on the effectiveness of any of these sanctions and indeed little information on the extent to which they are actually used. However, as in the UK, there appears to be a fairly widespread perception that punitive sanctions are not commonly used and/or that they are ineffective, inappropriate and even counter-productive, and are likely to harm the child. While this has prompted demands for judges to be less 'soft' it has also stimulated a search for more creative responses (eg in Australia, Canada, Finland, New Zealand and the US). Australia, notably, has attempted to pursue both paths simultaneously.

Although interventions aimed specifically at non-compliance cases are even thinner on the ground than those for the broader group of high conflict cases there are some interesting, if not proven, approaches.

Clarification of Orders

A key theme in the admittedly very limited research on non-compliance is that in many instances it flows from vague or poorly framed/understood orders, often originally made by consent (Australian Attorney-General's Department, 2003b; Pearson and Price, 2002). In Arizona research on Maricopa County's Expedited Visitation Services, which deals with breach applications, found that in 44 per cent of cases the order was made more specific (Pearson and Thoennes, 1998). Reflecting this recognition, in Sioux Falls, South Dakota, the first response to a complaint is for a court-contracted lawyer to restate the terms of the original order in simple terms, warning that failure to comply may lead to contempt action. As a preventative measure all consent orders are also being reviewed to clarify ambiguities (Pearson and Price, 2002).

Dedicated Systems to Ensure a Rapid Response

Several US states have established special processes to ensure a rapid response to a complaint, bringing the case before a specially designated officer of the court within a couple of weeks. There are examples in Arizona (Maricopa County's Expedited Visitation Services); Michigan (the Friend of the Court scheme) and Utah (the Expedited Parent-time Enforcement Program). After initial evaluation, the officer will attempt to resolve the dispute or refer to mediation or other services. Where a court hearing is needed, in Michigan the 'Friend of the Court' will bring the proceedings; elsewhere unrepresented litigants will usually be given assistance with the application. Court officers may be expected to provide recommendations to the court, including referrals to services.

Mediation

The UK Government has made it clear that mediation is not included as one of the contact activities to which, under the forthcoming legislation, defaulting parents will be ordered. In some jurisdictions, however, such as the US states mentioned in the previous section, and also in Finland, compulsory non-confidential mediation is the first step in dealing with cases where a breach of a contact order is alleged. It is also of note that something similar is envisaged under legislation currently before the Australian Parliament[2] (Australian Government, 2005). Before filing a breach application (with some exceptions) parents would be required to contact one of the new Family Relationships Centres (Parkinson, 2004) which would seek to settle the issues through dispute resolution techniques or refer the family, on a voluntary basis, to a specialist programme such as the Contact Orders Program in which a form of mediation is one of the services on offer (Australian Government, 2004).

Evaluations of existing mediation schemes in enforcement cases are sparse and limited in scope. In Finland a substantial proportion of cases have been reported to settle (52 per cent compared with 39 per cent without mediation) (Kurki-Suono, 2004). In Utah, 51 per cent of cases settle in full and 26 per cent in part, with 60 per cent of parents rating the service as good to excellent, and strong support reported from family justice professionals (personal communication with the programme director). Follow-up data is, however, lacking. The scheme in Maricopa County has been more extensively evaluated (see below) but only limited data is reported on the mediation element.

Educational Interventions

As reported earlier education classes for high conflict/non-compliance cases have been developed in a few US states, eg Maricopa County, Arizona, and Los Angeles, California. In Australia, where referral to parenting programmes was the most significant innovation in the new compliance regime, classes form an important element in service provision. These programmes are covered in more detail elsewhere in this chapter.

Monitoring

Monitoring was a key feature of Maricopa County's enforcement programme for many years, although this has now been abandoned because of funding problems. However, there are interesting examples elsewhere, which both offer more than simple checking up. In Greenlee County, Arizona, a third party is contracted to handle all the mechanics of contact, in order to ensure that parents do not have to interact over changes or cancellations. A report

---

[2] Now the Family Law Amendment (Shared Responsibility) Act 2006.

from each parent is obtained after every visit, records complaints and can be called on in any litigation. In Utah monitoring is part of a bundle of services (including education and supervised contact) designed to help parents address the problems impeding implementation of the court order. So far, neither of these programmes has been evaluated. Monitoring is also part of the role of some parenting co-ordinators (see section on services for high conflict families).

The Need for Realistic Expectations

As will be apparent, Maricopa County's Expedited Visitation Services combines a number of different enforcement elements. This scheme has been evaluated several times (albeit before the addition of the education class and while monitoring was still in place). A number of positive findings are reported. Punitive remedies and court-ordered custody changes are rare and although many orders are upheld, rather than made more specific or renegotiated, compliance rates are described as 'high' (though frustratingly no figures are given). Litigation rates tended to decline. Around 60 per cent of parents were satisfied with the process and 69 per cent of non-resident fathers reported their situation had improved (Pearson and Anhalt, 1994; Pearson and Thoennes 1998). Unusually there is also a study of children's experiences which reported a significant reduction in children's perceptions of conflict without any evidence that enforcement adversely affected child adjustment (Lee and Shaugnessy, 1995).

More negatively, one-third of parents reported no resolution of their difficulties and one year on 81 per cent reported they were still experiencing problems. Worryingly, 42 per cent of mothers cited concerns about safety. Moreover, any improvements are not necessarily attributable to the programme: the only study to use a control group found very little difference a year on, indeed on one measure, perceived improvement, the non-programme group were more satisfied. The only statistically significant difference was that resident mothers were less apt to complain children were upset at handover, that the father was unsupportive of their role and there were still disagreements about custody (Pearson and Thoennes, 1998).

Research on a variety of (US) enforcement programmes (Pearson and Thoennes, 1998) found substantial levels of user satisfaction, even among parents with more protracted disputes. However, parents did not consistently report significant increases in contact, reduced anger or alleviation of their problems. Moreover 'success' depended largely on the quality of the parental relationship and the severity of dispute. The researchers concluded that while education, mediation and monitoring interventions could work for families with fresher disputes and lower levels of conflict, high conflict parents with entrenched disputes were much more difficult to help and likely to need a variety of remedies, including therapeutic interventions.

The same conclusion is reflected in Australia's Contact Orders Pilot programme and in an earlier experiment in Canada, the Manitoba Access Assistance Project. Aimed at cases where mediation had failed to resolve access denial, this offered a combination of detailed assessment, case management, therapy, monitoring and, where necessary, legal action. Improvement was reported in one-third of cases, though there was no data on re-litigation. Unfortunately the project proved too costly and was abandoned (O'Connor, 2002). Even in this programme one-third of cases reported no improvement whatsoever. It is clear that, where non-compliance is a major problem, expectations about the proportion of families who can be helped even by intensive interventions need to be modest.

The Need for Planning and Resources

In 2000, responding to concerns about the failure of the family courts to enforce contact orders, Australia introduced a highly structured three-stage regime which moved progressively from preventative measures, through remedial action to punitive sanctions.

- Stage 1 (when initial order made): parents are informed of their obligations and the consequences of failing to comply; information is given about programmes to assist.
- Stage 2 (first breach without reasonable excuse): the court may change the order; require parents to attend a parenting programme, or order compensatory contact.
- Stage 3 (repeat breach or first time but showing serious disregard): if a parenting programme is not deemed to be appropriate, the court *must* order either community service, require a bond; impose a fine or commit the defaulting parent to prison for up to six months.

Draft legislation currently before the Australian Parliament[3] (Australian Government, 2005) additionally requires courts to consider awarding compensation for expenses; imposing a bond at Stage 2; and ordering costs. These proposed measures are aimed at 'strengthening' the enforcement regime, although an earlier government proposal to require courts to consider changing residence (Australian Government, 2004) appears to have been discarded.

At the same time, acknowledging that 'the current process of seeking enforcement orders from the courts escalates the conflict and often does not resolve the problem' the government is proposing to try a 'new approach'. Before filing a breach application (with some exceptions) parents would

---

[3] Now the Family Law Amendment (Shared Responsibility) Act 2006.

be required to contact one of the new Family Relationships Centres which would seek to settle the issues through dispute resolution techniques or refer the family, on a voluntary basis, to a specialist programme such as the Contact Orders Program (Australian Government, 2004). The Family Law Council has also been asked to work on developing better processes in the family law system for dealing with breach or variation issues.

These measures reflect recognition that the compliance regime has not been as effective as had been hoped (Australian Government, 2004) although data is very limited. There appears to be no published information on the use of Stage 3, though anecdotal reports indicate it is very rarely used. At Stage 2 major problems with the supply of suitable parenting programmes restricted the number of orders the courts could make (Family Court of Australia, 2003). Early research reported varying expectations of the regime and criticisms from: parenting programme suppliers (some of whom questioned the coherence of providing parenting support within a disciplinary framework); judges (some of whom preferred the more imme-diately punitive approach); and both resident and non-resident parents, the former resenting the implication that their parenting was inadequate, the latter seeing parenting classes as an inadequate response (Rhoades, 2003).

It remains unclear whether the new regime was ill-conceived or merely poorly implemented. One message, however, is unequivocal: there is no point in giving courts powers to refer to parenting programmes without ensuring a sufficient supply of appropriate services. Enforcement cases cannot simply be slotted into existing programmes for parents who seek help with post-separation parenting; they require specialised approaches which are time and resource intensive (Rhoades, 2003; Attorney-General's Department, 2004).

PROGRAMMES INVOLVING CHILDREN

The UK, in common with several other jurisdictions (eg Australia, Canada, Germany, US) has begun to develop community/school-based support pro-grammes for children experiencing parental separation or divorce (Fthenakis, undated; Hawthorne et al, 2002; O'Connor, 2004). Aims include provid-ing peer support, enabling children to gain a better understanding of their experience, and helping them develop coping skills. While research reports mixed results, a few versions, eg the CODIP skill-based programme in the US, have been consistently proven to have beneficial, if modest, effects on children's adjustment (Center for Families, Children and the Courts, 2004; Grych, 2005).

In the US (Geelhoed et al, 2001) and Canada (O'Connor, 2004) there are also some court-related, occasionally court-provided programmes, some using commercially available materials, and in a few places (including the whole of Florida) attendance is compulsory. While there appears to be no direct evidence of parental/child opinion about this, court personnel report parents do not object (Geelhoed et al, 2001). Research on court-related programmes is in its infancy though there are some positive findings: eg one study of a (voluntary) programme in Montreal (cited O'Connor, 2004) reports that 68 per cent of children were very happy to attend with only 5 per cent negative; 80 per cent found it helpful. Children in a mandatory programme in Kentucky (Oliphant et al, 2002) reported that the programme helped them cope with divorce-related problems; understand the effects of divorce on their parents' behaviour; and resulted in improved relationships with parents and others. Further research is needed, however, to ascertain effectiveness.

A feature of some children's programmes, which sometimes run in parallel with parents' groups, is feeding back to parents what the children have said. For instance in *Kid's Turn*, in California, children produce a 'newsletter' conveying their views. Group leaders report this has a powerful impact on parents, motivating them to examine their own behaviour (Kelly, 2002). Feedback, whether from group sessions or individual child consultations, is also used as a lever for change in the Alameda model of therapeutic mediation (see earlier section) and in the Australian Contact Orders programmes, again, it is said, to good effect:

> The most powerful activity of all in creating an impetus for change in the parents, is feeding information back to parents about what their children have said their worries and feelings are, and the effect conflict is having on them' (Attorney-General's Department, 2003a).

More broadly, there is increasing interest in involving children more in processes such as mediation and counselling. This is a key theme in Australia, where a nationwide professional development programme Children in Focus is said to have been a catalyst for change towards what is known as 'child-inclusive practice (Webb and Moloney, 2003; Smyth, 2004). One clear message from research on children's experiences of parental separation is that many children do not feel their views were canvassed or taken into account by either their parents or professionals (O'Quigley, 1999) and while professional views differ there is evidence that many children are willing to participate and find it helpful (McIntosh, 2000).

CONCLUSION

This study emerged from the convergence of two concerns. The immediate stimulus, as mentioned earlier, was concern that in the often febrile UK debate about contact unsupported claims were being made that other jurisdictions are dealing with the problems much more effectively than we are and that particular 'models' have been shown to 'work'. In reality, as this chapter has hopefully shown, the evidence is quite sparse. At the same time it was clear, from work done by this author, and others (Buchanan et al, 2001; Walker, 2001; Trinder et al, 2001), that the needs of separating families in England and Wales were not well catered for by existing services. Hence there was interest in looking to other jurisdictions for ideas.

While in some respects the poverty of the research evidence to date is disappointing, it would be a pity if this was used to justify doing nothing. Nor does it mean that there is nothing that can be learnt from other countries. There is a pool of promising ideas which can be usefully drawn on. But clarity is needed about the evidential basis on which new ideas are being promulgated and the criteria which are being used to assess effectiveness. Provided this is done then drawing on international experience can be productive, though principally through acting as a stimulus to the formulation of home-grown interventions, rather than as a source of off-the-peg interventions to be uncritically transplanted.

REFERENCES

Advisory Board on Family Law, Children Act Sub-Committee (2002) *Making Contact Work. A Report to the Lord Chancellor on the Facilitation of Arrangements for Contact between Children and their Non-resident Parents and the Enforcement of Court Orders for Contact* (London, Lord Chancellor's Department).

American Bar Association Family Law Section (2001) 'High Conflict Custody Cases: Reforming the System for Children—Conference Report and Action Plan' 34 *Family Law Quarterly* 589.

Arbuthnot, J, Kramer, KM and Gordon, DA (1996) 'Does Mandatory Education for Parents Work? A Six-Month Outcome Evaluation' 34 *Family and Conciliation Courts Review* 60.

Arbuthnot, J and Kramer, KM (1998) 'Effects of Divorce Education on Mediation Process and Outcome' 15 *Mediation Quarterly* 199.

Arbuthnot, J, Kramer, K and Gordon, DA (1997) 'Patterns of Relitigation following Divorce Education' 35 *Family and Conciliation Courts Review* 269.

Attorney-General's Department, Australia (2003a) *The Contact Orders program: a summary of the independent evaluation of the Contact Orders Pilot* (Canberra, Attorney's General's Department).

Attorney-General's Department, Australia (2003b) *Submissions to the Parliamentary Inquiry on Child Custody (www.aph.gov.au/house/committee/fca/childcustody/index.htm).*

Australian Government (2004) *A New Approach to the Family Law System: implementation of reforms.* Discussion Paper 10 November 2004 *(www.aph.gov.au).*

Australian Government (2005) Family Law Amendment (Shared parental responsibility) Bill 2005 (www.aph.gov.au).

Bacon, B and McKenzie, B (2001) *Best Practices in Parent Information and Education Programs after Separation and Divorce.* Report prepared for Family Mediation Canada.

Blackwell, A and Dawe F (2003) *Non-Resident Parental* Contact (London, Office for National Statistics).

Buchanan, A, Hunt, J, Bretherton, H and Bream, V (2001) *Families in Conflict: Perspectives of children and Parents on the Family Court Welfare Service* (Bristol, Policy Press).

Buehler, C, Betz, P, Ryan, CM, Legg, BH and Trotter, BB (1992) 'Description and Evaluation of the Orientation for Divorcing Parents: Implications for Postdivorce Prevention Programs' 41 *Family Relations* 154.

Center for Families, Children and the Courts (2004) Research Update, April 2004: Programs for Children of Separating Parents: Literature Review and Directions for Future Research (San Francisco, Center for Families, Children and the Courts).

Coates, CA, Deutsch, R, Starnes, H, Sullivan, M and Sydlik, B (2004) 'Parenting Coordination for High Conflict Families' 42 *Family Court Review* 246.

Coates, CA, Jones, W, Bushard, P, Deutsch, R, Starnes, H, Hicks, B, Stahl, P, Sullivan, M, Sydlik, B and Wistner, R (2003) 'Parenting Coordination Implementation Issues' 41 *Family Court Review* 533.

Criddle, MN, Allgood, SM, Piercy, KW (2003) 'The Relationship between Mandatory Divorce Education and Level of Post-divorce Parental Conflict' 39 *Journal of Divorce and Remarriage* 99.

DeLuse, SR (1999) *Mandatory Divorce Education: A Program Evaluation Using a Quasi-random Regression Discontinuity Design* (Dissertation Abstracts).

Department for Constitutional Affairs, Department for Education and Skills and Department for Trade and Industry (2004) *Parental Separation: Children's Needs and Parents' Responsibilities* Cm 6273 (London, The Stationery Office).

Department for Education and Skills (2005) Draft Children (Contact) and Adoption Bill, Cm 6462 (London, The Stationery Office).

Department of Family and Community Services (undated): 'Statement of Requirement' (for research tender) (Canberra, Attorney-General's Department).

Doolittle, DB and Deutsch, R (1999) 'Children in High Conflict Divorce: Theory, Research and Intervention' in RM Galatzer-Levy and L Kraus (eds), *The Scientific Basis of Child Custody Decisions* (New York and Chichester, Wiley).

Dyer, CA (1989) *The Effects of an Educational Orientation Session on the Efficacy of Divorce Mediation* (Dissertation Abstracts).

Ellis, D and Anderson, DY (2003) 'The Impact of Participation in a Parent Education Program for Divorcing Parents on the Use of Court Resources: An Evaluation Study' 21 *Conflict Resolution Quarterly* 169.

Elrod, LD (2001) 'Reforming the System to Protect Children in High Conflict Custody Cases' 28 *William Mitchell Law Review* 495.

Erikson, S and Ver Steegh, N (2001) 'Mandatory Divorce Education Classes: What Do the Parents say?' 38 *William Mitchell Law Review* 889.

Fthenakis, WE (undated) *Divorce as a Family Transition: Interventions for Divorced Parents and Children* (www.fthenakis.de/Vortrag_Interventions, pdf).

Fischer, RL (1997) 'The Impact of an Education Seminar for Divorcing Parents: Results from a National Survey of Family Court Judges' 15 *Journal of Divorce and Remarriage* 199.

Free, SH (1998) *Divorce, Parent Education and Litigation* (Dissertation Abstracts).

Geasler, MJ and Blaisure, KR (1999) '1998 Nationwide Survey of Court-Connected Divorce Education Programs' 37 *Family and Conciliation Courts Review* 36.

Geelhoed, RJ, Blaisure, KR and Geasler, MJ (2001) 'Status of Court-connected Programs for Children whose Parents are Separating or Divorcing' 39 *Family Court Review* 395.

Goodman, M, Bonds, D, Sandler, I, Braver, S (2004) 'Parent Psychoeducational Programs and Reducing the Negative Effects of Interparental Conflict Following Divorce' 42 *Family Court Review* 263.

Gray, C, Verdieck, MJ, Smith, ED and Freed, K (1997): 'Making it Work: An Evaluation of Court-mandated Parenting Workshops for Divorcing Families' 35 *Family and Conciliation Courts Review* 280.

Grych, JH (2005) 'Inter-parental Conflict as a Risk Factor for Child Maladjustment: Implications for the Development of Prevention Programs' 43 *Family Court Review* 97.

Hans, JD and Fine, MA (2001) 'Children of Divorce: Experiences of Children whose Parents Attended a Divorce Education Program' 36 *Journal of Divorce and Remarriage* 1.

Hawthorne, J, Jessop, J, Pryor, J and Richards, M (2002) *Separation, Divorce and Family Change: a Review of Interventions and Support Services for Children* (York, Rowntree).

House of Commons, House of Lords (2005) Report of the Joint Committee on the Draft Children (Contact) and Adoption Bill, HC 400-I, HL Paper 100-I (London, The Stationery Office).

Hughes, R, Jr and Kirby, JJ (2000) 'Strengthening Evaluation Strategies for Divorcing Family Support Services: Perspectives of Parent Educators, Mediators, Attorneys and Judges' 49 *Family Relations* 53.

Homrich, AM, Glover, MM and Blackwell White, A (2004) 'The Court Care Center for Divorcing Families' 41 *Family Court Review* 141.

James, A (1999) *Assisting Families with Post-separation/divorce Conflict: The Use of Family Assistance Orders in England and Wales* (York, Rowntree).

Johnston, T (1994) 'Outcome study on Special Master cases in Santa Clara County' (unpublished).

Johnston, JR (1999) *Developing and Testing GroupInterventions for Families at Impasse. Report to the State-wide Office of Family Court Services* AOC, Judicial Council of California, San Francisco (unpublished).

Kelly, JB (2002) 'Psychological and Legal Interventions for Parents and Children in Custody and Access Disputes: Current Research and Practice' 10 *Virginia Journal of Social Policy and Law* 129.

Kibler, S, Sanchez, E and Baker-Jackson, M (1994) 'Pre-Contempt/Contemnors Group Diversion Counseling Program. A Program to Address Parental Frustration of Custody and Visitation Orders' 32 *Family and Conciliation Courts Review* 62.

Kramer, L and Kowal, A (1998) 'Long-term Follow-up of a Court-based Intervention for Divorcing Parents' 36 *Family and Conciliation Courts Review* 452.

Kramer, L and Washo, CA (1993) 'Evaluation of a Court-Mandated Prevention Program for Divorcing Parents' 42 *Family Relations* 179.

Kramer, KM, Arbuthnot, J, Gordon, DA, Rousis, NJ and Hoza, J (1998) 'Effects of Skill-based Versus Information-based Divorce Education Programs on Domestic

Violence and Parental Communication' 36 *Family and Conciliation Courts Review* 9.

Krolczyk, BJ (2001) *Evaluating Mandatory Parent Education for Divorcing Couples with Children* (Dissertation Abstracts).

Kurki-Suono, K (2004) *National Report: Finland* (Committee of Experts on Family Law www2.law.uu.nl/priv.cefl).

Lee, CD, Shaugnessy, JL and Banks, JK (1995): 'Impact of Expedited Visitation Services, a Court Program that Enforces Access. Through the Eyes of Children' 33 *Family and Conciliation Courts Review* 495.

Leitz-Spitz, MA (2002) *Marriage may be Temporary but Parenting is Forever: Do Court-mandated Divorce Education Seminars for Divorcing Parents Reduce Litigation rates?* (Dissertation Abstracts).

Loveridge, K (1995) *Statewide Mandatory Divorce Education Program Evaluation Results* (Salt Lake City, Utah, Administrative Office of the Courts).

Maclean, M and Mueller-Johnson, K (2003) 'Supporting Cross-Household Parenting: Ideas about "the Family", Policy Formation and Service Developments across Jurisdictions' in A Bainham, B Lindley, M Richards and L Trinder (eds), *Children and their Families: Contact, Rights and Welfare* (Oxford, Hart Publishing).

Mayes, G, Gillies, J, MacDonald, R and Wilson, G (2000) *An Evaluation of the Parent Information Programme* (Edinburgh: Scottish Executive Central Research Unit).

McClure, TE (2002) 'Postjudgement Conflict and Cooperation following Court-connected Parent Education' 38 *Journal of Divorce and Remarriage* 1.

McIntosh, J (2000) 'Child inclusive Divorce Mediation. Report on a Qualitative Research Study' 18 *Mediation Quarterly* 1 at 55.

McIsaac, H and Finn, C (1999) 'Parents Beyond Conflict: A Cognitive Restructuring Model for High-conflict Families in Divorce' 37 *Family and Conciliation Courts Review* 74.

McKenry, PC, Clark, KA and Stone, G (1998) 'A Qualitative Evaluation of a Divorce Education Program' 4 *Human Development and Family Life Bulletin* 5.

McKenry, PC, Clark, KA and Stone, G (1999) 'Evaluation of a Parent Education Programme for Divorcing Parents' 48 *Family Relations* 129.

McKenzie, B and Guberman, I (1997) *For the Sake of the Children, A Parent Education Program for Separating and Divorcing Parents, Final Report* (Winnipeg, Manitoba, Children and Family Social Services Research Group, Faculty of Social Work, University of Manitoba).

Neff, R and Cooper, K (2004) 'Parental Conflict Resolution: Six-, Twelve-, and Fifteen-month Follow-ups of a High-conflict Program' 42 *Family Court Review* 99.

O'Connor, P (2002) *Child Access in Canada: Legal Approaches and Program Supports*, Department of Justice, Canada.

O'Connor, P (2004) *Voice and Support: Programs for Children Experiencing Parental Separation* (Canada, Department of Justice).

Oliphant, E, Brown, JH, Cambron, ML and Yankeelov, P (2002) 'Measuring Children's Perceptions of the Families in Transition Program: a Qualitative Evaluation' 37 *Journal of Divorce and Remarriage* 157.

O'Quigley, A (1999) *Listening to Children's Views and Representing their Best Interest: A Summary of Current Research* (York, Joseph Rowntree Foundation).

Parkinson, P (2004) 'Family Relationship Centres' (Presentation to the Family Court Conference, Brisbane, Sept 2004).

Pearson, J and Anhalt, J (1994) 'Enforcing Visitation Rights—Innovative Programs in Five State Courts May Provide Answers to this Difficult Problem' 3 *Judges Journal* 40.

Pearson, J and Price, D (2002) *Child Access and Visitation Programs: Promising Practices* (Washington, Office of Child Support Enforcement, Administration for Children and Families, US Department of Health and Human Services).

Pearson, K and Thoennes, N (1998) 'Programs to Increase Father's Access to their Children' in I Garfinkel, S McLanahan, D Meyer and J Seltzer (eds), *Fathers under Fire: the Revolution in Support Enforcement* (NY, Russell Sage Foundation).

Pedro-Carroll, J, Nakhnikian, E and Montes, G (2001) 'Assisting Children Through Transition. Helping parents Protect their Children from the Toxic Effects of Ongoing Conflict in the Aftermath of Divorce' 39 *Family Court Review* 377.

Pruett, MK and Johnston, J (2004) 'Therapeutic Mediation with High Conflict Families' in J Folberg and A Milne (eds), *Divorce and Family Mediation: Models, Techniques and Applications* (NY and London, Guildford Press).

Rhoades, H (2003) 'Enforcing Contact or Supporting Parents? Policy Aims in Confusion'. Paper presented at the Oxford Centre for Family Law and Policy.

Schepard, A (2004) *Children, Courts and Custody: Interdisciplinary Models for Divorcing Families* (Cambridge, Cambridge University Press).

Seippert, J, Lybarer, D, Bertrand, L and Hornick, J (1999) *An Evaluation of Alberta's Parenting after Separation Seminars* (Calgary, Canadian Research Institute for Law and the Family).

Smyth, BM and Moloney, L (2003) 'Therapeutic Divorce Mediation: Strengths, Limitations and Future Directions' 9 *Journal of Family Studies* 161.

Smyth, B (ed) (2004) *Parent-Child Contact and Post Separation Parenting Arrangements Research Report No 9* (Melbourne, Australian Institute of Family Studies).

Stacer, DL and Stemen, FA (2000) 'Intervention for High Conflict Custody Cases' 14 *American Journal of Family Law* 242.

Stone, G, McKenry, P and Clark, K (1999) 'Fathers' Participation in a Divorce Education Program: A Qualitative Evaluation' 30 *Journal of Divorce and Remarriage* 99.

Strategic Partners Ltd (1998) *Contact Services in Australia Research and Evaluation Project* (Canberra, Legal Aid and Family Services Attorney-General's Department).

Sullivan, MJ (2004) 'Ethical, Legal and Professional Practice issues Involved in Acting as a Psychologist Parent Coordinator in Child Custody Cases' 42 *Family Court Review* 576.

Thoennes, N and Pearson, J (1999a) 'Parent Education in the Domestic Relations Court: A Multisite Assessment' 37 *Family and Conciliation Courts Review* 195.

Thoennes N and Pearson J (1999b) 'Supervised Visitation: A Profile of Providers' 37 *Family and Conciliation Courts Review* 460.

Trinder, L, Beek, M and Connolly, J (2001) *Making Contact* (York, Joseph Rowntree Foundation).

Trinder, L, Connolly, J, Kellett, J and Notley, C (2005) *A Profile of Applicants and Respondents in Contact Cases in Essex* DCA Research Series 1/05 (London, Department for Constitutional Affairs).

VanHoy, J and Pitts, GE (1995) 'Children Cope with Divorce Program Evaluation from Marion Superior Court Records' (unpublished. Cited in Bussey, M (1996) 'Impact of Kids First Seminar for Divorcing Parents: A Three Year Follow-up' 16 *Journal of Divorce and Remarriage* 129).

Vick, M and Backerman, R (1996) 'Mediation/arbitration: Surveys of Professionals and Clients'. Paper presented at the Boulder, Colorado Interdisciplinary Committee on Child Custody. (Cited Sullivan, MJ, 2004).

Walker J (ed) (2001) *Information Meetings and Associated Provisions within the Family Law Act 1996: Final Report* (London, Lord Chancellor's Department).

Webb, N and Moloney, L (2003) 'Child-Focused Development Programs for Family Dispute Professionals: Recent steps in the Evolution of Family Dispute Resolution Strategies in Australia' 9 *Journal of Family Studies* 23.

Whitworth, J, Capshew, TF and Abell, N (2002) 'Children Caught in the Conflict: Are Court-endorsed Divorce Parenting Education Programs Effective?' 37 *Journal of Divorce and Remarriage* 1.

Wolchik, SA, Sandler, IN, Winslow, E and Smith-Daniels, V (2005) 'Programs for Promoting Parenting of Residential Parents: Moving from Efficacy to Effectiveness' 43 *Family Court Review* 43 at 65.

Index